Allen Graubard

FREE
THE
CHILDREN

*Radical Reform and the
Free School Movement*

*Vintage Books
A Division of Random House
New York*

To my mother and the
memory of my father

VINTAGE BOOKS EDITION, January 1974

Copyright © 1972 by Allen Graubard

All rights reserved under International and Pan-American Copyright Conventions. Published in the United States by Random House, Inc., New York, and simultaneously in Canada by Random House of Canada Limited, Toronto. Originally published by Pantheon Books, a division of Random House, Inc., in 1972.

Library of Congress Cataloging in Publication Data

Graubard, Allen, 1938–
  Free the children.
  Includes bibliographical references.
  1. Free schools—United States. I. Title.
[LB1029.F7G7 1973]   371'.02   73–5750
ISBN 0–394–71932–8

Grateful acknowledgment is extended to the following:
  Communications on Alternatives Newsletter, for use of excerpt from Newsletter #2, Fall 1971.

  Random House, Inc., for excerpts from *New Reformation—Notes of a Neolithic Conservative* by Paul Goodman. Copyright © 1970 by Paul Goodman.

Manufactured in the United States of America

CONTENTS

INTRODUCTION

The American system of public education is in very deep trouble. This is now so widely admitted as to be almost an official truth, especially in the great urban areas of the country. The so-called crisis of the schools shows itself in many ways. In the urban schools young people drop out or are truant in astonishingly large numbers. Despite years of official concern, education for poor and minority youth is as disastrous as ever. All across the country, parents and other taxpayers are so dissatisfied with schools and skeptical of what can be done that they are voting down bond issue after bond issue, with the result that large city school systems have been forced to close weeks early as well as cut down on educational programs. Lack of money worsens the problems, leading, for example, to long and bitter teacher strikes. But in a way, the disgruntled taxpayers have a point. More money doesn't make the schools more successful in important ways: the kids don't get less bored, the poor and minority youth don't find their life chances enhanced by new buildings with decorator colors and opaque projectors.

Increasingly, significant numbers of students and adults see the dominant school methods as destructive of intellectual curiosity and emotional growth. They see the authoritarian methods of discipline as degrading and harmful. They see the curriculum as archaic and irrelevant. Many young people are bored, apathetic, or even hostile toward school, and even with all the systems of discipline, punishment, and threats, they don't seem to learn very much; certainly, few acquire a deep and honest desire to learn.

These kinds of criticisms have been voiced for over a decade by the so-called romantic critics like Paul Goodman and Edgar Z. Friedenberg. In the past few years, this sort of critique has grown in volume and is heard coming from such unromantic places as the Ford Foundation, the Office of Education, the Carnegie Corporation, and the National Education Association. (I do not mean that these Establishment institutions officially take this position; simply that people in them are increasingly making rather romantic and progressive noises.) Of course, there is very little agreement on the analysis of the causes of the troubles or on the best paths to a cure for the ailing system; but the fact that the school system needs deep and far-reaching changes is very widely admitted, even by many public school people themselves.

The concern with reforming education has spread quickly and many people—parents, students, teachers, administrators, government and foundation officials—are working for reform of various sorts inside the public school system. But over the past few years, a small but rapidly growing number of people have despaired over the possibility of substantial changes within the public school system within a reasonable time. For them, the public schools as they now exist are not places they want their children to be, and there are students and teachers who have similar feelings. So, in keeping with a great American tradition of self-help, these few parents, students, and teachers have decided that if you want good schools and want them now, you'll have to do it yourself. These people do not see the traditional private schools, even the respectably progressive ones, as fulfilling their desire for real alternatives to the kinds of schools now dominant. Consequently, a phenomenon known variously as "free schools" or "new schools" or "alternative schools" has emerged. The founding during the past few years of several hundred "new schools" sharing to various degrees a commitment to libertarian methods, significant student and parent participation in decision-making, and an articulate opposition to the methods and spirit of normal public and private school education is sometimes called a "movement," though this word obscures as much as it illuminates. In any case, the development is something new and interesting.

In this book, the phrases "free school" and "new school" will be roughly interchangeable. During the course of the book, the meaning of the terms should become clear, as well as the subtle disputes that have arisen about the proper application (and desirability) of the term "free school." (It does *not* mean that the schools don't normally charge tuition.) The variety within this category as well as the difficulty in defining the category will be taken up in detail in Chapter 2. As will become clear, the range of these new schools is surprisingly large. Their significance is far greater than the very small number of people currently active might seem to indicate. Many experimental alternative schools within the public school system are now beginning, and many of these are free schools. However, they are necessarily enmeshed in the public school bureaucracy and are under various constraints and pressures because of this. In the private free schools (the subject of this book) one finds a situation of real independence. These institutions are built by people who have not asked educational "experts" to design or approve an "experimental program," people who have not waited for the educational professionals to form committees and study groups to evaluate by "cost-benefit" analysis the most efficient and realistic technique of reform.

By scraping together money from wherever, finding an old house or a friendly church, scrounging material, attracting teachers who are willing to work for room and board and little more because they believe in what is being tried, the people doing free schools have started several hundred small educational institutions which are startlingly (and often exhilaratingly) different from what most Americans think of as schools. There are parent-cooperative elementary schools, kindergarten-through-high-school communities inspired by the example of Summerhill, student-organized high schools, "community schools" for black children (run by parents and other community people whose anger at what the public schools so often do to minority children is understandably great), street academies for high-school dropouts—to name some of the main types of new schools. The key to these institutions is that they are almost always the result of voluntary grass-roots efforts to build schools where children and young people are not oppressed by the arbitrary discipline and total power characteristic of most public schools and where the possibilities for experimenting and searching for new and better ways for children to live and learn can be explored. The people doing this are acting on what a much larger number of people are feeling—that great changes in schools and methods of education are urgently needed.

In this book I try to give as accurate and complete a description of the free school development as I can, at a point in time when the movement is still growing rapidly and changing as it grows. I don't pretend to be a neutral observer reporting on an interesting cultural phenomenon. I have been and still am deeply committed to effecting radical changes in education, and I have been deeply involved in free school activities. But, although committed to the basic meaning of the free school development, I have tried to be as clear as possible about the serious problems that exist in these schools in theory and practice, and I have tried to analyze where these problems come from and how they might best be understood and confronted.

I do not claim to be speaking for the free school movement; no one honestly could. I want to tell people, whatever their views on youth and education, what these new schools are like, because I think they are of great symbolic significance. I also want to confront the people committed to radical reform in education—my associates, so to speak —with the difficulties and dilemmas that I have seen and experienced, because I am convinced that unless we face these problems honestly, our brave and hopeful talk of wonderful reforms will become rhetorical bravado, convincing very few and changing very little; and another vision of a better future will be distorted and ignored.

I don't think this has to happen. I think that the free school development represents in education the same spirit of radical critique that has appeared in many sectors of American society over the past decade, beginning with the demand for an end to injustice represented by the rise of the civil rights movement. In order to create a truly humane and liberating education, we must be in the process of creating a truly humane and liberating social order. I hope the free schools can be a significant part of the movement to accomplish both of these goals.

Given the nature of the enterprise this book represents, my debts are necessarily many. I couldn't possibly cite all of the free school people who have talked to me, shared experiences, let me visit their schools, ask questions, and argue; I can only offer an open thanks to the students, staff, parents, and others who have helped me even when they didn't know they were doing so. To the students and staff of the Santa Barbara Community School, where I spent a year as a teacher, organizer, and coordinator, I owe the inspiration that powered my growing commitment to working full-time for radical educational reform (they also helped me convince myself that I didn't really want to continue as a professor of philosophy, respectable as that ancient calling is). To one of this wonderful group I owe a particular debt. Jeremy Kramer was so central in my Santa Barbara work and was so integral a part of my work back in Cambridge on the New Schools Directory Project (which compiled the first detailed and fairly accurate directory of free schools) that I want to express my appreciation for all his help, his humor, his complaints, and his arguments.

An old friend who helped me in many ways in the research and writing of this book, and whose experience and good sense always moved me to revise whenever she made a suggestion, is Christopher Anne Boldt, formerly at the Santa Barbara Community School.

I don't think back at all kindly to my own public school education, despite all the honors and prizes my "performances" gained, but the experience of college and graduate school was more a mixture of good and not so good. After moving uncertainly through several fields of study, I somehow backed into the philosophy department at Harvard in my third year of postgraduate academic wandering; and though I seem to have forsaken—professionally, at least—the academic vocation of philosophy, the education I received has affected me in ways too complex and diffuse to try to describe. For this good kind of education and for being real teachers and friends to me, I want to thank Professors Stanley Cavell and John Rawls.

There are friends and comrades to whom one has a more general debt, not for reading particular chapters of a manuscript, but for years of discussions, suggestions, chance remarks, and personal support, and I want to express to them a very heartfelt and general kind of thanks: to Professor Marshall Cohen, Norman Fruchter, Rachel Fruchter, John McNees, Nancy Hoffman, Patricia Collinge, Jacque Goldfarb, Lillian Drasin, Richard Yoder, Diane Berman, Barbara Gates, Wayne O'Neil.

My greatest debt is to Tim Affleck. From almost the beginning of my interest and activity in free schools, Tim was my partner. We worked closely together at the Santa Barbara Community School, on the New Schools Directory Project, on the gathering of material for this book, and on the thinking and talking through of hard questions. In every way he has been a real collaborator, and without his help and encouragement, I would never have felt adequate to the task of attempting this book.

Whether I have succeeded in producing a useful work is for others to judge. Many people have made the book possible, but what is finally said in the book is my responsibility.

FREE
THE
CHILDREN

1 · "FREEDOM WORKS"
The Theory of Radical School Reform

A parent, after hearing a discussion of what a free school would be like:

> I don't think it's a good thing. The kids may be happy and having fun; but this is a tough world. When they grow up they'll need discipline and there's a lot of boring hard work they'll have to do. If they don't start learning how to suffer now, they won't be ready for it later on.

A dominant trend in modern sociology is to emphasize the contributions that various social institutions make to the stability of the "social system." The key idea is that society can be looked at as a system which has needs that must be met ("functions" performed by various institutional "structures," to speak technically), so that *it* (the social system) can survive and reproduce itself over generations. Emile Durkheim, the great French sociologist, was an early and very influential exponent of this "social system" approach. He was also particularly interested in education, since he saw education as a critically important institution for society's passing on its values and thus ensuring its survival and stability.

Durkheim, using this particular sociological point of view, characterized education as follows:

> Education is the influence exercised by adult generations on those that are not yet ready for social life. Its object is to arouse and to develop in the child a certain number of physical, intellectual and moral states which are demanded of him by both the political society as a whole and the special milieu for which he is specifically destined. . . .
>
> . . . Education, far from having as its unique or principal object the individual and his interests, is above all the means by which society perpetually recreates the conditions of its very existence. Can society survive only if there exists among its members a sufficient homogeneity? Education perpetuates and reinforces this homogeneity by fixing in advance, in the mind of the child, the essential similarities that collective life presupposes. But, on the other hand, without a certain diversity, would all cooperation be impossible? Education assures the persistence of this necessary diversity by becoming itself diversified and by specializing. It consists, then, in one or another of its aspects, of a systematic socialization of the young generation.[1]

A very different conception of complex societies like our own is one that conceives the society as primarily an arena of conflict among different groups. Rather than concentrating on the system and its needs, this conception (classically expressed in the works of Marx) emphasizes the divisions among groups, and the conflicts of all sorts—political, social, economic, and ideological—which are related to these divisions. From this perspective, the idea of the society's interests should be interpreted as the needs of particular dominant elites in whose interest the status quo functions.

From this "society-as-conflict" perspective, the "social

system" conception of education stated by Durkheim is essentially conservative. *The society* really means *the status quo,* and education as a social institution is intended to perpetuate this status quo.

The "socialization" of the new generation is accomplished through various formal and informal means. In industrial societies, formal institutions known as schools have assumed an increasingly central role. In the United States, the trend has been toward more and more young people being in school longer and longer. Schools are expected to teach basic intellectual skills, to develop proper social attitudes, and to train the children as hard-working, respectful, and patriotic citizens of our democracy. Schools are supposed to fit young people for jobs and to separate out the superskilled and talented for the specialized needs of technology, science, and social and economic management.

The idea that societies and cultures change is neither startling nor new. What is peculiarly modern is the widespread acceptance of the idea of deliberate social change—"reform," so to speak. The idea is now almost universally accepted and has become commonplace. But it isn't a very clear notion. One sense of reform accepts the society and its needs in the Durkheimian sense, and seeks to improve existing institutions in order to better fulfill the status-quo-supporting functions. Another sense of reform proposes to change existing institutions in order to achieve goals that seem to be generally acknowledged in the ideology of the society but are apparently thwarted by the actual workings of the institutions. For example, accepted opinion is against racism, so reforms directed to ending blatant racism get at least lip-service from all respectable people.

These generally accepted conceptions of reform imply a concentration on a fairly clear and definite malfunction of a basically approved institution. That is, the fundamental structures of the society are not questioned, nor are the general purposes of the particular institutions; the purpose of the reforms is to make the institutions live up to their professed aims. Prisons, for example, are to rehabilitate criminals—if they aren't succeeding, we should make changes in the prisons. And so forth, as regards delinquency, poverty, slums, welfare, medical care, pollution, and crime. The critical point that necessarily arises—and leads to a more radical analysis of social change—is that many problems seem not to respond much to even the most well-intentioned reform efforts. Accordingly, it becomes reasonable to consider the notion that the problems don't arise primarily from some ascertainable malfunction of the particular institution, but from deeper social conditions; and that real reform will necessitate fairly radical changes in the basic structures and values of the society.

This conflict of analysis is obvious, and provides most of the basic material of political dispute. At the radical extreme is revolution, either violent or nonviolent—the idea that large-scale structural changes and shifts of power are necessary in order to overcome social problems and that groups that are on top in the status quo will do their damnedest to prevent such a radical reconstruction of society, lest they lose what they have.

Often, it is in the process of trying to bring about modest reforms that people become aware of the knotty interconnections of social problems and institutions; and through painful experience, they move in consciousness and action to work for deeper and more far-reaching institutional changes than they originally thought necessary. (A particularly vivid and concrete historical account of the growth of a revolutionary consciousness among people who started off seeking moderate reforms is John Womack, Jr.'s *Zapata and the Mexican Revolution*.)

These very brief considerations are not meant to be an analysis of the political theory of reform and revolution but to raise some fairly elementary considerations about institutional reform in general which are obviously relevant to the whole question of educational reform.

Educational reform, in the very moderate sense of reform noted before, could mean improving techniques for accomplishing what are now the generally agreed goals of schools. In this sense, one would ask about audiovisual techniques, different approaches to teaching reading, techniques of classroom management, "new math," more attractive textbooks, and so forth. This approach does not question the basic forms and methods of schools and the kinds of socialization functions the schools help perform.

But the kind of educational reform represented by free schools is called "radical school reform" (which is also the title of a popular anthology of educational reform writings edited by Ronald and Beatrice Gross). An approach to school reform that can reasonably be called *radical* does not concern itself much with moderate changes of technique. The emphasis is on the process of socialization and the kinds of character traits and values that are encouraged; the functions like "tracking" children to fit along social class lines to future job possibilities; the detrimental effect of the authoritarian techniques of public schools on qualities like intellectual curiosity. To see that schools need *radical* reform depends on a perception of deep and pervasive harm that can be ascribed to the dominant structures, values, and techniques of the existing schools. The idea is not, as in the most moderate sense of reform, that we need to improve our techniques somewhat in order to better accomplish what is already being done fairly adequately (e.g., use improved laboratory equipment to enrich the physics teaching already going on). Such pedagogical problems are seen as only marginally important, and in fact extensive concern with such questions often serves as a diversion from the really serious criticisms of the basic aspects of the dominant system of American education.

The explicitly pedagogical questions are only one part

of a larger critique. Basic to this critique is the issue raised by the sociological perspective of Durkheim. To what extent does the system of education serve the interests of the status quo? If one opposes some of the basic values and institutional arrangements of a social order, then one certainly opposes socialization institutions that sustain these values and institutions and would obviously oppose a school system that fulfilled Durkheim's conception of the social role of educational institutions. But if one holds attitudes radically critical of the dominant values and institutions, how can one seriously expect public schools or any other official institution to represent or support attitudes that are significantly subversive of the status quo?

This is a serious issue for any conception of radical reform, and it offers no simple solution, in theory or in practice. I won't enter into a discussion of the issue here, but it should be seen as underlying the whole question of radical school reform, and it is part of the many confusions that beset the building of new schools, either inside or outside the public school system. This book will attempt to clarify some of these confusions.

The theory of radical school reform is not really a "theory," in a respectable philosophy-of-science sense. It would be more accurate to talk about a cluster of attitudes, assumptions, and interpreted experiences (not always consistent or clear) about the nature of children, the evaluation of the effects of dominant school techniques, and the relation of educational questions to larger social, political, and economic issues.

The theory of radical school reform and the new schools movement ("movement," like "theory," understood in a very loose sense) is expressed in a number of recent books. A relatively small number of these writings have been very widely read and discussed for the past several years. Works like John Holt's *How Children Fail* have been extremely important in inspiring people to action. The free school development sprang up almost from scratch so far as actual experience was concerned. Very few people who organized schools had actually seen or worked in a free school, so that what they had to go on was a concrete sense of what was wrong with public schools and an abstract hope of how marvelous "free learning" would be. In this situation the books of radical school reform became a prime source of inspiration and support. One often finds in talking to free school people about how they got started that they say things like: "We read John Holt and then called a meeting," or "A friend gave me copies of *Summerhill,* Herb Kohl and Joseph Featherstone's articles on the British infant schools, and then I talked to some other parents . . ."

The corpus of new schools literature can be divided into four basic genres. (Some works overlap genres and some are difficult to classify. I have not attempted to be comprehensive in this listing, but I have included the most widely known and I feel the selection is fairly representative.) (1) Critical analyses of the structure and function of the public school system—Paul Goodman, *Compulsory Mis-education;* Jules Henry, *Culture Against Man;* John Holt, *How Children Fail* and *The Underachieving School;* Edgar Friedenberg, *Coming of Age in America;* Miriam Wasserman, *The School Fix—NYC, USA;* Paul Lauter and Florence Howe, *The Conspiracy of the Young;* Ivan Illich, *Deschooling Society;* The Schoolboys of Barbiana, *Letter to a Teacher.* (2) Personal accounts of experiences of teaching in public schools and of sometimes attempting to try out free education ideas—Jonathan Kozol, *Death at an Early Age;* Herbert Kohl, *36 Children;* James Herndon, *The Way It Spozed to Be* and *How to Survive in Your Native Land;* Nat Hentoff, *Our Children Are Dying.* (3) Personal accounts of doing new schools—A. S. Neill, *Summerhill;* George Dennison, *The Lives of Children;* Sylvia Ashton-Warner, *Teacher;* Elwyn Richardson, *In the Early World;* Peter Marin, "The Open Truth and Fiery Vehemence of Youth" (much anthologized). (4) What could very loosely be called theory of free education and advice on how to translate theory into practice, either in new schools or in public school classrooms—George Leonard, *Education and Ecstasy;* Neil Postman and Charles Weingartner, *Teaching as a Subversive Activity;* Herbert Kohl, *The Open Classroom;* John Holt, *How Children Learn* and *What Do I Do Monday?;* Carl Rogers, *Freedom to Learn;* Robert Greenway and Salli Rasberry, *Rasberry Exercises;* Joseph Featherstone, articles on British Infant Schools contained in *Schools Where Children Learn;* Jonathan Kozol, *Free Schools.*

Although these works (and others I haven't named) are often listed together as a kind of united front against the authoritarian system of public school education, there are substantial conflicts among them, and these conflicts reflect the tensions of theory and practice within the new schools movement. In this chapter I want to describe the theory by discussing some of the most prominent of the books just named, while raising some questions and criticisms. The emphasis will be on the "positive" pedagogical theory, that is, the conception of libertarian pedagogy and the conception of human (and child) nature that underlie the theory. I won't directly discuss the "negative" analysis, the critiques and analyses of the workings of the public school system, nor will I try here to give a fair description of how the more traditional approaches try to justify themselves. The political and social dimensions of the critique will emerge throughout the book, especially in the last chapters which deal with dilemmas of curriculum and with the politics of educational reform and the possible future development of the new schools movement. Also, in the chapter on curriculum, the reader will find an extensive discussion of the public school approaches and their justification, based on the works of social scientists who study education professionally and basically support the system, openly rejecting much of the critique and analyses of the "romantic" writers.

The central concept of the theory is, naturally, the messy notion of "freedom." Although some people doing new schools have come to find the term misleading, and reject it as a description of their particular new school, the phrase "free school" is still the most common name for this new wave of experimental schools. "Free" applies to the pedagogy, and not, as some people think when they hear it, to the tuition—which is often quite unfree.

The most widely known example of the free school is, of course, Summerhill in Suffolk, England. Neill's book about the school and its philosophy has been read by millions of people, and the school, now fifty years old, has had countless visitors. Although Neill has never claimed to speak for a movement, and although many people involved in the new schools would disagree with much that he says (especially his explicit Freudianism), Neill's conceptions of "freedom" and of "free children" express definitely and clearly an important part of the core assumptions of many new schools. Also, the emphasis on the *inherent* nature of the child and the image of social change through the development of happy free children by means of a free school environment are an important strain in free school thought.

Neill states boldly what is derogatorily called the "romantic" view of children:

> My view is that a child is innately wise and realistic. If left to himself without adult suggestion of any kind, he will develop as far as he is capable of developing.[2]

This seems to be as straightforward and uncompromising an expression of this view of children as is possible. As is often the case with a position that radically opposes the generally accepted views, there is an appeal to a "natural" child that is quite different from what most people would say is their experience with real children. There is an expression of faith which attributes all of the obvious observable troubles of children to the almost universal existence of bad adult interventions.

There are many questions that one could raise about Neill's faith, even when one is sympathetic. For example, it is revealing to substitute the word "adult" for "child" in the first sentence quoted. Would one want to say that an adult is innately wise and realistic? What would this mean? That only good things, emotional and intellectual, are natural and innate, while any bad things are the result of bad upbringing? So the child is the naturally good and wise creature before he becomes a defective, damaged adult? And what reason do we have to believe that a child will develop as far as he is capable of developing if there is no adult suggestion of any kind? Does this mean that where there has been adult suggestion, the child is always cut short of his fullest development, or that even when not cut short, the effort is at best redundant? Does Neill mean "develop in all ways"—intellectually, emotionally, artistically, whatever?

Clearly, these are some of the objections that could be made. But this really isn't the point. The importance of Neill isn't the challengeable wordings but the spirit behind the claims, for it is this spirit that has generated sympathetic vibrations from hundreds of readers, even those who could raise detailed objections to the particular formulations and the theoretical foundations of Neill's conceptions.

Neill states elsewhere in the book:

> Possibly the greatest discovery we have made in Summerhill is that a child is born a sincere creature. We set out to let children alone so that we might discover what they were like. It is the only possible way of dealing with children. The pioneer school of the future must pursue this way if it is to contribute to child knowledge and more important, to child happiness.[3]

Neill's school aspires to be a total community. Since Neill is interested in child-rearing, and in education proper only as it fits into the development of free, happy children, his chief concern is with the effect on the psyche of various ways of treating children. Coming out of a modified Freudian and Reichian perspective, Neill emphasizes the conditions of repression: the bad effects of imposing discipline in an authoritarian manner and frightening children about religion and morality, especially with respect to questions of sexuality. For Neill, personal difficulties and unhappiness, of which learning difficulties are only a manifestation, stem from repressive environments in the home and at school. Accordingly, Summerhill is not merely an attempt at a better school, pedagogically speaking; the goal is a community that acknowledges and supports the principle of protecting the child from the repressive effect of the coercive treatment of children found in the existing society. Neill says, *"A loving environment, without parental discipline, will take care of most of the troubles of childhood"* (his emphasis). He continues, "This is what I want parents to realize. If their children are given an environment of love and approval in the home, nastiness, hate, and destructiveness will never arise."[4]

Finally, Neill's simple answer to the question of how happiness can be bestowed is, *"Abolish authority. Let the child be himself. Don't push him around. Don't teach him. Don't lecture him. Don't elevate him. Don't force him to do anything."*[5]

With respect to the contemporary movement for radical school reform, Neill is rather idiosyncratic in his Freudian emphasis on the supreme, almost exclusive, importance of sex repression and his rationalistic faith in the relation of the elimination of sex guilt to the disappearance of religion and mysticism. (How Neill would deal with the hip free school adolescents whose sexual openness and apparent lack of guilt are far greater than anything he could have seen in the young people of Summerhill, yet who seem to be deeply absorbed in Yoga, Tarot cards, astrology, Zen, and even Jesus, is an intriguing question.) However, his optimistic view of the simplicity of love and its effects and his principled ignoring of the political, social, and economic conditions of the surrounding society are more representative. Neill avoided dealing with problems of social change, partly on principle and partly from prudence. He was afraid the society would close him down if he gave them a good excuse. This is still characteristic of much free school theory, though the tendency is to raise the banner of principle and deny the less satisfying but more realistic prudential motives.

Neill's conception of the function of education emphasizes the effect of freedom on the child's personality. The hope (and claim) is that free children will be self-motivated, integrated, able to seek out the learning they need in order to pursue interests that are truly their own, and, when they become adults, capable of choosing a way of life and work on the basis of considerations flowing from inside, rather than being ruled by externally imposed standards and goals.

In the new wave of radical school reform, the emphasis is more explicitly on the school proper and its structure and methods, rather than on the broader issue of child-rearing and emotional repression. (For example, very few of the new schools are boarding schools, which is a natural tendency for a Summerhillian school.) But, as Paul Goodman pointed out several years ago in *Compulsory Mis-education,* the emphasis on the child's freedom of choice, the challenge to the compulsory character of American schooling (and the conception of children implied by the emphasis on compulsion) was a crucial Summerhillian idea which was appealing to more and more people. As Goodman noted, the Deweyite "progressive schools" left over from that movement for radical school reform did not represent this principle and did not really challenge what

were more and more being perceived as crucial questions
—such as compulsory education.

A strong sympathy, if not close agreement, with the spirit
Neill expresses is shared by almost all radical school reform theory, and it follows quite obviously that there
should be a profound opposition to the dominant characteristics of the traditional public and private education
systems. The critical analysis and documentation of this
opposition have been provided during the past few years
in the listed works of John Holt, Paul Goodman, Jules
Henry, Jonathan Kozol, Herbert Kohl, and Edgar Friedenberg. Their works describe in detail the typical authoritarianism of the classroom, the obsession with order
and discipline, the motivation by induced fear and invidious competition for prizes and grades, rigid and irrelevant curriculum, pressure for conformity, systematic
denial of the importance of independence, originality,
spontaneity. Further, these works developed a social and
cultural analysis to try to explain why the situation was
as it was.

These writers were considered by many as romantics
and Pollyannas (see Chapter 4). They were accused of
exaggerating and misrepresenting, even of slandering one
of the great institutions of American life. But two years
ago a mammoth documentary study was released which
seemed to back up the critique these writers developed
(although disagreeing with them on basic issues of analysis
and solution). Charles Silberman could not be considered
"romantic" or "radical." In the beginning of *Crisis in the
Classroom,* he wrote:

> ". . . the most deadly of all possible sins," Erik Erikson
> suggests, "is the mutilation of a child's spirit." It is not
> possible to spend any prolonged period visiting public
> school classrooms without being appalled by the mutila-
> tion visible everywhere—mutilation of spontaneity, of joy
> in learning, of pleasure in creating, of sense of self. The
> public schools—those "killers of the dream" (to appropriate

a phrase of Lillian Smith's)—are the kind of institution one cannot really dislike until one gets to know them well. Because adults take the schools so much for granted, they fail to appreciate what grim, joyless places most American schools are, how oppressive and petty are the rules by which they are governed, how intellectually sterile and esthetically barren the atmosphere, what an appalling lack of civility obtains on the part of teachers and principals, what contempt they unconsciously display for children as children.[6]

The obvious import of such an analysis is that American schools are failing. This broad judgment is accepted by much of radical school reform theory. But, although the failures of the schools can appear as starkly as Silberman makes out, the issue of what is failure is not so simple. To the extent that one looks at schools purely as places that should nourish joyful, self-motivated, and active learning, both of mind and emotions, then the judgment of general failure is understandable. But, if one remembers Durkheim's sociological perspective described earlier, then the issue appears as more complicated. Looking at the schools as serving the functions he described, one might consider that apparent failures might be quite functional to the preservation of the status quo social structure; that a less purely pedagogical view of education would require a more subtle analysis of what would count as success or failure for an educational system. This issue will be developed at length throughout this book.

For most radical reform theory the concern is not with a political and social analysis of the functioning of the educational system, but with the kinds of pedagogical failures that the passage from Silberman's book summarizes. The theory is based on the conception of the child represented in its purest and most extreme form in the quotations from Neill. On the basis of such a conception, it would follow that the dominant public school methods violate the nature of the child and lead to the boredom, apathy, hostility, stupidity, and other negative effects which are observed so generally in American schools. The positive side of reform theory is that new schools based on the realization of the truth of the "romantic" conceptions of childhood and the process of learning would have results far superior to the standard public schools, not just in the area of emotional development which is so central in the Summerhillian conception of child-rearing, but also in the intellectual areas, with respect to the development of qualities like intellectual curiosity, initiative, self-motivated learning, and the quality of "learning how to learn," so prized now for our age of "knowledge explosion."

The most widely read of the recent radical reform writers is John Holt. His first book, *How Children Fail,* was truly startling, portraying in a vivid and concrete way the schools' effect of creating stupidity. Somehow, although almost everyone sees or experiences what Holt describes, no one had been able to see so clearly the process of how children fail and present it so convincingly; and the book deeply affected many people. In this and later books, especially *How Children Learn,* Holt also expresses some considerations of the good approach to education, a formulation of some principal themes of the "freedom" approach to learning.

He writes: ". . . when they learn in their own way and for their own reasons, children learn so much more rapidly and effectively than we could possibly teach them. . . ."[7] At another point Holt says:

> The child is curious. He wants to make sense out of things, find out how things work, gain competence and control over himself and his environment, do what he can see other people doing. He is open, receptive and perceptive. . . . What is essential is to realize that children learn independently, not in bunches; that they learn out of interest and curiosity, not to please or appease the adults in

power; and that they ought to be in control of their own learning, deciding for themselves what they want to learn and how they want to learn it. . . .[8]

I would be against trying to cram knowledge into the heads of children, even if we could agree on what knowledge to cram, and could be sure that, once crammed in, it would stay in. . . . For it seems to me a fact that, in our struggle to make sense out of life, the things we most need to learn are the things we most want to learn. . . .[9]

Most emphatically, like A. S. Neill, Holt claims:

What we need to do, and *all we need to do,* is bring as much of the world as we can into the school and the classroom; give children as much help and guidance as they need and ask for; listen respectfully when they feel like talking; and then get out of the way. We can trust them to do the rest.[10]

Such remarks are about the natural, which also means the ideal. One could not confirm their truth by looking at a random group of children. Holt's descriptions clearly do not apply to many actual children. And of course, Holt and all other radical school performers do not deny this. The theoretical claims contain an analysis of how the bad techniques prevalent in our society can distort and crush the natural capacities of children.

As is the case with such natural characterizations, much that is normative is contained in what appears to be only descriptive. "Natural" is about the trickiest word in the philosophical vocabulary, and there is a strong tendency in our thinging to consider that what is natural is also good and right. One way of claiming that something is good without having to make an argument to support an obvious value judgment is to describe it as "natural." This is an especially important point where "human nature" is concerned. The "is" that appears in theoretical conceptions like Holt's almost inevitably means in large part "should be" or "can be." At the high level of abstraction on which

Holt's remarks are offered, there would be a much more extensive acceptance of their general tone today than there would have been a half-century ago, although his actual position might seem a bit extreme to more moderate advocates of restrained "permissiveness." The "original sin" conception of human nature is not very popular today. Except for some moralists of the far right (often religious in a fundamentalist way) almost no one claims that children are essentially slothful, sinful, recalcitrant, etc., in need of the traditional kind of stern discipline to transform their lazy and rebellious spirits, in the manner of the Calvinists or Dickens's memorable schoolmaster of *Hard Times*, Thomas Gradgrind.

Holt's image abstracts from the social and cultural world in which the natural child becomes a real individual child. The description of the child expresses what *should* be—concerning the expression of interest and intelligence, curiosity and self-motivation; and it is implied that it *can* be—when bad interventions don't happen (which always happen, to some degree). For example, Holt says that children "learn out of interest and curiosity, not to please or appease the adults in power." But it would seem that what he means is that children *ought* to learn out of interest and curiosity; that, as in other areas of human activity, some motivations are morally superior and are related to morally preferable situations in other areas in life. It is clearly true that children often learn—quickly and deeply—in order to please adults in power. Love is complicated and children are naturally motivated to gain the love (and approval) of relevant powerful adults. It would be very difficult to isolate pure "interest" from the complexity of other motives like desire for approval or good self-image. (This, of course, applies to adults too.) Thus, if one child notices how pleased a parent is by his "self-motivated" interest activities, like learning to read or making a pot, or, later on, reading history or physics books, and he also notices that he can surpass his sibling by doing it, I think it would be natural to find the child working hard, learning fast, retaining well.

None of this is to say that what might be called "intrinsic interest" can't be part of what happens. But it is true that the natural child, like the natural person, appears purely only as a concept, while real children are always a mixture of the pure natural capacities and the effects of a particular world—a family, parents and siblings, a history of experience, responses from adults, the effects of a complex cultural environment which creates motives or at least warps the so-called "natural" motives. Even in Holt's terms, there is a crucial ambiguity in "giving children as much help and guidance as they need and ask for and then getting out of the way and trusting them to do the rest." In the ideal conception, nature will lead them to ask for what they need, but with real children what they ask for and what they need may not be identical, and often it will be necessary for adults to make judgments. We all know that, with our own adult friends, we don't always think their beings are so harmonious that they naturally choose well—emotionally, intellectually, nutritionally, politically, or what have you. It is true that there are moral reasons for not imposing our own judgments on other adults except in extreme circumstances, and that these moral reasons, along with the idea of nurturing moral attitudes of justice and freedom, should be applied (in a complexly modified way) to adolescents and even younger children. But this is not the same as claiming that nature does it.

The idea of a "nature," modified badly by unnatural external pressures, can be misleading in that it can misrepresent the meaning of culture. Cultural norms, social personality traits, and typical value clusters are not accidental shapings added on to an essential human nature, at least not in any interesting sense. The human being is always a cultural creature, and always part of a particular culture. The rationalist monarch who several centuries ago kept an infant from hearing any particular spoken language to see what language would be spoken naturally was making a tragic error. It isn't that there may not be a specific language-using capacity in all humans, but that the content of the category arises from a real and specific cultural experience. Similarly, to talk simply of interests and curiosity can obscure the fact that these are categories whose content is always being created and affected by obvious and not-so-obvious cultural influences. Adults cannot avoid being an important part of the environment, both in the sense of consciously creating part of it and trying to oppose the harmful influences of other parts of it. Therefore we should admit that just letting children alone with the expectation that "nature knows best" is quite complicated. Holt's and Neill's observations need a good deal of explication and they lend themselves to misinterpretation in thought and action when stated dogmatically or too theoretically (pushed often by the polemics of the situation).

Given the questions I have raised concerning the theoretical formulations of Neill and Holt, it would be misleading to imply that opposition to radical reform theory aligns one with John Calvin, Thomas Gradgrind, or Max Rafferty. Defenders of the public school system or of the traditional methods (reformed, of course) base their defense primarily on a claimed realism—about children, learning, and the needs of society—which they feel the "romantic" critics lack. (That's why they are called "romantic.") As was noted before, much of the radical reform theory concentrates on pedagogical questions, and does not attempt to broaden the critique politically so as to confront directly the sociological function of making children loyal and well-functioning members of the society. This argument shall be dealt with at length in Chapter 4.

At this point, what needs emphasizing is that the mainstream of radical reform theory concentrates its attention on the *educational* improvements that can be brought about by reform, improvements that could right the failure of the educational system so as to make things better for both individuals and the society. Conscious of the accusation of being romantic and unrealistic, a strong trend in the theory is to throw the charge back at the established system, to accuse it of being unrealistic (though not romantic) because it fails so consistently, even in preparing young people to work in this society—which might have been thought to be its purpose. The claim is that, in radically reformed schools, learning, even traditional academic learning, will go well; that children will learn to apply themselves on the basis of intrinsic motivation; that they will retain and develop their natural creativity and originality; that they will be especially good at being independent and creatively adaptable to new situations. Rather than being at a disadvantage in the "real world," free children will be *better* off than those undergoing the damage of traditional schools because they will be good at choosing freely and performing well, whatever career and work decisions they make. They will have much less anxiety and fear drummed into them while they are growing up and going to school, and consequently they will be happier and more integrated and emotionally healthy when they are adults. Moreover, the needs of the society (the same one defenders of the system are talking about) will be better met by freeing education. For example, engineers, product designers, and corporation planners will be adaptive and creative human beings who will be more capable of meeting the challenge of the accelerating pace of change, rapid obsolescence of skills, and heightened uncertainty about the future. Our society, our corporations, our government, our institutions need flexible and creative people. Our present school methods are old-fashioned; they don't use all the understanding we have now about children and psychology; they don't prepare for the new technological society; they aren't relevant. As a result, they alienate students, they bore students; this generates discontent and alienation in young people who then strike out blindly, burning and rioting. They see their schools as jails. Let us recognize that they have legitimate grievances; let us help them to reform things. Two very popular works which express this spirit are Neil Postman's and Charles Weingartner's *Teaching as a Subversive Activity* and George Leonard's *Education and Ecstasy*.

In the introduction to *Teaching as a Subversive Activity*, Postman and Weingartner summarize in brief the list of complaints about public schools, in a revealing way:

> The institution we call "school" is what it is because we made it that way. If it is irrelevant, as Marshall McLuhan says; if it shields children from reality, as Norbert Wiener says; if it educates for obsolescence, as John Gardner says; if it does not develop intelligence, as Jerome Bruner says; if it is based on fear, as John Holt says; if it avoids the promotion of significant learning, as Carl Rogers said; if it punishes creativity and independence, as Edgar Freidenberg says; if, in short, it is not doing what needs to be done, it can be changed; it *must* be changed. It can be changed, we believe, because there are so many wise men who, in one way or another, have offered us clear, intelligent, and new ideas to use, and as long as these ideas and the alternatives they suggest are available, there is no reason to abandon hope.[11]

This passage is revealing in several ways of the kind of reform spirit I am attempting to describe. First, there is that ubiquitous reformist "we." There is no mention of class structure or class interest, no sense of the dominant historical considerations in the development of public education which help explain the forms and purposes of the school system. The important social, political, and economic ways in which the system is successful are not discussed. The standard complaints are listed without qualification (for example, public school may shield children from some reality, but as in the working of the "hidden curriculum," there is an abundance of significant reality in the school); these complaints are given punch by citing as eclectic a bunch of authorities as one can find, from McLuhan to Goodman to Gardner. (The idea is that "everyone" sees the failure—so if you're dubious about "romantic radicals" like Goodman and Holt, you can trust a pillar of the Establishment like former HEW Secretary Gardner; and if Friedenberg is soft and humanistic, you certainly can believe respectable scientists like Wiener and Bruner. Of course, McLuhan isn't as "hot" these days as he was when Postman and Weingartner wrote *Teaching as a Subversive Activity,* which is a little dampening for the "with it" tone of the book, since McLuhan is a prime intellectual inspiration.)

No explanation is given of why the schools are as bad as the authors claim they are, other than that "we" made them that way. Also, almost all of the specified defects have to do with the effect of the dominant school methods on creativity, intelligence, and originality. The authors see the old education as creating "passive, acquiescent, dogmatic, intolerant, authoritarian, inflexible, conservative personalities who desperately need to resist change in an effort to keep their illusion of certainty intact."[12] This seems to me a curiously superficial characterization in the face of the obsessive American search for a certain sort of change and newness—moving to new places, the "democratic-relativist" attitude which makes it very bad taste to appear dogmatically certain or not agree that one person's opinion is as good as anybody else's.

But, whatever the range of personalities that actually emerge from the schools, the kind described is certainly a bad way to be, especially when our technological age with "its drastically changing future" will demand all sorts of intellectual flexibility and new concepts—"intellectual strategies for nuclear-space-age survival."[13] The "new education" aims to develop nothing less than a "new kind of person, one who—as a result of internalizing a different series of concepts—is an actively inquiring, flexible, creative, innovative, tolerant, liberal personality."[14]

The "super-reformism" of this perspective consists in the great scope of the claim concerning the fantastic effects that will result from a particular *educational method change*. Postman and Weingartner find this elixir of "new kinds of persons" in "new ideas"—which turn out to be a pretentious gimmick called the "inquiry method," theoretically (so to speak) grounded in a pastiche of bad philosophy and pretentiously phrased common sense taken from McLuhan and general semantics. (The inquiry method seems to be the idea that teachers should teach by asking good questions which they themselves don't know the answers to, and letting the curriculum develop from that.)

George Leonard's *Education and Ecstasy* does not focus on talking to teachers as *Teaching as a Subversive Activity* does, and is even more sweeping in its pretensions and its vision, but it offers the same conception of a fantastic transformation to be wrought by changes in education proper. Leonard, a former *Look* magazine editor and Esalen Institute vice-president, offers a similar critique of public schools, similarly ignoring any analysis of the social and historical roots and functions of the system. His vision is learning as the goal of life; but learning that will be constant ecstacy, helpfully defined as "ananda, the ultimate delight." (If this doesn't help, try the idea that solving a mathematical problem and making love are experiences in the same order of things, sharing common ecstacy.)[15]

His gimmick is a combination of groovy technology, brain-wave controls, teaching machines, and encounter groups. Postman and Weingartner claimed for their "inquiry method," that "like the locomotive, light bulb, and radio, its impact will be unique and revolutionary."[16] Leonard, approving Friedenberg and Goodman for their cries against dehumanization (although never confronting the social and political dimensions of their critique) faults them for not seeing the marvelous opportunities for unlimited transformation. He writes: "Distrusting science, they often fail to credit recent experimental work in human learning that shows real reform is practical, not visionary."[17] (It should be noted that the terms "practical" and "visionary" have no connotation of limits imposed by political power, class interest, indeed, the state of our knowledge of psychology, but only of electronics technology and what Leonard extrapolates wildly from some highly questionable biological and psychological experiments which he reports uncritically, unknowledgably, and breathlessly.[18])

The claim is that some fairly simple and easily "doable" reforms can universally transform education. Leonard offers us the hope that six successful experimental schools along with a lot of publicity "could transform education everywhere." (And I hasten to add, don't forget the old Yiddish proverb "If God wills it, even a broom can shoot." However, without God, maybe we better just sweep.) But more than this, it won't be just some better education that will result, but "new kinds of people" or the combinations of Archimedes, Handel, and Nietzsche which Leonard says is the way every child starts out—and presumably will remain, with a life "of an endless series of ecstatic moments stretch[ing] before him."[19]

From the height of such cosmic visions, the conception of educational reform represented by the two-year existence of the First Street School in New York, whose story forms the content of George Dennison's marvelous *The Lives of Children,* might seem a bit unimaginative and lacking in daring. Dennison shares the general critique of the public schools that is voiced by the entire radical reform spectrum. Perhaps because the school Dennison worked in was in a poor urban area and was composed of "failed" children, many of whom came from poor black and Puerto

Rican families, the author is able to give a concrete feeling of the complexity of the lives of children in a real America, not in some projected magic land of electronic learning, constant ecstacy, and new kinds of people resulting from an "inquiry method." The damage he found wrought on his students was only more extreme than usual, not qualitatively exceptional. He expresses a sense of reform in education which seems realistically limited but hopeful.

> Life in our country is chaotic and corrosive, and the time of childhood for many millions is difficult and harsh. It will not be an easy matter to bring our berserk technology under control, but we *can* control the environment of the schools. It is a relatively small environment and has always been structured by deliberation. If, as parents, we were able to take as our concern not the instruction of our children, but the lives of our children, we would find that our schools could be used in a powerfully regenerative way.[20]

The question for all reform that aims to have truly radical effects is how practical such aims are. The reasons why the structuring of schools is as it is, and what forces are opposed to the kinds of radical liberating transformations Dennison asks for, are important to understand, and this entails an inquiry into the complex relation of school reform movements to larger movements for social reform within the whole society. (This point will be greatly expanded in the discussions in the last chapter.)

Dennison does not attempt to analyze the historical and social roots of the dominant system or the relation of education to the social structure. He looks directly at the experience of one small school which lived the kind of libertarian education theory this chapter has described. To that extent, Dennison's main concern is with the actual pedagogy and theory of free school methods, rather than the social and political analysis of reform.

He emphasizes the obvious failures of the school system,

partly because so many of the children in the school were "failures." The public school system is faulted for its most definitive characteristics.

> Testing, grading, seating arrangements according to the teacher's convenience, predigested textbooks, public address systems, guarded corridors and closed rooms, attendance records, punishments, truant officers—all this belongs to an environment of coercion and control. Such an environment has not consulted the needs of normal growth, or the special needs of those whose growth has already been impaired.[21]

The ideal theory of a free school is stated simply and clearly by Dennison in terms of what was actually done at the First Street School.

> We made much of freedom of choice and freedom of movement; and of reality of encounter between teachers and students; and of the continuum of persons, by which we understood that parents, teachers, friends, neighbors, the life of the streets, form all one substance in the experience of the child. We abolished tests and grades and Lesson Plans. We abolished Superiors, too—all that petty and disgusting pecking order of the school bureaucracy which contributes nothing to the wisdom of teachers and still less to the growth of the child. We abolished homework (unless asked for), we abolished the category of truant. We abolished, in short, all of the things which constitute a merely external order; and in doing this, we laid bare the deeper motivations and powers which contribute to what might be called "internal order," i.e., a structuring of activities based upon the child's innate desire to learn, and upon . . . the needs of children, the natural authority of adults, the power of moral suasion . . . and the deep attachment and interest which adults inevitably feel toward the lives of children.[22]

Several very significant points about free school theory are brought out by Dennison's perceptions of what happened at his school. One crucial area of dispute in reform theory is the role of adults. Some formulations of the theory seem to deny any significant active role to adults or any place for authority and direction. (The response to the authoritarianism of the public schools often generates bad conscience about any sort of influence, especially when a simple conception of the notion of the child naturally tending toward his own good in all aspects of life dominates.) It is especially this area of free schools that generates the most anxiety, even from libertarian-inclined teachers and parents. The Pollyannaish quality of some free school talk which critics emphasize arises largely from impressions observers receive from both theory and practice in this area.

Dennison catches the reality of the world underneath much hopeful rhetoric about "freedom" and "love." Perhaps his training as a Gestalt therapist and experience with severely disturbed young people as well as his experience as a teacher with the poor and "disadvantaged" children of the First Street School have deepened his realism in comparison with the breathless and naïve optimism often reflected in free school theory. Dennison's sense of real and gritty difficulty is a most salutary theoretical tone, and, turning the accusation around, makes much of the official rhetoric of public school defenders seem Pollyannaish in its own right.

In a passage referring specifically to sexual freedom but more generally applicable, Dennison observes that the search of troubled young people is for *wholeness*.

> They do not want to lie and evade and suffer guilt, but to affirm themselves in the largest possible harmony of self and society, passion and intellect, duty and pleasure. . . . They know very well . . . that where sanction is involved, the attitudes of a few teachers are mere grains on a sandy shore. The problem begins in infancy and runs through the whole of society. . . . All he [the teacher] can do is

cease to attempt to control the young. Beyond this he can ally himself with the student's quest for wholeness. Here the teacher's own quest for wholeness is extremely valuable. Life being what it is, there is no man who can stand before the young and acclaim himself an exemplar of liberated energies. . . .

At best, the libertarian can demonstrate reason, faith, generosity, and hope, struggling against the damages he himself has already sustained and which he hopes to mitigate in the lives of his students.[23]

Love, one of the favorite concepts of free school theory and of the counter-culture which finds the Summerhillian philosophy so congenial, is another problem for the theory of radical school reform on which Dennison speaks in a refreshingly unsentimental manner. He stresses the importance of conflict, its inevitability, and even its desirability. This is far from that part of the free school spirit that minimizes conflict, avoids hostility, and, indeed, any form of "negativity"—which sometimes seems to mean all disagreement, criticism, openly voiced antagonism, or passionate dislike.

Dennison's view is

that frequently, the "love" of such enthusiasts is actually inhibited aggression. But this is by the way. The point itself is worth making: we cannot give love to children. If we do feel love, it will be for some particular child, or some few; and we will not give *it,* but give ourselves, because we are much more in the love than it is in us. What we *can* give to all children is attention, forbearance, patience, care, and above all, justice. The last is certainly a form of love; it is—precisely—love in a form that *can* be given, given without distinction to all, since just this is the anatomy of justice: it is the self-conscious, thoroughly generalized human love of humankind. This can be seen negatively in the fact that where a child (past infancy) can survive, grow, and if not flourish, do well enough in an environment that is largely without love, his development in an environment that is largely without justice, will be profoundly disturbed.[24]

Combining these theoretical observations with Dennison's remarks on the "natural authority" of adults, I want again to point up a comparison of this tough free school realism with accusations of romanticism coming from public school "realists" who, even while admitting the need for some improvement, defend the system, its compulsory attendance and curriculum, the need for some form of "hidden curriculum" socialization. A graphic way of doing this will be to quote Dennison's account of his beginning to teach reading to José, an illiterate thirteen-year-old Puerto Rican boy who had a record of six years of failure in the public schools (and who can represent the millions of other children who, to a greater or less degree, sustain damage within that system).

After explaining the human relation that had grown up between José and himself, and noting how his own and José's relatives' desire that he learn to read were openly expressed, Dennison writes:

And so I did not wait for José to decide for himself. When I thought the time was ripe, I insisted that we begin our lessons. My insistence carried a great deal of weight with him, since for reasons of his own he respected me. Too, his volition, in any event, could arise only from a background in which I myself already figured, with my own interests and my own manifestation of an adult concern he was accustomed to everywhere but in school. He did *not* feel that his own motives were no concern of mine. No child feels this. This belongs to the hang-ups of adolescence and the neuroses of the hippies. To a child, the motives of adults belong quite simply to the environment. They are like icebergs or attractive islands: one navigates between or heads straight for them. The child's own motives are similarly projected outward, they become occasions for dissimulation or closer contact. It is because of this that both affection and straightforward conflict come so easily. They come inevitably, and they belong together, to the teacher-learning experience.[25]

An account like this expresses in a concrete way necessary modifications to the abstract formulation of free school theory which is prevalent (this point will appear graphically in the next chapter's descriptions of theory and practice in the variety of existing schools). It also begins to raise some of the dilemmas about authority, the difficult question of curriculum (Is there anything not totally subjective to be said on what is worth learning? Is the *experience* of "learning" all that counts?), and the associated question of "relevance." (These problems will be discussed in detail later in the book, especially in Chapter 4, which deals with issues of curriculum and methods.)

One further point to note concerning disputes and differences of emphasis within radical school reform theory: Dennison doesn't claim to have discovered a new method. He doesn't proclaim hot new ideas, new theories of the mind or the spirit, or the fantastic results to be expected from new electronic equipment. He credits old John Dewey, Neill, the anarchists, and Tolstoy for sound insight into the relations of education and freedom.[26] This isn't to say that there are no new insights to be gained, nor that experience and increased scientific knowledge can't help us understand more. A point worth making is that education is not the sort of problem amenable to a sudden new discovery, either of theory or of techniques. This is crucial to understanding the differences among the various reform perspectives. If problems of education and youth were like the problems of finding a cure for cancer, then the search for a new idea or new technique or a new theory or a new discovery in psychology would make sense as a path of reform. This is the preferred American way of seeing problems—as accessible to a concentrated input of new ideas and new technology (good old American ingenuity and know-how). That education is not this kind of problem is part of the import of Dennison's book, in sharp contrast to the spirit of George Leonard's book.

I think this is a very important point, worth clarifying at some length. Speaking roughly, we can divide problems into two broad classes. One is the class of those problems about which we have a good idea of a solution, perhaps not the very best possible, but one that meets the value criteria it is reasonable to impose. The difficulty in reaching the goal comes in implementing the solution or solutions. The second class includes those problems for which we know of no solution that is even satisfactory, let alone ideal or best. We may not even have a good idea of what the solution *could* be like. An example of the first class would be the problems of starvation and serious malnutrition which exists for millions in the United States. We know what good nutrition is; we know how to raise enough food. The problem is one of social, political, and economic causes of poverty, distribution of income and wealth, social conscience, economic interests. We know how to solve the starvation problem. The existence of the problem does not come from lack of satisfactory ideas concerning the causes or possible solutions. Examples of the second sort of problem are the explanation (before the twentieth century) of the sun's action of giving off light and heat in the quantities we know or the capacity of young children to learn their language in the way they do. Before the development of the theory of nuclear physics and Einstein's discovery of "$E = mc^2$," no process known in our experience could even begin to explain what the sun does. Only the development of the new concepts and theory of nuclear and thermonuclear reactions made a solution possible. As for children learning language, we simply don't know and are only beginning to be able to move toward an adequate formulation of the problem. For reformers like Dennison, experience and knowledge leads them to place the problem of education in the first class. This isn't to say that new ideas aren't always helpful or that there need be no more progress in learning theory. The point is simply that education is a very human activity and human experience in this area is extensive; that, as Dennison writes, "our system of public education is a horrendous, life-destroying mess"; and that we know "solutions," like the First Street School and the knowledge and dedication and personal care that informed it. This doesn't mean there weren't any problems or that each child became an Einstein or a Jane Austen; simply that compared with what happens to most children in normal public schools, what happened at the First Street School was much, much better.

Some reformers like Leonard or Postman and Weingartner seem to conceive the problems as more of the second class (the comparison isn't exact, just significant). As with Postman and Weingartner's insistence on all the new ideas (like McLuhan) that *now* give us reason to change and create a wonderful education for everyone, and Leonard's super-psycho-electronic "learning domes" of the imagined John F. Kennedy School of the year 2001, it is only *now* that we have the real possibility of solutions. Really good education was waiting until these great discoveries came along.

This is not simply a theoretical point. A personal experience of mine is a good indication of how some free school people share this "new idea" sense of the problem and its solution. A group of free school publicists were setting up the first large national gathering of free school people, and naturally a planned program would be anathema to the spirit of free education. Someone connected with the *Whole Earth Catalogue* (whose spirit matches that of a large part of the free school movement) suggested greeting everyone with the announcement that the conference would be run as an "alternatives in education" game. People would be assigned to teams (they would be able to

defect, of course); the "gurus" expected at the conference
—Holt, Dennison, Goodman, etc.—would be the judges.
Each team would "brainstorm" and come up with its solution—the perfect school. They would act it out, and the
winning team would remain for a day to perform its solution for the media. A protest was made to the effect that,
as I just laid out, education is much more a "class one"
than a "class two" problem, that we have had for many
years very good conceptions of how libertarian schools
could exist, and that we have had good reason to think
that they would be far superior in many ways—even if
not perfect—to the badness we saw in the public school
compulsory authoritarian method. When it comes to acting
out solutions, we all know how groovy a perfect free school
would be—freedom, initiative, self-motivation, good personal relations, creativity—plus joyous learning of reading,
science, etc. The superiority of libertarian schools rests, as
Dennison points out, on the morality of the issue and on
our restrained sense of how much better the situation
would be, rather than on the perfection of it. In fact, as
with an issue like starvation in America, the real problems
of educational reform are social, political, economic, and
ideological. The constraints on having the reasonably good
learning situations that are possible are deep-rooted in the
needs of the particular social, economic, and political
structures of our social order. Therefore, the fundamental
issue for educational reform is the understanding of and
struggle with the hindrances to putting into effect the not
terribly complicated or cosmic or new radical reform ideas
which have been around for a good while. The answer to
this was that the game would "overleap" all those political
and social problems (the concept of "overleap" was
ascribed to Buckminster Fuller by the adherent); that is, as
Leonard claimed, if you showed people the *new* solution,
the groovy, perfect school, everyone would just *do* it,
"overleaping" all those depressing political-social-economic-
ideological "hang-ups." Presumably, the idea was that, like

the problem of the sun's action, once people were shown a solution that worked they would just accept it because it would be so obviously the answer.

One theme in this chapter has been to emphasize the context of the educational reform problem; to ask about the extent to which one must go beyond specifically pedagogical discussions. Even Dennison sometimes appears to short-cut this underlying question, as when, emphasizing how simple the running of a primary school is, provided it is small, he writes: "The present quagmire of public education is entirely the result of unworkable centralization and the lust for control that permeates every bureaucratic institution."[27]

This is importantly wrong. If the implication is that public education is an egregious failure, then there is room for debate. Until we get clear on why centralization took place, and whether the forms and functions of public education are significantly different where there is less centralization (the experience of New York is somewhat traumatic), and on why public education can be seen to have done very well a particular job (socialization by the "hidden curriculum") and is still doing this job, although experiencing mounting difficulties, we will be misconceiving the significance of radical school reform and its potential.[28] To ascribe some abstract "lust for control" to all bureaucracies can obscure the analysis of who gets controlled and who does the controlling of the bureaucracy and for what purposes and in whose interests. It does often seem that bureaucracies have a life of their own and develop within themselves job interests, petty tyrannies, and the like, but this truth should be placed in the perspective of a broad social rationality.

It is more sound to observe, as Dennison does elsewhere in his book, that "the more one pursues this thought [that no school at all is better than a bad school, but "no school" amounts to neglect], the more it becomes apparent that the deeper problems of primary education cannot be solved in the schools."[29] This observation is just as pertinent when applied to high-school age people, on whom the society and its roles, jobs, wars, etc., impinge so immediately. The implication of this perception is to emphasize the limitations of thinking of educational reform primarily in terms of pedagogy and methods, as many reformers, even radical school reformers, prefer to do. After all, such people are involved in educational institutions and feel most comfortable there. But comfort and good analysis are not often found together in our world, and understanding the limits and possibilities of educational reform means confronting directly that aspect of reform theory that goes beyond education proper into the social realities—war, racism, poverty, sexism, alienation, power, wealth, and so forth.

Having discussed the "freedom" theory of school reform, I want to go on to a description of the free school movement as it actually exists, what the schools are like in their variety, their aspirations, their achievements and failures, and the dilemmas as they appear now in the period of rapid growth and change of the young movement. Finally, at the conclusion of the book, I will return to an extensive discussion of the basic political questions just touched on.

NOTES

1 EMILE DURKHEIM, *Education and Sociology* (New York: The Free Press, 1956), pp. 71, 123.

2 A. S. NEILL, *Summerhill: A Radical Approach to Child Rearing* (New York: Hart Publishing Co., 1960), p. 4.

3 Ibid., p. 111.

4 Ibid., p. 161.

5 Ibid., p. 297.

6 CHARLES SILBERMAN, *Crisis in the Classroom: The Remaking of American Education* (New York: Random House, 1970), p. 10.

7 JOHN HOLT, *How Children Learn* (New York: Dell Publishing Co., 1970), p. 107.

8 Ibid., pp. 184, 185.

9 Ibid., p. 187.

10 Ibid., p. 189.

11 NEIL POSTMAN and CHARLES WEINGARTNER, *Teaching as a Subversive Activity* (New York: Delacorte Press, 1969), p. xiv.

12 Ibid., pp. 217–18.

13 Ibid., p. 218.

14 Ibid.

15 GEORGE LEONARD, *Education and Ecstasy* (New York: Delacorte Press, 1968), p. 21.

16 POSTMAN and WEINGARTNER, *Teaching as a Subversive Activity*, p. 27.

17 LEONARD, *Education and Ecstasy*, p. 215.

18 For example, Leonard reports, without critique or qualification, some experiments of several years ago that made claims about the connection of RNA and memory. Referring to the same claims, the recent volume *Biology and the Future of Man*, ed. Philip Handler (New York: Oxford University Press, 1970), a survey report of the National Academy of Sciences on the current state of the sciences, states: "These claims are presently regarded with great suspicion and are taken seriously by only a small group of investigators" (p. 415).

19 LEONARD, *Education and Ecstasy*, pp. 232–33.

20 GEORGE DENNISON, *The Lives of Children* (New York: Random House, 1969), p. 6.

21 Ibid., p. 97.

22 Ibid., p. 98.

23 Ibid., pp. 103, 104.

24 Ibid., p. 116.

25 Ibid., p. 112.

26 Tolstoy's writings can be found in the volume *Tolstoy on Education* (Chicago: University of Chicago Press, Phoenix Books, 1968), and a good selection of anarchist writings on education can be found in the anthology *Patterns of Anarchy*, ed. Leonard Krimerman and Lewis Perry (New York: Doubleday & Co., Anchor Books, 1966).

27 DENNISON, *Lives of Children*, p. 9.

28 For an important discussion of this question, see the recent book by Michael Katz, *Class, Bureaucracy, and Schools: The Illusion of Educational Change in America* (New York: Praeger Publishers, 1971).

29 DENNISON, *Lives of Children*, p. 213.

2 · LET A HUNDRED FLOWERS BLOOM
Free Schools in America

McKinney School believes that children want to learn and strives to ensure that the child's natural enthusiasm for learning doesn't atrophy and die. Adults often get in the way. Their role needs to be one of providing atmosphere and means. We respect the child's desire to learn and be responsible for himself by including him as a partner in the learning process. He is free to participate in choice of subject matter and learning projects. . . .

Children are naturally quite capable and even extraordinary human beings. We believe that a minimum amount of encouragement will add up to an overall sense of freedom and purpose.

So we appeal to each student as a resource guide as well as a learner for he is the best source of information about himself. We emphasize that he learns to do something well in which he is interested. This is how we strive to help him to build a positive self-image, establish an identity and gain a feeling of adequacy and competence. All of this takes place in an atmosphere of community in which students and teachers learn from each other.*

* From the brochure of the McKinney School, a free school in San Mateo, California for students aged five to sixteen.

Through hundreds of variations, this message is conveyed by almost all free school brochures. In practice, this means doing away with all of the public school apparatus of imposed disciplines and punishments, lock-step age gradings and time-period divisions, homework, frequent tests and grades and report cards, rigid graded curriculum, standardized classrooms, dominated and commanded by one teacher with 25 to 35 students under his or her power. It also implies a rejection of the standardized forms of teacher training and credentialing, a desire to experiment with new types of buildings and space arrangements, and serious attempts to involve parents and other community people in all phases of teaching and school governance.

Five years ago there were about thirty schools that could be classified as free schools. These included some very progressive schools founded during the "progressive education" movement (e.g., Peninsula School in Menlo Park, California, founded in 1925); some Summerhillian schools (e.g., Lewis-Wadhams, in Westport, New York), and some recently founded black community schools (e.g., Roxbury Community School, in Boston). Then, as now, the black community schools are characterized by considerably more structure and more concern with directly teaching traditional skills than are the typical free schools (exemplified in the brochure just quoted). Despite this emphasis these schools are clearly part of the alternative school development because of their determined and articulate opposition to the public school system and its effect on black children and because of the political movement toward "open education" (even if this pedagogical movement is not as total as in the white-middle-class-based free schools). (For an insightful analysis of this particular question of new schools attempting to meet the needs of poor minority groups, see Jonathan Kozol's recent book, *Free Schools*.)

In 1967 and 1968, 20 to 30 new schools were started annually. Nineteen sixty-nine saw the beginning of the surge of free school growth with the founding of around 60 to 80. Over 150 were founded in 1970, and the figure for the 1971–1972 school year should be well over 200. (It should be noted that this rather remarkable growth comes at a time when there is an actual decline in the number of traditional private schools, and when the number of applications to even very prestigious places like Phillips Andover Academy has declined noticeably.)

The growth of the schools has been accompanied by the development of several regional switchboards and a national New Schools Exchange in Santa Barbara, California, which publishes a bimonthly newsletter. Regional newsletters are distributed, and there have been regional and national conferences and "festivals of alternatives." Most indicative of official recognition, courses on alternative schools have begun to appear at schools of education throughout the country. (Kozol's book contains an extensive listing of regional switchboards and other free school resources.)

Some aggregate statistics on free schools:[1]

91% are day schools; 9% have boarding students. (Most of the boarding schools are explicitly Summerhillian.)

51% are elementary; 29% are high schools; 20% are combination elementary-high schools. (Some elementary schools, especially those started by young parents, contain only a small age range, say, six- and seven-year-olds, with plans to let the range of the school grow with the children.)

The average size for free schools is approximately 33 students. About two-thirds of the schools have enrollments of less than 40; and most of the small number of schools that have enrollments of more than 100 are minority group community schools or street academies. The small size is explained mainly by the conscious commitment to an intimate community, something that can only be achieved in small groups. Many free school people value the idea that everyone in the school knows everyone else fairly well; that staff people can relate to each other and to all of the children. Often, free schools refuse to expand beyond 30 or 40 students because of the feeling that some of the most valued qualities of the free school atmosphere would be diluted.

For the community schools, like Michael's Community School in Milwaukee (290 students) or the New School for Children in Boston (140 students), being a force in the community and involving relatively large numbers of people is a much higher priority than in the more typical free schools, and so the importance of the warmth and intimacy of the very small community is lessened.

Income and expenditure:

The main source of income, as one would expect, is tuition. Four-fifths of the schools charge tuition, mainly on a sliding scale. Because of this sliding scale idea, the concept of "scholarship" is rather fuzzy in most schools. Usually people pay what they say they can afford; and the hope is that there will be enough high tuition payers to balance the people who can pay little or nothing. This is important since free schools do not want to be elite private schools providing a special form of education for the class of people who can afford to pay the very high expenses characteristic of most traditional private schools. The normal sliding tuition range is about 0 to $800 per year.

The schools that do not charge tuition are almost all community schools and street academies based on poor and minority group constituencies. The intention of the organizers of such schools is to involve people who couldn't consider paying a real tuition. It is an important goal that the schools be true alternatives to the public system, rather than alternatives only for the wealthy who have traditionally had alternatives. Some of these schools have gotten substantial foundation help; others have successfully tapped state, federal, and local sources—poverty program agencies, youth services, Model Cities, and the like; others have gotten help from church groups, corporations, or local private gifts. These sources are difficult to obtain and very chancy. Some free schools started with the hope of getting outside support so that they could eliminate tuition and be true community schools, but have found this impossible and have had to begin charging tuition.

The money that does come in goes mainly for staff. Most free schools make do with astonishingly little. In terms of money expenses (as opposed to true value of services), approximately 30% of the schools have a per student yearly expenditure of below $300, with about 12% actually below $100 per student. The average yearly expenditure per student is a little below $600 per year. (This includes rent expenses, which are not included in the public school figures usually quoted.) Since the free school teacher-student ratio is around 1:5 rather than 1:25 to 1:30 as is common in the public schools, these expense figures are both impressive and depressing. What explains them is that many teachers work for almost nothing, many volunteers are used, and parents take on many functions of maintenance and administration that cost money in public school systems.

Of course, such aggregate figures don't tell anything about the variety and character of the actual schools. The really important dimensions of description can only be approached through concrete accounts. For example, since free schools are generally grass-roots efforts of the consumers of education, so to speak, rather than institutions organized by state-approved professionals, the processes and difficulties of free school formation are of great interest to anyone interested in how people can form and manage their own institutions. Related to this is the issue of governance. In the public school system parents, students, and teachers are ordinarily not involved in the actual governance of the schools. An administrative structure of principals, vice-principals, and on up through supervisors, superintendents, and elected or appointed school boards is common. Parents, along with all other eligible voters, may help to choose the school board, but this is not meaningful participation. At the school level, it would be naïve to consider student councils and PTAs as participants in governance. In free schools, parents, teachers, and students share and exercise real power. How does this work?

As described in Chapter 1, free school theory is especially critical of the "hidden curriculum" of the public schools: the forms of control and regimentation which manifest themselves in the various discipline and punishment systems, the system of grades and tests, competitive rewards, etc. In theory, freedom should take care of questions of motivation, content of curriculum, discipline, and organization of time and process. In practice, how do free schools handle these issues?

In the United States there has always been a small part of the population that has opted out of the public school system. The parochial (mainly Catholic) schools take by far the largest number of these. But there has always been a clientele for secular private schools, usually middle, upper middle, or upper class families that want superior education to prepare their offspring for the good colleges as well as to ensure that they meet the right people and develop attitudes befitting an elite. (The spirit of Groton, Exeter, St. Paul's, or Choate, to pick the most prominent examples, has an obvious and important social dimension.) The people who start free schools are generally not in the group that traditionally has supported private schools for reasons of social position or social mobility. By the very nature of the free school philosophy, it could be safely inferred that most people drawn to free schools are liberal to radical in their political, social, and/or cultural orientations. They tend to hold the kind of egalitarian, anti-elitist views that in America have been strongly supportive of the public school system, at least in its ideal form.

The fact that an increasing number of people with this perspective now find themselves founding their own schools in direct philosophical confrontation with the public school (a very different situation from traditional private schools) is a sign of a profound and growing disillusionment with the public school system, a disillusionment not confined to groups like the urban blacks who can clearly see the hurt done to their children—the obvious failures of the school.

The past fifty years have seen the formation of a number of private progressive schools. In terms of progressive ideas on pedagogy, this older progressive movement has a good deal of overlap with the contemporary free school development. (The discussion in Chapter 4 of some of John Dewey's analysis of the disputes that arose during the early progressive movement will show this clearly.) It is quite remarkable how the current educational arguments echo those of over sixty years ago. But the progressive schools that grew from the Deweyan movement were in the main started by professional educators, just as the movement to make public schools more progressive received much of its support within the profession. (A good history of this development is Lawrence Cremin's *The Transformation of the Schools: Progressivism in American Education 1876–1957*.) The distortions and corruptions that happened to originally progressive ideas that were adopted by some public schools is a sad subject. The private progressive schools, it can be claimed, did achieve high educational standards, and with the liberal and progressive pedagogy which the movement espoused. But the support for these schools came from a small segment of the middle class, and the schools eventually became well established and respectable, providing quality education and college preparation at very high cost. Then, as now, facilities were excellent; teachers were highly qualified and well paid. The schools are not grass-roots operations; they are very professional in all ways. They do not publish journals or have conferences to challenge the public schools and attempt to convince more and more people about the damage young people sustain in them. (Some examples that I have in mind are Putney School in Vermont; Shady Hill School in Cambridge; Walden School in New York City; Miquon School in Philadelphia.) These schools, though much more progressive than the traditional private academy, serve a small and affluent class, and they have not made significant efforts to change this situation. Therefore, although there is a significant overlap between the older progressive spirit and the new wave of free schools, and although some of the older schools are in a process of significant change (e.g., Miquon School has opened a "free high school"), the older established progressive schools are not included in the development that is the subject of this book. (Whether the free school development will take the path of the old movement which had a comparable crusading spirit in its younger days is a serious question to keep in mind.)

How Free Schools Begin

The New School in Plainfield, Vermont, founded in 1966, is an elementary school (ages 5–13) in a lovely rural setting, and is one of the oldest of the current free school wave.

The school was started by a half-dozen families in response to a despair about the local public schools. The original group of interested families was very large—perhaps twenty or thirty couples. Many of these were not actually interested in starting an alternative school, but rather in working within the public school system for more interesting and humane education. At that time private schools were under the supervision of the local school boards, and the parents proposed to the board that they become an "experimental classroom" within the public school system. Though the plan had the backing of the State Department of Education (which has been consistently forward-looking and liberal in its official policies if not in their actual application), it was turned down, out of hand, by the local board. It's possible that no board in the state would have accepted it, but in Plainfield the effort to liberalize education was simply another battle in the long town-gown fight. Viewed as an adjunct of Goddard, the parents were treated rudely, harassed, and ultimately threatened with truancy suits. Ironically enough, when they turned to Goddard for support, they were also rejected. The administration and education faculty at the college all felt that it was proper to work within the structure of the public schools for educational change.

In despair, the half-dozen families, which had been at the center of the effort to start the school, met together to decide what to do next—abandon the enterprise or find a new strategy. During that meeting of six or eight people, one family donated its garage to house the school, another offered to meet any budget deficit up to three thousand dollars, and the group decided that if there were fifteen children who wanted to attend the school, it would be worth starting. At some nadir in the planning process that minimum number dropped to nine, but when the school actually opened, there were twenty-six students.

The founders of the New School had sharp differences of opinion, but circumstances prevented a split.

One of the parents suggested that had the school been in

a more populated area, it would have split into two schools fairly early, one following old-fashioned progressive school lines (Dalton, Putney), the other applying some sort of mixture of the principles of A. S. Neill, Leicestershire schools, and the romantic anarchists in education. Plainfield, however, could not support two alternative schools, there was not—and still is not—any alternative to public school other than the New School, and so parents with differing points of view were forced to adjust their differences or leave.

The Community School in Santa Barbara, California, is another example of a parent-teacher organized elementary school, charging tuition and based on a progressive white middle-class group of mainly young parents. Its origins were somewhat different from the New School's since the founders were already involved in a free school in the city when they decided to start their own school. This situation shows something about the process of participation in free schools. People often have differing ideas about the school, even within the generally shared free school framework; and these differences frequently lead to serious conflicts which can result in splits within schools and the spinning off of new schools.

A teacher in the Community School describes its beginning:

The Santa Barbara Community School was conceived in the spring of 1969 by two parents who were involved with another free school. One of these parents was the secretary for the school, the other taught dancing there. They were dissatisfied with the free school they were in for two reasons. The first had to do with the fact that the school was attended by children from four to sixteen. It happened that many of the older children, the high-school aged students, were what might be called "problems." They were "into drugs," they had serious emotional problems or problems with their families, and/or they had had such bad experiences in the public schools that they were determinedly unmotivated towards anything academic or even active. It was felt by some of the staff, and specifically the two parents mentioned above, that this group of the older students created a bad atmosphere in the school, that they were undesirable as models for the younger children, and that they absorbed too much of the energies of the staff, to the detriment of the younger children. The second reason that these parents, and several of the staff members of the free school were dissatisfied with the school was the director. They felt that his personality was divisive and that, largely due to him, the staff was not able to function well and deal with the problems that faced it. So these two decided that they would try to form their own school which would be for younger children only, with the idea that as these children got older the school would gradually develop a high-school program.

They approached the kindergarten teacher who they felt was a good teacher and one of the few people there who was able to function despite the chaos and bad feelings. She agreed to come along and suggested two other teachers, one of them the free school's art teacher. The five women proceeded to hire four more full-time teachers (all men) and three apprentice teachers. Of the full-time teachers three had previously taught in the free school, three had taught at the college level, three had taught in public school, and one was a professional carpenter. Responsibilities were divided in this way: one teacher and one apprentice for the preschool and kindergarten children; one teacher and one apprentice for the first, second, and third grades; one teacher and one apprentice for the fourth, fifth, and sixth grades; two teachers for the junior high aged students; one art teacher; one shop teacher; and one science teacher. The school was funded by a combination of tuitions and donations which had been made by the founders and other members of their family, so the teachers and the teacher aides were all able to be paid. The teachers were guaranteed $450 per month and the apprentices $200.

The Second Foundation School is a kindergarten through twelfth grade urban free school in Minneapolis, Minnesota. It was founded by teachers from local public schools and colleges in 1970. Judy Vincent, one of the founding teachers, describes its origins in an interview:

Q: Who were the people who started the school?

JV: The people who started the school were Bob and Judy Vincent, Chuck and Judy Sigmund, Mary Lunde, and another couple we knew.

Q: How did you meet these people?

JV: Well, I taught at Edina Senior High School with Mary Lunde. Chuck and Bob both taught at North Hennepin Junior College. Mary Lunde and I decided we were tired of taking the garbage we had to take from the administration. We had the first meeting. There were five of us and three other people who lost interest after the first meeting.

Q: How did you decide what kind of school Second Foundation would be?

JV: We had read John Holt's books and a lot of other things, so we had an idea of what we wanted to do. We didn't want to have grading, mandatory attendance, detention hall, passes and bells and all that jazz.

We decided to set up as a nonprofit corporation so that we would have legal status in the state of Minnesota. We looked into the state laws for private schools. Then we found a sympathetic lawyer who incorporated the school as a nonprofit corporation.

Initially it was just going to be a junior high and high school, because that was the group with which most of us had dealt. But then the Sigmunds had two boys who were then four and five years old and they wanted to send them to a free school. They weren't thrilled about the other schools in the Twin Cities area. Then we decided to make it the entire spread from preschool through high school. We visited Wilson School where they have K through twelve and we were very much encouraged by that because it seemed to work very well —so we decided then.

In Santa Barbara, the organizers of the Community High School were already working in the free elementary school, but they had been especially interested in problems of high-school age young people. The school beginning is described by Tim Affleck, one of the founding directors.

In connection with Vietnam Moratorium activities, one of the organizers met the activist student body president from a local high school. The Community School building was offered for use as a "Moratorium Meeting Room." The success of this activity suggested to the students that it would be really valuable having a comfortable place for regular meetings of high-school people for discussing problems and socializing without customary adult supervision.

The directors of the Community School offered the students the steady use of the Community School facilities, as well as their own personal support. The small group decided to meet regularly on Friday nights. They called this weekly gathering the "American Dream Coffee Room" and hand-printed flyers encouraging other students from the city's schools to come and participate in "general meetings, some films, discussions, making a newspaper, coffee and whatever. Bring friends."

Attendance, fifteen or twenty at first, rapidly grew to forty or fifty (some nights up to eighty) in a few weeks. A loose structure to the evenings emerged. First there

would be announcements and discussion of school problems and issues like ecology or the eighteen-year-old vote
or other political questions, then films (the directors
helped the group procure these and supplied the pro-
jector) or speakers, and later music, folk dancing, and
talk around the fireplace, with coffee, cider, and cookies.

Out of the Friday night meetings came a seminar one
afternoon a week, Education and Society, in which the
students and the Community School directors tried to
put school problems into some perspective. Students
read and discussed books by John Holt, Edgar Friedenberg, Paul Goodman, and others. In addition, the directors talked about some of the ideas behind the founding
of the Community School (elementary) and how the
experiment was working.

By February, the fifty or so regular Friday night people had organized an after-school "free high school"
program. From the whole range of students' preferences
for subjects not available (or not adequately explored)
in their public schools, came this schedule:

Monday: 3:30 Drugs (some films)
         5:00 Sex Education

Tuesday: 3:30 Education and Society
         4:00 Women's Studies

Wednesday: 3:30 American History and Foreign Policy
           7:30 Ecology Meeting

Thursday: 3:30 Theater
          5:00 Strategies of Change and Nonviolence

Friday: 3:30 Religion
        6:00 Philosophy
        7:30 American Dream Coffee Room

Beginning at 3:30 PM each weekday, following the end of
our school day, the Santa Barbara Community School
offers a program open to all of the high-school students of
Santa Barbara. This program is entirely free of charge.

Its content reflects the interests of those students now participating.

The classes were taught by the directors and other interested people from the community. A former nurse taught sex education, a volunteer from the city Ecology Action Committee led the ecology class, and a woman instructor from University of California at Santa Barbara who was teaching a university course on Women's Studies helped start a high-school "women's group." Public school teachers were invited to participate (and occasionally did) in the education seminar. One teacher from the local Continuation School (a euphemism for the school where dropouts and trouble makers are sequestered until they are eighteen years of age) participated on a regular basis.

The guerrilla theater class presented a theater piece, which they themselves conceived and improvised, on the lawn of one of their high schools. The presentation dramatized (and protested) the administrative dismissal of a student member of the students' elected legislative council, and caused much consternation on the part of the school administration.

After a month or so of after-school classes, a small group of ten students felt they wanted a full-time alternative school program. This wish matched the directors' feelings that the Community School should include high-school aged students. However, the lower school facilities were plainly too small to accommodate more students and there was also the problem of no money readily available for such a project.

One of the directors had visited the much-publicized Parkway Project in Philadelphia, an experiment which confirmed the director's sense of the great possibilities of using the city itself as a classroom. By renting a small office for little money per month, the group felt they would have sufficient facilities. They could use the office as a central meeting place to arrange classes and have all-school gatherings, and then have classes in various other locations in and around the city.

Still, salaries for a paid staff would have made necessary a substantial tuition which would have excluded many students who expressed interest in joining the school. Since sources of private funds for radical school experiments are difficult if not impossible to come by, the directors felt it would be worthwhile to try to do a school with a predominantly volunteer staff. In order to achieve this, a university-Community School exchange program was proposed by the directors. Expenses involved would be minimal (gasoline, supplies, etc.) and volunteer tutor-teachers would receive academic credit from various departments at the university for their work at the school. The possible use of university facilities, the laboratories, recreational facilities, craft equipment, and meeting rooms, could be an important part of the "community as classroom."

The idea was presented to a sociology class on educational change at the University of California at Santa Barbara taught by Richard Flacks, a sociologist who had recently come to Santa Barbara. Over sixty students volunteered to tutor before there was any official announcement of solicitation of staff people. This number exceeded not only expectations but also the immediate need in as much as at the beginning there were few students. Two sociology seminars were organized, one for the twenty tutors actually to work in the school, and one for the new people who still wanted to be part of the project. The seminars were for credit and in them students discussed theoretical and practical problems of education and society as experienced through actual work in the project. Having this weekly class was considered important in developing staff unity and overcoming some of the obvious difficulties that a volunteer staff would necessarily present.

A storefront in the downtown area of the city was rented (the lower school building was uptown) and the high school officially opened on April 7, 1970, with an enrollment of twelve. By the end of the month the enrollment had jumped to forty-four, even though the school year was almost over. Four of the students were seniors in public high, having only a month to go to graduate.

Free schools, especially at the high-school level, often see themselves as exemplary. Although the numbers of students involved in any one school is tiny compared to the average public school, the participants in the free high schools definitely see themselves as developing a *model* that could be used by others, not simply doing a nice thing for themselves. They think that their ideals and dissatisfactions are shared by many other people, and that there would be a good response to the demonstration of the feasibility of starting and maintaining new schools expressing the ideals of free education.

In an account of the beginning of the New Community School, a high school in Oakland, founded in 1969, Steve Fisher, a staff member, expresses this theme clearly.

Insights into the nature of alternative community schools are best gained by conceiving these schools as organizing processes in which human and social problems are confronted and dealt with; simply to list courses or describe curricula misses the point. Course lists may be exotic, but they are no substitute for a community honestly facing social issues. The history of New Community School is as much a matter of what happens outside regular classes as inside.

New Community School opened for classes in a rather dingy but rent-free West Oakland YMCA in the fall of

1969. For more than half a year preceding this opening, staff and students met to formulate the philosophy and structure of the school. It was in this early formulating and organizing period that the basic character of the school was outlined. Also in this period some of the staff carefully surveyed other local efforts at alternative schools to assess their strengths and weaknesses. As the school later passed through times of difficulty the insights gained and the documents produced in this period would provide welcomed anchor points. In California there are few laws regarding secondary education. The freedom a new school has is wonderful; but it can also lead to endless internal squabbles and discouraging breakdowns of responsibility, to the detriment of the educational process. A recent report from the school states that:

> In a community school the quality and continuity of the program will depend first upon the dedication, skill, and maturity of the staff, secondly on constant efforts to set forth official policy in detail and in writing, and finally upon the involvement of key parents and students in decision making. Where discipline has few economic sanctions to support it and no established tradition, an experienced leadership and mutually agreed upon codes and contractual arrangements are the only substitutes.

This need not necessarily lead to inflexibility; at its best, a carefully structured community school encourages serious decision-making from all its members.

A significant factor in this period was the social and political climate out of which the school arose. Studies released in the late sixties (and confirmed again in 1971) revealed the ineffectiveness of education in Oakland, particularly in the Black community. At the same time, student protest on secondary and college levels was prevalent in the country, and involved large numbers of white students. Analysis after analysis pointed to many of the root problems in education: bureaucratic structures, built-in racism, blindly held middle-class attitudes, and poorly trained teachers.

In this period of educational ferment it seemed appropriate for as many people as possible to develop actual models of what education might be. As a model school, New Community School attempted to anticipate the problems that might destroy the educational process. Recognizing the great cultural differences between Black and white students, the school organizers decided to set up two departments meeting the special needs of the groups. The Black Studies Department would be staffed by Black personnel, and have charge of a special curriculum, as well as interview, counsel, and advise Black students. There would be courses particularly designed for Black students such as history, literature, and there would be courses designed for any student in the school —languages, math, and crafts, for example. Since this decision was made the school has traversed the spectrum from total integration to almost total separation. It may be impossible to find the ideal situation, but the structure at least gives recognition to the fact that there are crucial cultural and psychological differences between certain groups at this time in history. It enables these groups to get together and to some extent determine their own destiny. Our experience has confirmed the wisdom of this decision; in fact, the school has found it important to make room for various interest groups, including women and men, poor whites and wealthy whites, and sexual minorities. Education arbitrarily brings together vastly different people, and if the process is to function well at all—in fact, if people are to learn from one another—the very structure that unites them must acknowledge their differences.

Other decisions in the early phases of the school were important. Community organizing was seen as a way to develop a student body. In the Black community, students but especially parents were contacted regarding the possibility of a new school. Community relations, community service, and publicity immediately became important aspects of the new school. The early organizers saw too many alternative schools which had left the established system only to end up reflecting it at its worst points by becoming upper-middle-class white-controlled introverted sanctuaries, accountable to no one, and scorning evaluation. Within the school, a careful administrative structure was designed. The Board of Directors would meet monthly and have student, staff, parent, and community representatives. A proportion of the Board would always have to come from the local community. A Steering Committee would meet weekly and handle interdepartmental matters. It is sometimes difficult for the people of an alternative "free" school to see the value in these structures, but they have enabled New Community School to deal with the most explosive issues which divide our society and our educational institutions—racial conflicts, age gaps, authority and responsibility problems. To confront these issues squarely is the supreme need in education today.

When the school opened it was clear that feelings were strong. The Black Studies Chairman wrote:

The emphasis on Black Experience is necessitated by the fact of the unique position of Black Experience in the White World. The problems that confront Black People are different from problems that confront whites, because of the history of political and social oppression of Blacks. This oppression of Black People continues to the present day; it is the reality of police brutality systematic suppression of truth with regard to education, as well as political and social discriminations.

One of the students wrote the first week:

Things were new and different . . . this was a school definitely prepared for "us." The students who were not adjusting properly to the role of the public schools were placed in a place just for them. Change became of the essence but many times irrelevant psycho-philosophical discussions were on ego-hip-levels rather than the down-to-earth jive. But all this is a part of real learning.

This same student wrote the second week:

Racism is a heavy thing and so far this has occupied the main interest in this new school. People on their own trips were many times forced to let reality come to their heads. Brothers and sisters ran-it-down since from here is where revolution began, comes and will come, jive, bullshit, put-ons, fronts, and other devices for surviving in today's society exist prevalently and will continue to exist but the comunication is becoming more down-to-earth and hopefully will continue to do so.

One of the poorer white parents wrote after the first couple of months:

While my sons attended the public schools, I was concerned that what and how they were learning was neither sufficiently stimulating nor particularly relevant to them. They appeared to be generally unenthusiastic about school. The NCS has generated distinct changes in their attitudes. They are developing a real "school spirit" for the first time. And as a result of true learning, they are beginning to experience themselves in relation to the real world, causing their centers of interest to expand.

The emphasis on problems of racism and relation of the school to the larger community is often characteristic of staff organizers of free high schools. Such organizers understand the political, social, and economic context of educational reform and hope their schools will be relevant to the problems they see. But not all schools are as successful as the New Community School.

The staff of the Santa Barbara Community High School writes:

> The student body (ages 13–17, half female) was and is comprised of students from families of lower-middle- to upper-middle-class backgrounds, and remains chiefly middle-class in constituency, despite serious and conscientious attempts to have the school represent a real cross section of the Santa Barbara community. It's still extremely difficult for an alternative experimental school (and the new school movement in general) to relate to problems of education as perceived by people of poor and minority groups. In Santa Barbara the largest minority group by far is Mexican American (Chicano). These people are painfully aware of the various forms of oppression which their children must face in this society and they are realistically apprehensive about getting involved with an "experiment." Chicanos suspect that the Community School will not prepare their children for the problems they will have to deal with later in life. They are afraid that the young people in the school will have difficulty in acquiring skills and gaining standard credentials. Even if they are tempted to try an alternative school they feel that their kids may be held back (penalized) when re-entering public school. In the case of the Community School, re-enrollment has often been difficult.

A recent development in free schools, one without significant parallel in the previous progressive school reform movements, is the formation of high schools based on white, working-class constituencies. A high proportion of the student body in these schools are "dropouts" or "pushouts" from the public schools. Young working-class people are very frequently tracked into the "loser" slots of the society or become dropouts at a rate much higher than is characteristic of middle-class youth. While the civil rights movement of the last decade brought to public attention the plight of the black youth (and now, increasingly, Puerto Rican, Chicano, and Native American youth), the white working-class youth have not received the same sort of public sympathy. Schools mainly for black dropouts like Harlem Prep and CAM Academy in Chicago get wide attention (e.g., in Silberman's *Crisis in the Classroom*). Esso and other corporations have donated funds to Harlem Prep and have brought public attention to their own deep "social concern" by showing TV ads of Harlem Prep commencements, pointing out Esso's contribution. But the problems of white working-class youth have not seemed to have a similar appeal, even if only for public relations.

Several free high schools with this constituency have begun in the past couple of years, and the staff organizers almost invariably display the same high level of political sophistication and sensitivity to the complexities of the situation that the account from the black-oriented New Community School in Oakland shows.

A fine example of this group of free schools is Independence High School in Newark, New Jersey. The school grew out of a youth center project which was organized in 1970. The organizers felt that there was a great need to develop new institutions for working-class youth.

The group's account of the beginning of their school:

The Ironbound Youth Project, Inc., was created by a group of young adults living in Ironbound who were interested in helping to establish a range of social, educational, and recreational programs needed by teenagers and young adults in the neighborhood. The Project strives to involve the people who will benefit from these programs in the development, implementation, and control of each program. During the summer of 1970 members of the Project and several teenagers from the neighborhood put on a series of rock concerts in

Independence Park. This experience produced a group of about thirty teenagers who met regularly on Wednesday evenings through the month of September. Early in October a storefront was rented at 108 Wilson Avenue with funds previously raised by the Project.

Throughout the winter months this center was the source of recreational activity for approximately 200 teenagers and young adults. In addition, the volunteer staff worked constantly to alleviate scores of individual problems. These included: medical, legal, and psychological help for people suffering under the use of drugs; educational counseling and assistance in making applications to college; tutoring teenagers with particular problems in high school; meetings and seminars on the problems of drugs in the neighborhood and possible solutions; counseling on the variety of personal problems affecting young people, and special programs of counseling and self-defense for teenage women. In addition, the center provided the impetus for a tutoring program for twenty-five elementary school children held at a neighboring church during the recent teachers' strike; a youth newspaper, *Gimme Shelter,* aimed at explaining the problems of youth and suggesting solutions to the larger neighborhood; the creation of a neighborhood print shop to train youth in the various printing skills; and the location of fifteen volunteers who are presently spending nine to fifteen hours per week working inside East Side High School and Wilson Avenue School for the duration of the school term.

Immediately prior to the beginning of the recent Newark teachers' strike, seven teenagers, two Vista volunteers assigned to the Youth Project, and one teacher from Essex County College began meeting to talk about the possibility of establishing an independent, experimental school for dropouts in the Ironbound community. The group held discussions on the problems students have in high school, made several trips to experimental schools in New York City, White Plains, Philadelphia, and Cambridge, and the number of potential students rose to thirteen.

After visiting the Division of Curriculum and Instruction at the State Department of Education in Trenton in early March, the group began planning its own school.

The deep social and economic problems that characterize the neighborhood are well understood by the staff as crucial to understanding the situation of the young people who come to the school. (This is a different emphasis from that of the middle-class free schools where the stifling of creativity and joy in learning are the leading accusation, as in the books by Leonard or Postman and Weingartner discussed in Chapter 1.)

The organizers note that the local public high school has a dropout rate of 33 percent.

The young people on the streets and in the parks are vulnerable in a way their parents rarely understand. They quarrel with their parents' values, they hate school, they don't want to work at dead-end jobs—so instead they grow their hair long, they wear raggedy bell-bottomed pants and loose shirts. They are hated by a neighborhood bred on hard work; a neighborhood which still sees leisure as something indulgent. And on the streets, drifting unsure of what they believe in or where they're going, in flight from tension at home and scared of what seems to be bad futures, the young people who crowd Ironbound's streets drift in an endless empty present from which the only escape almost inevitably becomes drugs.

Young people are increasingly conscious of the inadequacy of life in the neighborhood. The older generation suffers under a myriad of personal, social, and economic problems as well, but seems bent on ignoring the problems which work on both generations. It remains unclear how the tensions caused by the change in life style and values of young people hitting up against the hardened traditions of the older generations will be resolved.

The Students

The free schools for working-class dropouts like Independence High start off with young people who could be considered damaged, at least in the sense that they are already being labeled as "failures." Almost always these young people have done poorly in high school, although the relation of this fact to actual intelligence is of course very questionable, especially when one sees the quality of their work when they get turned on in their own new schools.

In the more middle-class free schools the students are not predominantly dropouts. In elementary schools it is usually the parents who make the decision and commit themselves to the new kind of school. Sometimes the child is unhappy in public school; and, even though the parents may have serious doubts about the libertarian and unstructured free school method, they decide to try it. Sometimes the child is unhappy *and* the parents believe in libertarian methods, the ideal combination, so to speak.

Judy Vincent, teacher-founder at Second Foundation School explains why people send their kids there. There is a variety of reasons.

Among high-school kids the most common response is that they don't have any alternatives—either they go to Second Foundation or they drop out of school. With most of the high-school students, it's the kids who decide they want to come, not the parents—they kind of get dragged into it. Few are the high-school parents who really agree with what we're doing. The elementary kids who came, they were, for the most part, kids who were having troubles in public schools, and the public schools wouldn't have them, or the problems they were having in the public schools spilled over into the family, the home. One little boy who came wouldn't stay in the public schools, he kept running away—he was only eight —and so his parents would be subject to prosecution. So they had to find a school he would stay in.

Among the parents of the elementary kids there was one set of parents who really believed in what we are doing.

On this topic, a teacher at the Santa Barbara Community School writes:

Our parents are mostly young people (white) with middle-class backgrounds but without middle-class aspirations. None of them have very much money unless they happen to have inherited it. We have a couple of fathers who teach at the university, a couple of carpenters, a couple of store owners (a leather shop and a "head shop"), several elementary school teachers, a printer, a woman who makes clothes for a living, a few who are students at the university and city college, one lawyer, a couple of housekeepers, a waitress, a woman who works in a record store, a man who does astrological charts, a few women who work part-time at the university, a man who works for the county in an alcoholic rehabilitation program, and several mothers on welfare. A few of them might be described as politically radical; most of them are apolitical, but these share with the radicals an alienation from the middle-class value system implicit in the public schools. They send their children to the Community School either because they truly believe in what we are trying to do or because they are dissatisfied with the public school in their district. One parent took her boy out of the local public school after they insisted that he take tranquilizers if he was to attend there. Occasionally we have parents who put their children in the Community School not because they themselves are dissatisfied with the public school but because their children are truly unhappy there. This was the case this year with one woman who had managed to enroll her child in probably the most progressive of the Santa Barbara public elementary schools even though she did not live in the district. The little girl, however, did not like the school (she thought her teacher was "mean"). She managed to spend long hours out of several days in the bathroom and one morning she managed to convince her teacher that her mother was going to pick her up at eleven o'clock and spent the entire rest of the day waiting outside for her. This is how it was brought to her mother's attention that her child was unhappy at the school; and now she sends the girl to the Community School, where she already had several friends and is quite happy. The mother, however, like several of our parents, is still not altogether sure that we don't go "too far."

As the Second Foundation teacher mentioned, in high schools it is almost always the case that the students themselves make the decision, although the decision needn't be a committed or enthusiastic one. Often the young person wants *out* of public school, and basically out of school in general; and the free school is the best way of approaching this goal, within the compulsory school attendance laws. Parents almost always want their high-school age children to be studying seriously in a disciplined way, preparing for college or jobs. They worry that being in free schools may hurt their chances of getting into college or of transferring back into public school at the right grade level, and these anxieties are not entirely baseless, as I shall show later. But many high-school students want a freer situation, students who are doing well inside the system as well as those who are doing poorly and/or dropping out. The Community High School director describes his students:

> In terms of public school standards of success and failure, the students represented the whole range: those who had been given mostly D's and F's to class Valedictorians, with a median roughly similar to the public school appellation "average student."

Some students had bad experiences early on in their schools:

> Q: Jennifer, when did you first realize you weren't too fond of public school?
> J: When I was in the fourth grade. But I started right out in the first grade. My mom sat me down before I ever started school. OK. She taught me how to write, to read, to add, and to subtract. I could write my name in the first grade. Not print it. *Write* it. So I come to class and I sit down. I got all these other kids around me. So I sit there and I'm doing everything like she said, but because I wrote my name instead of printing it, I got nothing but D's and F's all the way. The first report card I got they flunked me in the first grade. I didn't dig that at all. Right after that I just said, "You know where you can put this school." After that, that was it.

A fifteen-year-old woman honor student:

> J. B. I never liked public school because if a person gets caught smoking or ditching a class, they say, "Did you do it?" If you say no everything is fine. If you say yes you're suspended for a couple of days. So it just teaches you that if you lie everything is fine. If you tell the truth you really catch the rap. They teach you how to be a crook.

From a "problem student":

M: For my part I don't especially like being *made* to do anything. And especially something I have no interest in at all. I can't stand the way he says "DO IT." Its more of a general type thing and its kind of hard to explain.

And this from a serious minded "academic" student:

Q: What were your criticisms of the public school at the time you were in it?

D: Well they involved disagreements about the way the public school was structured in terms of discipline, classes, student-teacher relations, and also curriculum—actually what is taught and how accurate it is—say how accurate history classes are about the United States. Or any classes for that matter. There's a lot taught in public school that's just lies.

The students at the Second Foundation School are mainly white and middle-class, and they express their reasons for wanting to leave public school in the following ways:

I was stagnating in public school because I wasn't enjoying what I was doing—spending seven hours a day doing nothing, just doing the necessary assignment to get by. In fact I got very depressed. I found out about this school, decided to come, convinced my parents, and that's why I'm here.

They make you take courses that you don't want to take. You don't learn from them but you have to take them for the credits. They don't interest you. You're just there because you have to be. You are forced to do things fast. They make you go through all their rules, which really cramp a person up.

Any person with any intelligence whatsoever, ends up wasting the majority of their time in public school. The things that they make you do are, for the most part, worthless. I found myself, after the first two weeks, after I found out what all my classes were, walking around in a daze. I didn't think about what I was doing because I had to go through the same fixed routine, day after day. Your mind wasn't turned on. Anything that broke the routine—people would jump at the opportunity to go up to the office and bring back leaflets—that broke the routine of the day. It's not every day you get to go to the office.

From the New Community School in Oakland:

Students come to the school for countless reasons. Some come because they felt lost in the large crowds at public schools, others were asked to leave public schools because of their outspoken political views or because they did not conform to the proper dress codes; everything from loneliness to politics to boredom might be given as reasons. One student wrote in her application:

I feel that the last couple of years I spent in school have been a waste of time and energy for both myself and the teachers . . . instead of sitting around complaining about school I think trying out a new and different type of learning would help everything . . . a good school to me would be a school that was interesting, educational, and has a feeling of togetherness. Also, a good school should always be aware of the student's needs and try to meet these needs, because if the school doesn't work with and around the students it is hard for the students to maintain their interest.

Another student wrote:

. . . Berkeley High is too big and impersonal. It depresses me just to set foot on the campus every morning. New Community is really different. I really enjoy it because people are more down to people and care more about each other. The whole atmosphere is just much more relaxed.

It is much easier to communicate feelings to other people. The things you learn in B. H. S. seem irrelevant and boring. . . . Here you get a feeling of learning, not just accomplishing.

In general, the students that come to New Community School are mature, socially aware, articulate, independent. They have a scorn of put-ons and fakeness, and are particularly concerned that they feel they are being respected—respect: one of the words that comes up most frequently when students are expressing their needs. One of the teachers described New Community School students in the following way:

These students in general feel cramped, stifled, or overprotected by restrictive public high schools. They feel denied a "real" or relevant role in society, and reject the "abstractions" and academic focus of high school. . . . Such students demand a holistic approach to their education, and involvement and depth in their learning experiences and personal relationships. Eager to experiment and engage in real tasks, they prefer to do their own thing rather than study what others have done or made. They are vitally concerned with the values of freedom and justice and look to the histories of oppressed groups for their identification. . . .

New Community School students also have a marked tendency to saturate themselves in extracurricular activities . . . their active school life may involve each student in an additional four to ten hours of attendance per week.

The energy of the students is amazing; the pace of the school is frenetic. One day recently a large group of students began the day with a 4 AM photography trip and ended the trip at 10 PM with a guest speaker.

The breadth of student interest and personalities is as amazing as their frenetic pace. Black students are frequently quite clear about their identity and direction. As one student put it:

. . . wake up and realize that the day of the mammy and burned head-scratching Negro is over. And to all those beckoning, sissy, piggy, wiggle white people the hell with you yo mommie and yo Daddy if you ain't hip to the *Black People* way of things.

Among the students there is also the inner searching, a desire for a more peaceful existence:

the task of getting outside myself, just long enough to see the sunshine, I've been planning, dreaming, scheming, and hating far too long. beyond me, the sky of gulls or ancient trees. absorb. my upbringing cries absorb. What becomes of those I absorb. They are not gone. But I have been absorbed.

One of the most difficult but important tasks for all these students (as well as staff) is understanding their common rebellion, yet maintaining their separate identities with pride and self-assurance.

When the school is attended by dropouts the question of parents is not very pressing. Whether or not the parents sympathize with the spirit of the free school (they usually don't) they are somewhat thankful that their children are in some school rather than on the streets or in trouble. The reasons the young people from Newark give for disliking the public high school and wanting an alternative are:

As students at East Side, we are told that our school is one of the best. One of the best what? We certainly hope they don't mean school. Maybe prison, or a zoo, but not a school.

A school like East Side is an insult to Ironbound. The books are dated as far back as the late thirties and forties, and most of them are handed down from other schools. These are history, English, science, health, and business books. How could a student even be half-interested in something that doesn't have anything to do with what's happening today. How can you relate to the history of the past if there's no attempt to connect it with what's going on today?

Most of us don't fail because we are stupid, but because we're uninterested and many of the teachers don't keep our interest. When we ask questions, we are told it's in the book or it was on the board. If this is true, why are the teachers here? Or aren't they supposed to answer questions? You're graded on your attitude before you're graded on your work. How can you blame anybody who has to go to school in a zoolike atmosphere for having a bad attitude?

A seventeen-year-old describes why he dropped out and how he got involved in starting a free school, an account that is marvelously revealing about the humiliations young people are subjected to by the "system."

I'm a former student at Harrison High School located in Harrison, New Jersey. I dropped out of school for several reasons. When I first tried to enroll the principal demanded that I wear a tie and jacket. I said that was unconstitutional and that he had no right to make me do it. He told me to get out and not to come back until I was willing to obey his dress code. I refused to do it. I soon received a summons to appear before a judge in juvenile court where I was placed on probation for two years. The judge also said if I still refused, I'd be sent to Secaucus detention home. I submitted to their dress code with resentment and was labeled a trouble-maker. I sat in class and did nothing. The results—I learned nothing except that school and the school system doesn't work and I ended up leaving school when I was of age.

I later moved to Newark. When I tried to enroll in East Side High, I was given a run around story about their being overcrowded already. I went to the Board of

Education for guidance and they told me I could go to another school on the other side of town. I inquired about this school and found it to be one of the worst schools in New Jersey. The results—I was out of school and had to wait at least till next year to try again.

I recently got involved with the Ironbound Youth Project. Some of us looked into the problems of dropouts and after careful thought and consideration, we decided there was a need for an experimental school in Ironbound. I want to see this school begin because it would be the first time I'd be permitted to learn and express myself the way I want to. And maybe then I'd be able to function the way I was meant to, to be an independent thing. Thinking and doing for myself.

Some of the concerns and mixed feelings parents often have about free schools are well illustrated in the following remarks made by a mother whose two daughters went to a free high school for a year and are now back in public school. The woman and her husband are both scientists, and both daughters have always done brilliantly in school. A problem arose when the older daughter was chosen as valedictorian of her graduating class at the local junior high school and was not allowed to deliver her speech because she discussed and criticized administration censorship of the school paper.

Q: Did you have any reservations about her going to the free school or were you pleased with the idea?

A: Well, it was like an emergency situation as far as Deborah going to the public school was concerned. She was not happy to the point of being ill. It was really ruining her whole life, and as she was a year ahead of her peer group anyway, it seemed to be a reasonable idea just to give her a holiday. So the choice was either to take her out of school for a year and have her just do nothing which seemed at the time not a good idea, or to send her to something experimental. Like this part of the philosophy which I agree with, the other half of which I was noncommittal about. I really believe that you have to be happy while you're learning. Teachers have got to make work you're doing at school either exciting, stimulating, or fun. It's got to be something that has some joy in it. School's got to be a happy place, not destructive. What I was committed on, and what now after a year of their going to the school and my having read more about it, I have great reservations about, the lack of discipline in the sense that they didn't go to classes if they didn't want to and that often there aren't many classes at all. . . . It seems like there were a lot of programs in the beginning they could join into, but when it actually came down to practice there weren't very many lessons that they attended and I think that for kids that weren't very well motivated, it was a waste of time. . . . I've been kind of negative in my criticism. I do feel still that the major feeling of having happiness learning, however, was there at the school. It's not a destructive school. It's a school where one makes great friends obviously, with people of all ages, up to about 30 anyway, and they're friends that mean a great deal and there's no holds barred, and I think that this is wonderful.

The School in Operation: Methods and Curriculum

A random sample of public schools would look much more alike in organization, classroom structure, curriculum, and physical plant than would a random group of free schools, even though the number of free schools is minute compared to the number of public schools. This section gives a sense of how philosophy becomes practice, what a day in a free school might be like, how different schools attempt to cope with their problems, what gets taught and how.

The first long account, written by Christopher Boldt, a full-time teacher, covers two years of the Community School in Santa Barbara. Important themes that emerge are how to have freedom while avoiding chaos or, in free school language, the "structure vs. non-structure" discussion; the importance and difficulties of using volunteers and parents; field trips as a vitally important element in the program; and the variety of teaching styles that coexist within a single school.

Of the thirty or so children in the school that year about half of them were returns from the first year. They ranged in age from four to twelve. Unfortunately all of the junior high group from the year before had graduated and there were very few new enrollments in that age group. There were, therefore, considerably more younger children than older children. The great majority of the children were white, from low-income, middle-class families. All of the staff was white. There were two black children (who had attended the year before) but they were taken out of the school by their parents after Christmas, largely because their mother thought that the school did not emphasize academics enough and that her boys should be with other black children. There were also two Chicano children, also brothers; they stayed in the school the whole year but did not come back the next year. Their parents gave financial reasons as the cause of their withdrawal but it was believed that this was not the whole story.

Activities the second year included academics (reading, math, and creative writing) art, folk dancing, sports, ceramics (there were several pottery wheels and a kiln), sex education, film making, jewelry, welding, science, carpentry, Aikido, and no doubt some other things which I've forgotten. Cooking was done at the school and there was a lunch time store which sold things cooked, yogurt, milk, fruit, etc. (no candy) until the kitchen was closed down by the Health Department for lack of three porcelain sinks and a self-defrosting refrigerator. After that, cooking classes were done by one of the parents at her home. There was no regular drama class but plays were done at Halloween and Christmas and in the spring the children did a movie of *Romeo and Juliet*.

At the beginning of the year, the children were generally free to do as they liked all day, although occasionally some pressure would be put on certain students to do some reading, math or something of that nature. This was minimal and only applied to those children who rarely or never participated in these activities voluntarily. Likewise it was considered important that children should have the experience of making something that pleased them and of carrying out activities that required planning and follow-through; and so if it was observed that some child shied away from ever participating in arts and crafts projects he or she was sought out and encouraged to try something of this kind. After about a month and a half most of the staff noticed that there was a lack of cohesion among the students and that there was a group of boys who rarely participated in any school activities, but mainly roamed around the building (and the neighboring art institute) causing trouble. The staff debated at length what to do about this. An Arizona trip and a more well-coordinated sports program were two proposed solutions. Both were helpful. Also it was suggested that since the school's activities were not appealing to these boys someone should seek them out and find out what it was that they would like to do. The result of this was that after the Arizona trip work was begun on an underground fort, a project that continued throughout the whole year. Christmas also had a good effect on the school. It was decided to do a

Christmas play. Everyone in the school collaborated, either by acting in it, building sets and props, or making costumes. This play and preparations for an all-school Christmas party helped to bring everyone together in an atmosphere of productive, mutual cooperation. After this it was decided that the staff should try to continue to work more closely together and should divide up the responsibility for the students more equitably (the majority of the teachers had formerly been working with the older students, a minority of the children in the school). Some improvement was made in this area but not much.

Not long after school reopened in January it was felt that more action was needed to lessen the chaos factor in the school. It was suggested, and the suggestion adopted, that the children and the teachers should fill out daily schedules. They would be free to choose whatever activities they wished, even to write "Play" in every one of the time slots if they chose to, and they were free to change their plans if they indicated the change in their schedule, which was posted in the hall.

This experiment was fairly successful (if not overwhelmingly popular), especially for the younger students. For one thing it caused the children to ask what was going to be available each day; and once they knew in advance what their choices were and had to spend at least a few minutes thinking seriously about how they would like to spend their time, they usually decided that they would like to participate in at least some of the offered activities. Thus both communication and participation were improved. Another feature of the schedules was that they presented certain things as being available at specific times. Thus instead of different children wandering in and asking to do some reading at all different times of the day, the children understood that reading would be happening at 10:00. This made it easier for the teachers to plan their days to include more activities. Of course every child's inclinations did not always fit the schedule and if a child wanted to read at 11:00 or at 1:30 there was almost always someone available to help him or her. The schedules were less popular with the older group than with the younger groups, and after a few months the oldest children stopped filling them out altogether. However since this group was much smaller and tended to stick together more this was not regarded as a problem by any of the staff.

Different teachers worked in different ways. Some liked to plan their days or even their weeks in advance and prepare work for the children to do. Others worked more spontaneously, picking up on the interests of the children as they were manifested. There was a lot of science taught during the year, for instance, but never a regularly scheduled science class. The children worked independently with batteries, wires, bulbs, bells, etc. The science teacher built rockets with the children: they designed them and made the fuel themselves. That teacher also worked on the underground fort. When the diggers struck two enormous rocks, he and some of the kids attempted to make an explosive to blow them up. Unfortunately (or perhaps not) they were not successful. Various methods, including leverage, were tried to remove the rocks. Eventually a portable hoist was rented.

Several field trips were taken during the second year. The first was a visit to Arizona by a group of the older students. The second trip was for a group of the seven-, eight-, and nine-year-olds. They spent a week in Death Valley, where they visited an old gold mine, an operating steotite mine, the Ubehebe craters, Zabriskie Point, a hot springs, Salt Creek and the sand dunes. One particularly cold and windy day was spent in the several Death Valley museums. The children were especially interested in the historical exhibits because they had, in preparation for the trip, been reading the history of the first explorers to cross the valley. Several parents who were familiar with the area and knew quite a bit about geology (as well as camping techniques) accompanied the three teachers who went on the trip. This turned out to be the beginning of closer relationships between the teachers and the parents. Not only did the group of parents who went on this trip become good friends with the teachers, but the success of the trip opened the teachers' eyes to the value of parent participation in the school.

A third trip was made (for the older students) to the Mother Lode area in the Sierra foothills. Again some parents came and were a great help. In this trip the kids were especially interested in learning techniques of outdoor living and survival. They had a good opportunity to test their skills when they found themselves caught in an unexpected snowstorm. They also had an interesting experience with police harassment.

The first, second, and third grade teacher took a group of her youngest children for a week-long visit at a ranch school in the Sierras. Here they had the advantages of a country setting, such as creeks to swim in, a lake to fish, horses to ride, and the comforts and conveniences of the indoor facilities, the kitchen, beds to sleep in, and the pottery shed. Interestingly enough, some of these children became more interested in academics on this trip than they ever had before. Reading stories by the fireplace at night and writing stories or doing math together in the afternoons, after swimming, fishing, and exploring were over, proved to be for them a more natural and comfortable mode of learning than classes at school had been.

There was one other trip, for two days, which was also

a visit to another free school, the Exploring Family School in San Diego. The children went to the zoo the first day and to a crafts fair the second. On the way down they stopped for a visit at the Los Angeles Museum of Science and Industry. In San Diego they did their own shopping and made their own meals and in between excursions they used the host school's leather shop, rode its donkey, and played with the various games, books, and learning devices available there. The adults on this trip were one mother and one teacher.

The picture of the first two years of the school has been sketchy. It has been a retrospective view and in general the things I have chosen to emphasize have been chosen because I felt they would be useful as springboards for comparison with the third year, 1971–1972. In this next section I will try to give a more complete picture of the daily life of the school, which is the best way I can think of to make clear what we are all about.

At the end of the 1971 school year the lease ran out on the building the school had been using on the Brooks Institute property. Since the Institute now wanted the building for its own use we had to find a new location. It was thought for a while that someone might finance the down payment on a house or some property if something suitable could be found and therefore various parents and teachers spent the summer looking for a place to buy. By late August nothing had been found and it furthermore became clear that our potential benefactor had had second thoughts and was no longer willing to commit himself beyond a (possible) $5,000—not enough to make a down payment. So it was decided to open school in a public park and to solicit the use of various parents' homes for rainy days. We were all a little apprehensive about how school in the park would work out. Where would we keep our supplies? Would our arts and crafts program be severely limited? Could the children be expected to do any academic work at all in this setting? None of us guessed that it would be as successful as it was.

The facilities of the park turned out to be quite adequate—a lesson in how little was really needed. There is perhaps a little more than an acre of flat, well-tended, grassy ground with lots of large trees, picnic tables, fireplaces, electric outlets, sinks with running water, and open spaces for sports. There is also a playground with swings, a slide, and some merry-go-round type equipment. There are bathrooms, a public phone, and plenty of parking space.

The great virtue of the park has turned out to be its openness, which has greatly improved communication among and between the teachers and the students. Everyone can see everyone else; we know where the students are and what they are doing and they know where we are and what we are doing. This has eliminated the need which we felt last year for schedules. Furthermore the teachers, instead of each being sequestered in his or her room, with his or her group of students, are now all together, in the equivalent of one big room with all the students. The result is that we tend to work more closely together, to plan together and coordinate our efforts much more than we ever did before. We don't, moreover, have to pay the price usually paid by large groups of people together in a big room: noise. The children who want to run can run, the children who want to be noisy can be noisy. The sound floats off into the trees and rarely are the activities of a boisterous group disturbing to the peace of a quieter group. The teachers and parents who work at the school are all very pleased with this arrangement which we feel allows every child, the quiet and the lively, maximum freedom to do whatever he or she chooses, and also allows the teachers to work with small groups of children at a time while having under their supervision all the other children in the school. I am not sure how the advantages of this arrangement could be duplicated in a school which, because of climate, had to spend most of its time indoors. Perhaps large (auditorium sized) carpeted rooms, extensive use of acoustic tile, movable room dividers, and glass walls looking onto courtyard play areas would have the same results. Of course this would be much more expensive.

There are, of course, certain disadvantages to school in the park. The biggest problem is storage. Each of the children has a cardboard box ($9'' \times 11'' \times 3''$) in which to keep his or her papers, pencils, books, and the work she or he has done or is going to do. (Not many books can be kept in these boxes but since we generally don't use textbooks this is not a problem. Instead of textbooks the children work on worksheets designed for each child individually by the teachers.) These boxes, together with others containing all of the various supplies which we need (we have a paper box, several book boxes, several paintboxes, boxes containing equipment for printing, leather work, animation, yarn crafts, and tools for carpentry, and a couple of boxes of lost clothes) have to be packed in the teachers' cars every afternoon and unpacked again every morning. It is not possible for us to do any arts or crafts activity that cannot be completed in one day unless it is small enough and durable enough to be stored and transported. We cannot use our pottery wheels; we do not have our darkroom. We cannot have aquariums or terrariums or set up any long-term scientific experiments. We cannot have a garden or keep any animals. We cannot display any arts or crafts that we have done—everything has to be taken home immediately. We cannot show movies or slides at school. We cannot do any cooking or sewing (on a machine) at school. Our science teacher is also a skilled jewelry maker. Last year he brought his tools to school and set up a shop where many of the older kids made jewelry. This has not been possible this year.

These problems have not seriously bothered us, however. We have found other places to show movies and slides and we use various teachers' and parents' homes for cooking, welding, sewing, and piano lessons.

Some parents have voiced another objection to the school in the park which is that their children are not learning the restraints and self-discipline that are necessary for living and working with other people indoors. This came up at a parents' meeting. One father in particular complained that after his son (age five) comes home from school each day it takes an hour or two for him to lower his voice level to an acceptable pitch for indoors. This objection was not widespread however. In the upcoming cold and rainy months it is projected that we will be spending more time indoors, at various people's houses and perhaps at the university or in the Community Union building, and that this will give all of us the opportunity to learn how to function well indoors as well as out.

Despite our apprehensions and the various limitations mentioned above both our academic and our arts and crafts programs have been, if anything, more successful this year than last year; and in general our curriculum has been expanded and improved. We operate on a general plan of academics in the morning, followed by sports, with arts and crafts and trips in the afternoon. One aspect of our working more closely together is that all the teachers follow this schedule. That is, the art teacher will participate in the reading, writing, and math activities in the morning; all the teachers take part in sports, all plan trips together, and all participate in the arts and crafts activities.

We gather at 9:00 in the morning and unpack the cars. If it is chilly we may build a fire, make cocoa or have a warm-up game or jog around the park. Academics usually start at about 9:30, generally at the instigation of the children. There is always a group (varying from one-third to two-thirds of the whole school) that is interested in doing math, reading, or writing. This group will not always be the same; that is, one child may be very interested in this kind of thing for a week or a month and then his or her interest might decline for a week or a month; meanwhile some other child, not formerly interested in doing any "work," will have developed an enthusiasm for it. The large number of adults (teachers, parents, and friends) who work at the school makes it possible for us to work with the children in small groups, and to develop individualized programs for each one. Math is done on worksheets written by the teachers (or sometimes by the older students). The content and sequence of these worksheets is more or less the same as that in the state-adopted textbooks (we have a couple of copies which we use for reference). We prefer using our own worksheets, rather than textbooks, because they enable us to control the rate at which each child moves from one idea to the next. For instance, one sequence of problems we do starts with $10 + 10$, $10 + 10 + 10$, etc., and moves on to $10 + 10 + 5$, then $20 + 20$, $22 + 10$, and finally into problems like $23 + 34$, and even $25 + 27$. Some children progress through this sequence very quickly, needing perhaps only one page of each type of problem. Other children are less secure or perhaps just slower learners and need to repeat each new step, and review all the previous steps, before moving on to what looks like a harder type of addition. By watching the children as they do the work we are able to decide how fast they should go and write papers for them accordingly. Also some children particularly enjoy doing a certain operation (such as multiplication or "carrying" or "borrowing") and put in requests for that specific type of work. By writing the papers ourselves we are able to accommodate them. When time permits we like to decorate these papers with pictures drawn either by the teachers or by the older students.

Reading is also taught in an individualized way. We do not have a group of children sit in a circle and take turns reading from a textbook. Most often we work one to one with the children; sometimes small groups will form, not necessarily of children the same age, and will read storybooks that have been given to us or picked out by the children at the library. Sometimes children will read with a teacher, sometimes alone; sometimes the older children will read to or teach the younger children. Teachers often write stories for the children to read and the children write stories for and letters to each other.

We use phonics worksheets for reading and spelling. Some of these are designed by the teachers and illustrated by some of our more artistic parents. Others are dittoed or xeroxed from published workbooks. We have not found any of these that really pleased us, however (with the possible exception of the Sullivan workbooks which we have used occasionally).

The older and more advanced children, those who can already read quite well, read independently or write stories. We have a school newspaper which comes out about once every two weeks and this has motivated quite a few children to do writing.

Some of the older children work almost exclusively with the science teacher. He does various experiments with them, examines specimens under a microscope, does dissections, and reads with them from various natural history sourcebooks. Often he has them do research to answer specific questions (such as "What is the difference between a dog and a cat?" or "What is the difference between a bird and a bat?"). He has been trying to help them follow their natural bent for scientific investigation and at the time use this as a basis for learning reading and writing. Recently he has been collaborating with some of the other teachers to develop small books, worksheets, and coloring sheets about animals which will hopefully encourage some of the other children in the school to use their natural interest in reading and writing as a basis for learning some natural science.

As I have indicated, the teachers spend a large amount of time, both inside and outside of school, preparing books and worksheets for the students. There are some advantages to this: (1) the quality of the result is, generally, better than what is commercially available; (2) it allows us to tailor the work to the interests and needs of the children and also to our own interests and areas of knowledge (as in the case of the natural history workbooks mentioned above); and (3) it is cheaper than buying ready-made materials. There are also some disadvantages: (1) it is extremely time consuming; and (2) we feel sometimes, because we do spend so much time and energy preparing these papers, we tend to become overreliant on them or perhaps shortsighted as to the many other ways of learning. No doubt, if there were available good, versatile, stimulating, and inexpensive materials ready-made we would want to use them and thus free ourselves to explore other techniques of learning and teaching.

I have said that the first part of the morning is generally devoted to academics and have tried to give a picture of the nature of this academic activity. This does not mean, however, that all the children participate in this. Some will be on the playground, others will be socializing or playing games with each other. All the teachers do, however, devote their energies to these academic subjects at this time. This was a decision that was made at a staff meeting before school opened. It was felt, and it has proved to be the case, that if all the adult energies were directed in this area for two or three hours each morning, the majority of the kids would follow suit. This idea was based on our belief that children are naturally curious and eager to learn and that if they are given a stimulating environment and are not seduced away from it by other types of activities, they will voluntarily choose to work and to learn, and that this work and this learning will be more important to them for having been chosen voluntarily. Further we believe that they will probably learn better if they are able to choose what they are going to learn, i.e., if they can read what they want to read when they want to read it, do the kind of math they feel like doing when they feel like doing it, and not when they don't.

Sports activities go on all day long. There is almost always someone playing soccer, kickball, snake in the grass, whatever. Usually, however, at about 11:00 there is a "big game" involving children of all ages and several of the teachers or parents who are there. Soccer has been especially popular this year. Last year, when we had the facilities, it was basketball and kickball. Sports have been very important in creating a happy, friendly, and cooperative atmosphere in the school. In my own memories of my grammar school days sports stand out as a highlight. This was the thing that I and most of my friends enjoyed most at school. It seems that the energy level of young children is naturally geared to the high pitch of excitement of sports and to the running around and the challenge to physical coordination. However when I was in school the only teacher that participated in the sports activities was the gym teacher, and all she did was blow the whistle. It is very valuable, I feel, for all the teachers, at one time or another, to be involved in these games as participants rather than supervisors. It is part of the reason for the close relationship between the children and the adults in our school, a relationship that is essential to a school such as ours. The games are also valuable because they are one of the activities that all ages in the school can do together. The children are never segregated by age, but natural separations do take place, even in arts and crafts projects, based on differences in skill and coordination. In sports children of all ages and abilities play together and learn to cooperate and coordinate their efforts. It is interesting that although the youngest ones are usually not the ones chosen on a team, the older children have never objected to including them. Nor is there any discrimination against girls in our sports activities. Women teachers as well as men teachers play all the games and it has never been suggested by any of the students that any game be limited to boys.

There is no formal lunch hour. The children eat their lunches (which they bring) whenever they are hungry. The teachers usually eat at about 12:00 and then set up for the afternoon activities.

These afternoon activities may be field trips to the museum, library, botanical gardens, or tidepools, or to somebody's house for cooking, sewing, or some other special activity. Or they may be arts and crafts projects in the park. The schedule for these events is made by the children at an all-school meeting held on Monday mornings. Usually the teachers come to the meeting with some suggestions which they have talked over the week before in a staff meeting. These are sounded out, and to them are added the ideas of the students. If an activity must be limited to a small number of students, the children sign up for it at this Monday meeting. If there is anything that they must bring to school in preparation for a project, they are told about it at this time.

As with academics all the teachers try to cooperate and concentrate their energies on whatever trips or art activities are planned for the afternoon. Sometimes we break up into several different groups, sometimes we all participate in one activity; but whatever we do has usually been planned in advance by the whole group.

As I have indicated, the park has been responsible for reshaping much of the organization of the school. It necessarily brings us all closer together. And since we found ourselves working together more than ever we began planning together more than ever. Furthermore the openness of the park has made it more accessible to the parents. They feel more comfortable staying late in the morning, coming early in the afternoon, or just visiting during the day. This has led to more parent involvement in the school and more parent contribution to the curriculum. These two factors, more and better coordinated planning on the part of the teachers and increased parent participation in the school, have made it possible for us to expand our curriculum considerably as compared to last year. In the first three months of this year we have had regularly scheduled classes in swimming, welding, sewing, piano, cooking, animation, computer programming, Spanish, French, diving, and food gathering and we have done extensive work on an individual basis in reading, math, spelling, writing, and science. Furthermore we have had special group projects involving carpentry, linoleum block and other types of printing, leather work, clay, candle making, moviemaking, collages, Christmas decorations, and stained glass.

This account illustrates concretely some of the free

school concepts that have been discussed before in more abstract terms. The importance of improvisation and experimentation, the constant self-examination and self-criticism of the staff, the ingenuity needed to cope with severe financial constraints (such as finding that being forced to use a park for a school was a boon in disguise—it should be noted that not many places can match Santa Barbara's splendid, warm, and clement climate); the dedication of staff who during the period described received very little pay (per capita student expenditure for a year was on the order of $370), the ease with which trips could be taken and parents involved (a function of the small size and intimate atmosphere), and the ability to have several concerned adults aware of each child's special circumstances and able to deal with the children often on a one-to-one basis—all these are characteristics of free schools and will emerge in varying forms in the accounts of the other schools.

The New School in Vermont describes its program in the following way:

The people involved in the school any given year determines what the curriculum will be. That is to say, the paid staff tries to provide all the subjects or activities in which the kids are interested either by teaching themselves or finding parents or college students who will teach them. Sometimes the curriculum is heavily weighted in one direction or another. Sometimes the kids themselves determine how they spend a lot of their time. For example, at different times the kids have been interested in model building (ships, motorcycles, planes), building shelters in the woods, playing capture the flag, playing soccer, cooking, beading. These activities, and many like them, have taken some help from adults but they were basically child-initiated and child-organized. Other activities, like the production of several plays (*13*

Clocks, Oedipus, A Midsummer Night's Dream, The Tempest, etc.), the production of a school literary magazine, the building of the pond and the bridge across the brook, the preparation of concerts and an opera, dance classes and recitals, and an advanced math program were all initiated and organized by adults. (One of the plays was done primarily by the children with some adult help.) There are a lot of other activities which are a sort of combination of child and adult input. Skiing, for example, was an adult idea (most of the kids ski one day a week) but the kids have participated heavily in the administrative work involved such as getting transportation together, making arrangements for cut rates with ski areas, etc. Crafts are a sort of combined effort, with kids making suggestions and adults contributing skills. Social studies is similar. Sometimes a child says, "I want to study Indians," or "I want to study Egyptian writing," and if a few more children are interested a course is put together. Sometimes a parent comes in saying that she is reading Chinese or that he is studying Russian and would anyone like to join, and Chinese history or Russian becomes part of the curriculum. Activities for a term are usually decided at a series of meetings.

Basic skills are always taught, because both children and adults recognize their necessity and because most of the kids want to learn to read, write, and reckon. All the children at the school learn to read and write, even those with severe reading disabilities (dyslexia or deafness), though in two instances outside tutors were employed. All kinds of techniques are used to teach reading, depending on the preferences of the teachers involved. They all work. Some kids learn more slowly than others; some years seem to be better for reading than others, but again all children learn to read. The same is true of math—a variety of approaches has been used and continues to be used—math games, math ac-

tivities, cuisinaire rods, new math textbooks and workbooks, old fashioned work sheets. All the kids eventually
learn basic math and usually some algebra and geometry.

The concept of curriculum is more complex when applied to high schools. For elementary age children, basic
skills and the nurturing of curiosity, self-confidence, and
the ability to get along with others are the obvious curriculum. For high-school age, the questions of what is
valuable to learn, what prepares a young person for adulthood in a complex and confusing society, how humanities
and science can be related, etc., are important and hard to
answer. (This issue will be dealt with at length in Chapter
4.) Even many public high-school systems are admitting
that the traditional required curriculum might not be
intellectually nourishing or relevant to the lives of many
students today. There is a growing interest in creating
electives, claimed to be a big reform (though why it is only
now, after much student agitation including "voting" by
dropping out and truancy, is a question worth considering). This is one indication of the spreading questioning
of the old pedagogical wisdom. The programs of the new
experimental public high schools like Parkway Project in
Philadephia, Metro High in Chicago, or Other Ways in
Berkeley are others.

Most people in free high schools realize that simply saying "noncoercion," "choice," "self-motivation," and "participation" doesn't solve any problems. But they often do
honestly admit their problems, and are both willing and
institutionally flexible enough to confront the dilemmas of
the education of young people with a capacity to experiment that few (if any) public schools can match. In fact,
much of the time and energy in free high schools is involved in discussions about what the school is and should
be. In an important sense, this is the core of the curriculum because the subject is not simply the organization of

an institution, but the conceptions the students have of their own interests, concerns, ideals, values, and future expectations. They are at an age when in many cultures they would be fully active as members of the society; while in the U.S. they are compelled to attend a high school where almost everything about education and behavior, including when one can go to the bathroom and when one can argue with a teacher, are prescribed by adults backed by a set of powerful punishments (as well as promised rewards like good grades, recommendations, etc., which can be taken away for "bad" behavior). The typical high school is neither a "good" one, like Metro High, nor a horrendous ghetto or slum school like East Side High in Newark (described in sections from the Independence High account) or George Washington High School in Manhattan, schools where teachers and principals admit that truancy is rampant, the dropout rate is greater than 50 percent, and the danger of sporadic violence and even riot generate constant anxiety. Those who haven't been in an average high school, between the extremes, should see Fred Wiseman's film *High School*, which, although banned inside the Philadelphia school system by irate school people who felt they were slandered, was defended by Superintendent Mark Shedd as a good representation of the typical world of the American high school.

The Community High School, as described before, was attempting to develop a model for a free high school which could use the surrounding community and nearby university as learning resources. There were constant difficulties and deep concern (though doubtful success) in confronting these difficulties. A former coordinator gives the following account of the first two months of school operation:

The first week of the new school was taken up almost completely with planning how the school would be, what the students wanted to learn, how the university tutors would function in the school, and how the school would be organized. The first structure attempted was essentially modeled after the public schools and the university; scheduled classes of the traditional kind (algebra, geometry, biology, creative writing, U.S. history, etc.), meeting two or three times a week for hour durations. While some classes met in places in the community (the Botanical Gardens, neighborhood back yards, coffee shops), many happened at the storefront.

Scheduling problems were difficult; university tutors had to make their own class schedules and college activities mesh with their teaching commitments. There was general confusion as to the nature of the roles of "student" as well as "teacher." It became immediately clear that the new school was going to be as much a learning experience for the tutors from the university as it was to be for the students. After a month of trying to make the school work, students and staff came to the decision that, as a report stated:

. . . all involved had failed to learn from our experiences in the public school system, that we had simply modeled our school after the public school only without the threat of punishment or expulsion which allows the public school system to appear as if it were functioning properly.

After days of discussing and planning, the students and teachers came up with a new plan of class organization; classes (organized around a general topic which could be broken down into more specific interests), tutorial groups (seminars which were to serve as a floating "counseling" group for discussing school problems), and individual tutorials.

The main "curriculum" during the first two months of school operation was "how to make your own school."

The whole school met weekly to evaluate ideas and practices. Students and staff alike suggested changes in scheduling, classes, transportation arrangements and in general struggled to make the school serve their needs.

Formal classes were started then abandoned or changed to a different topic of study altogether. Kids dropped into classes and then stopped coming. Some classes struggled on despite a lack of continuity due to students dropping in and out. One very intelligent and active woman student wrote:

I also had a Shakespeare class at Windell's Donut House. I'm getting to be quite profound on the happenings in the first act but I may forget the rest of the play before we're through with the first three scenes. The reason is because people in the class keep changing and I'm the only one who read and more or less understood it.

The activities which were most successful (other than attending special activities, lectures, films, and plays at the university) were the independent, student-initiated projects: sitting in and observing the local courts (some students did this for days at a time to follow the progress of interesting cases), attending city council meetings, and making an urban community organic garden.

The new experience of self-determination was the big experience for the young people. Sharing in decision-making, chores, and in the taking of responsibility for the whole effort was extremely meaningful and exciting for most of the students. Parents were especially impressed with this aspect of the venture, reporting that their kids, for the first time, "wanted to go to school." Local psychologists and probation officers referred their problems to the school, and the school became fairly well-known in the community in its first two months.

During those first months the volunteer university

tutor program was, if chaotic, generally workable. Several of the tutors became very deeply involved with the school and formed a core group to serve as an organizing-coordinating committee for the following year. Several of the core group had graduated from the university and were able to devote full time to the project.

At the all-school meeting at the end of the year it was decided that more effort was needed to implement the in-community aspect of the program, and that more staff should work on that part of the curriculum. In addition, the core staff organized a week-long orientation session for the new university volunteers who would work at the school the following autumn. Ken Cruze, an ex-public school teacher who had taught in the Santa Barbara system, was hired as coordinator. The group moved into a larger storefront, and the new school year began.

Concerning staff problems, Ken Cruze wrote:

Of the seventeen staff people, there were but five or six who really had a grasp of the knowledge in their field of interest and some idea of how to work with it in a teaching situation. Of the other staff people, some were very good at establishing warm relationships with students, others were mainly disorganized, coming late or dropping out altogether. This of course made the already limited program (no science experts) even more limited.

Although the planned classes and tutorials were not overwhelmingly successful, the curriculum of participation remained intact. The organizers felt that the continuing lack of community involvement was due primarily to the fact that the majority of the staff did not come from Santa Barbara proper, but rather from the university community of Isla Vista, ten miles away. Cruze, over the course of the summer, had made contacts in Santa Barbara where he lived and proceeded to set up connections to the community. During Christmas he set up an interaction program with a Black community project, Operation Solidarity. There was one class a week with them where aspects of the Black experience were discussed. Also a Chicano history class was organized which involved contact with Chicanos and Chicanas Cruze had met over the summer.

During the next summer seven of the staff people moved into Santa Barbara. An ecology expert decided to become (at the school's prompting) a regular staff member in order to initiate a school-community project, a community urban farm. Two women staff members took an auto mechanics class and prepared plans for an auto shop.

Ken Cruze's description of the school organization:

We decided to require staff interviews with students who intended to come to the school. These interviews would enable coordinators to explain the operation of the school to prospective students and to establish interest areas which would be known to the coordinators, who could help link up students with appropriate staff people. It was felt that during the previous year some students were never able to discuss their program in detail with anyone.

When the interviews began we had established a basic core program including math, chemistry, history (Black, Chicano, U.S., China), auto mechanics, carpentry, French, Spanish, biology, organic farming, drama, reading, and writing. The people in these areas were better prepared and qualified as a whole than the staff from the year before. During the interviews, student interests were noted on cards, so that by the beginning of the year the interests of all the students would be known to the coordinators. When the school opened the class meeting times were put on a board and the students were encouraged to make up written schedules, leaving one copy with coordinators. . . . our position was that if a student signed up for a class, and failed to show up, we should find out why.

Thus the staff assumed a more formal way of evaluating and coordinating classes.

Students who were not interested in any of the formal classes being offered could make a special arrangement for independent studies and would have to report in every two weeks to let us know how their activities were progressing. The coordinators felt that they should make some evaluations as to what a student might need, rather than simply asking what a student wanted. For example, I encouraged students to take history and took some pains to explain why I felt it was important, rather than taking a neutral position.

The next description is from the New Community School in Oakland. As with other free schools, problems of attendance, responsibility, and trust have to be faced constantly, as there are no set institutional and bureaucratic frames like those which exist in a public high school. According to staff member Steve Fisher:

The entire New Community School operated for the first year, paying four full-time staff and several part-time staff, for a fraction of what one single administrator in the Oakland Schools receives for an annual salary. Much was learned the first year. By asking for letterhead endorsers we met many people involved in education in the Bay Area. Faced with many difficulties, internal and external, from poor attendance to encounters with police, we learned the extreme value of meetings, getting people together to talk things out face to face. Meetings still remain the heart of the school. The courses were heavy on the academic side. Our two-rooms-and-a-gym facilities allowed little experimentation with elaborate classes.

We also came up against our particular limitations and problems. While we found help evaluating the administrative side of the school, we could not find, and have not yet found, adequate help in evaluating either the emotional growth or intellectual development of the students. We found attendance to be a problem, and felt the potential conflict that could arise between Black parents wanting a structured, thorough education for their children and white students wanting a free and spontaneous form of education. Located in a YMCA, we hardly looked like a school; publicizing ourselves to the community proved to be difficult. Part-time staff and student volunteers made staff communication and continuity difficult. Tuition income was low, since most of the students came from middle and lower income families. The end result was that we spent that first summer structuring the school more thoroughly, dropped students we could not handle, raised tuition, and set up student-staff-community committees to screen staff more carefully. Most disheartening was the loss of some strong Black families in the school who were dissatisfied with the appearance of the YMCA and the relaxed nature of the classes. It is hard to imagine anything more difficult than setting up with minimal funds a school in a generally lower or middle-class neighborhood that will almost immediately look substantial and appealing.

One problem alternative schools rarely seem to face is that of whether or not to become a lasting institution. The second year at New Community School was spent asking and answering that question. Application had been made to the San Francisco Foundation, and the Foundation responded with a one year grant of $20,000. It was the conviction of the administrative staff that to appeal to poorer or Black families the school had to look like a school, and possess a good deal of stability and structure. By the end of the second year many things had been accomplished. A building was purchased for the school; land in the High Sierra was purchased for a camp site; the school got its own truck. At the same time, committees were restructured and employment standards were raised. A report on Black Studies reveals some of the difficulties that department was facing:

The Black Studies Department was clearly lagging at the beginning of the (second) year, largely due to the problem of employing a Chairman who was also part-time student with no time to spare. Most of the students in Black Studies were public school dropouts (in contrast to the first year), which caused the staff an additional burden. . . . It is the growing consensus of the administrative staff and Personnel Committee that along with ethnic and racial factors, matters of efficency and competence must play a very large role in the development of a community school.

The problems arising in an alive interracial school are, of course, complex. White staff in any school will probably display some degree of racism, making staff relations and decision-making difficult. At the same time, it is difficult to find Black educators willing to work for subsistence wages. It takes an enormous amount of persistence and commitment to overcome these problems which affect educational institutions as much as any other parts of our society.

Students, staff, parents, and community must grow with and understand the school. An enormous amount of time at New Community School is spent in meetings discussing the future of the school and the application of its philosophy to present realities. Administrative information in a school must be readily accessible and passed around. Yet there are many schools where students and staff cannot even get hold of budgets. The decision to purchase a building for New Community School was one of the most important decisions the school ever made, and a good deal of staff time was spent discussing it. A foundation report describes part of the process:

> Prior to the reception of the San Francisco Foundation grant it had become apparent to administrative staff at New Community School that a changeover from a careful but spontaneously energetic organization to a stable institution had to be made . . . it is particularly important in an alternative school environment to have a sense of stability. . . . However, "institution building" is often an unwelcome concept to the young and rebellious staff and students who are naturally attracted to an alternative school. There is a strong feeling for the transitory and even the apocalyptic in the youth ethic. Thus the prospect of additional funds to work with was carefully and frequently presented to and discussed with staff and students. The matter was discussed thoroughly at a weekend staff retreat held in December of 1970. At that time, a major consensus was reached in a staff decision to seek a building as a permanent location.

This process of decision-making has been focused on here because it shows not only the creation of long-term commitments at the school, but also because each decision, each crisis, each success and failure are part of learning for the whole school community. Many staff at the school would agree that one primary function of a community school teacher is to grasp and crystallize moments of human encounter and expression and point out—in as forthright a way as possible—the underlying meanings. Discussing a major purchase may get into the way money works in America, or the significance of commitment; random student complaints about a boring conference may get into the public fronts that people and organizations put on, and whether or not a student wants to take on a "public" life. So much learning in the school occurs outside of classes!

The direction of innovation at the school is influenced by a number of factors. Staff desire considerable stimulation and challenge; students desire involvement in a real world and depth of encounter with others. It is important that the school respond to the needs of the future of the young people, and at the same time respond to the immediate needs of the local community. In general, the program at New Community school is college-oriented, so that the students will at least have a fair chance to choose whether or not to go to college. Along with the academic stress, there is a stress on learning real skills that will aid students in their future lives. Such skills include construction, mechanics, printing, community organizing, and research. Almost every student in the school has the independence and energy to become a community leader of some sort, and the staff views itself as training leaders. Since many of the students are choosing to work in organizations which are alternatives to the traditional ways of doing things, or are choosing to someday work in poverty communities, their education must be practical as well as academic. This is a key theme in the curriculum of the school.

Science programs have included survival "live-ins" at the Lawrence Hall of Science in Berkeley, setting up laboratories from scratch, and developing the twenty acres of land the school purchased in the Sierra. Encounter sessions are held at the school from time to time, and outside people are chosen to assist the school in these sessions. At the present time, students and staff are involved in interracial encounters. "Marathons" or intensive twenty-four hour learning sessions always appeal to the students. The school's applied technology class has set up a fix-it shop for the local community, and repairs everything from TV sets to automobiles. The "research team class" is an experiment this year. The team consists of three staff and twelve students doing often original research on a topic—this semester the Eastbay shoreline—with the intention of publishing the material as curriculum guides for other high schools. These efforts to direct the curriculum outward are often precarious, for everything of this sort involves organizing, asking for funds and support, and we cannot always succeed. The danger of total discouragement always looms ahead—what if we can't find any more free films for the Saturday morning children's film series? What if the Sierra Club refuses to help us publish the Bay guide? Yet these are real life problems, and perhaps secondary education need not be the sheltered sanctuary that many people would like to see.

Each school develops its own courses, special projects, and tutorials. There is no standardized list of "major" subjects, no "academic" and "commercial" tracks, no set sequence of requirements (such as "Sophomore English— the Classical period" and "Junior English—the Romantic period"). Since there are no grades and no final examinations or anything of this sort, there is little "objective" data of academic achievement, very narrowly defined. What can be usefully noted is the way learning is approached, the varieties of curriculum offerings, and the sense of how the different sorts of classes and projects arise from the interaction of student interests and choices and staff capacities and interests.

As the descriptions from the different schools show, many people in free high schools express constant dissatisfaction with their own efforts. They know that often classes don't go as well as they had hoped; that often not much work is done and efforts peter out without much intellectual gain. (The following descriptions and curriculum lists can give some sense of what is being attempted.)

Free high schools based on a white middle-class constituency often reflect the concerns and values of the current youth counter-culture, especially the emphasis on "getting one's head together," concentration on the "spiritual," and sometimes a kind of anti-intellectualism or at least an opposition to the systematic scientific approaches to knowledge that have come to be associated with aspects of contemporary society that are intensely opposed—the authoritarian public school methods, for example. Although the youth culture is present in working-class and community-oriented high schools also, there are important differences in emphasis, as a comparison of the curricula will illustrate. (For example, note the sample week schedule from a middle-class free high school compared with the course lists from the Santa Barbara, Oakland, and Newark schools.)

Curriculum

The Santa Barbara Community School describes the curriculum for its third year:

Now, in the third year, Ken Cruze writes, the class program includes: auto mechanics, organic farming, art (held at Casa De La Raza, which is a multi-racial community center and taught by combined Chicano and Anglo staff), algebra (taught on different levels with some individual tutorial), Chicano history (now held at La Casa), French, German, drama (taught by a professional drama person at the Park Theatre), women's health (at the Women's Center), music theory and practice, early Santa Barbara history, photography, and reading.

There are four on the job training situations: a student learning carpentry at a local shop; a student working at a health clinic; law in a law office and printing at a print shop. The woman student working in the print shop has been a part-time employee now for almost a year and is paid for her now skilled work. In addition, two students are being paid for their work in the community farm project.

From our observation of these classes we have found that the staff is consistent and prepared with only a couple of exceptions.

Ken Cruze offers these descriptions of some courses and some comments on them:

Auto Mechanics: Taught by Dale, Patrice, Barbara, and Dave. There are seven students. They use a residential garage which has a number of old car parts which can be used for explanatory purposes. It is not highly equipped and is not a place where advanced work can go on. A very positive aspect of the program is that it is taught in part by women and there are woman students in the class. This is a conscious attempt to break down the traditional role of mechanics as a field appropriate only to men. We feel this is important since women are often pressed into having roles in the society which do not match their real needs and desires.

Student Rights: Initiated by Jeremy Kramer, a recent high-school graduate and former president of the public high school, the group did research on sex discrimination in the public schools. They then presented their findings to the school board. There was a great deal of learning in doing the legal and sociological research necessary for the preparation of the proposal. They used the research in a real situation.

U.S. History: We are attempting to examine U.S. history through the eyes of various ethnic and economic groups: Blacks, Chicanos, Indians, white working-class and ruling groups. For example, we will discuss the points of view within the labor movement, then take the same period of time to study the policies and experiences of people in the ruling class. We feel this method puts societal problems in clearer perspective.

We find that as we examine the material, there is a definite bias within the public school history classes on the same topics. In fact we have been coming to the conclusion that there is something terribly significant about the misrepresentations and distortions we have ourselves been taught in public school history classes. To have us believe that the Alamo battle was a glorious battle between the good people (the white Americans) and the evil people (the Mexicans) helps us to justify the Mexican-American War, which means we accept the right of the United States to take land away from another country. (No serious scholar will dispute the injustice of that war, that is, unless one can accept the statements of the American General Emory who wrote in 1859 that the "white race" was "exterminating or crushing an inferior race.")

After students have studied a view of history which depicts Chicanos as enemies, less enterprising and inferior, it becomes more difficult for those students to view Chicanos favorably today.

In concluding this section, I want to emphasize something that these curriculums represent. They emerge from discussions among teachers and students. Students participate in shaping both the form and content of the more formal aspects of their education; and, as has been noted in all of the reports, this participation itself is seen as a crucial part of the educational process. Another aspect of the freedom of free schools is the lack of constraint on subject matter. Public school teachers are often politically restricted as to subject matter and materials—books and subjects that are seen as politically dangerous from the point of view of powerful groups in the community are often avoided; and there are numerous cases of protests

Spring Schedule: The New Community School

	Monday	Tuesday	Wednesday	Thursday	Friday
8:00–9:00	Physical Education	First Aid	Physical Education	First Aid	Physical Education
9:00–10:30	Ethics and Change African Studies History and Community Involvement	Black Studies, Drama, and Poetry Sociology Photography	Ethics and Change History and Community Involvement African Studies	Black Studies, Drama, and Poetry Sociology Photography	African Studies Love and Sex
10:30–12:00	Creative Writing Modern Literature World Literature Black Literature Comparative Literature	Geometry Philosophy of Art Black Literature Comparative Literature Film Making	Creative Writing Modern Literature World Literature Algebra	Geometry Sociology Black Literature Comparative Literature	Creative Writing Modern Literature World Literature Algebra
12:00–1:00	Political Collective School Presentation	Staff Meeting Films	Committees School Meeting	Films	Steering Committee
1:00–3:00	Languages: Français Espanol Deutsch Public Communications Workshop Native American Studies	Languages General Math Native American Studies	Life Science Arts and Crafts Automotive Maintenance and Repair Public Community Workshop	Languages General Math Native American Studies	Life Science Arts and Crafts General Math
3:00–5:00	Karate	Karate	Karate		
7:00–10:00				Women's Liberation Philosophy of Art	

Independence High School, Newark, N.J.

CURRICULUM

	1st quarter Sept 6–Nov 9	2nd quarter Nov 22–Jan 28	3rd quarter Feb 7–April 14	4th quarter April 24–June 23
SOCIAL SCIENCES				
PROBLEMS	Youth Culture	Organized Crime—Drugs	Vietnam and Foreign Policy	Ecology
INSTITUTIONS	Education	Legal System	Economy	Political System
WORLD HISTORY	Far Eastern	African	European	Latin America
U.S. HISTORY	Colonial and Revolutionary	Westward Expansion	Civil War and Reconstruction	20th Century
MINORITY HISTORY	Indian History	Black History	History of Women	Working-Class History
	Psychology and Sensitivity Workshop	—	—	—
	Independent Study			
EXPRESSION				
	Basic Reading	—	—	—
	Basic Writing	—	—	—
	Creative Writing	—	—	—
	Independent Reading	—	—	—
FINE ARTS	Drawing	Painting	Ceramics	Sculpture
GRAPHIC ART	Photography	Silk Screening	Printing	Video Tape/Film
	Drama	—	—	—

	Folk	Blues	Soul	Rock
MUSIC	———	———	———	———
LANGUAGE	Conversational Spanish			

SCIENCE—MATH

Folk	Blues	Soul	Rock
Basic Math	———	Chemistry	———
Algebra	———	Biology	———
Health-Medicine	———	Geology	———
Astronomy	———	———	———
Independent Study	———	———	———

PHYSICAL EDUCATION

Folk	Blues	Soul	Rock
Roller Skating	Ice Skating	———	Horseback Riding
Horseback Riding	Bowling	———	Tennis
Tennis	Dancing	———	Camping
Camping	———	———	———
Swimming	———	———	———
Exercises	———	———	———
Independent Activity	———	———	———

SKILLS

Folk	Blues	Soul	Rock
Auto Mechanics	Plumbing	Bike Mechanics	Record Keeping
Carpentry	———	Electrical Work	Masonry
Appliance Repair	Driver's Education	———	———
Cooking	———	Fashion Design	———
Typing	———	Drafting	———
Shorthand	———	———	———
Musical Instruments	———	———	———
Independent Study	———	———	———

against teachers or even dismissals because they used "obscene" or "radical" material. Within free schools there is no political harassment and no dismissal for overstepping any lines of what is considered appropriate. The listing of courses illustrates the serious attention to subjects like women's history and working-class history, an attention based on the perception that there are groups in our society that have suffered oppression and that this situation is not honestly or adequately recognized or even acknowledged in the public schools and in their approved curriculums and textbooks.

Schools keep experimenting with different ways of organizing classes: sometimes classes, sometimes "projects," sometimes individual tutorials. Often the schools try to make incidental education a reality by finding work in the community for students. But it is not clear how accurately this emphasis expresses where many young people are at today. (The idea is very appealing to many staff people, especially those with a political perspective.) The problem of whether the curriculum should be in any sense structured or "required" (with the participation of the students) is a constantly debated subject. For example, the New Community School requires each student to participate in a given number of projects of his own choice, while the Santa Barbara Community School made no such requirement though, as the school got older, the staff and students tended to emphasize more participation in academic endeavors. Many students and staff became increasingly dissatisfied with the general tone of the school when there was a large number of students mainly hanging around.

The argument is not simply one about the most useful form of organization or the proper kinds of pressure to be exerted. The basic questions are about the real purposes of schools and what is worth learning, why, and how. (This will be the subject of Chapter 4.)

A Week in the Life of Community School
(Minneapolis, Minn.)

Monday	Tuesday	Wednesday	Thursday	Friday
Beginning of the week meeting. 10:00 Organizing for math with Sharon Organizing for history with Marja Cheesemaking with Steve	Philosophy 10:00 with Doug School Paper 11:00 Jim upstairs co. room	Yoga 10:00 (only with people with blanket, candle, and incense are admitted) Bread baking 9:00	Astrology 10:00 with Meri Lehtiner Future with Tom 10:00 Drawing class with Carol 11:00	Speaker from U of M admissions 10:00 "Happy, sad" Film with Jim Heliotis and other movies 11:00
Lunch 12:30	Lunch 12:30	Lunch 12:30	Lunch 12:30	Lunch 12:30
Improvisational workshop 1:30 Brooke at the pottery studio 827 Ashland 1:30 Sky-divers meeting at Lanath Wells' 7:30 Kathy Carrier	Slideshow of art work by high-school students. (Mrs. Belvo) 1:00 Greening of America 1:00 upstairs co. room	Improvisational workshop 1:30 Brooke at the studio 1:30 Decision making meeting: admissions, graduation requirements. 2:00 Volleyball at Macalester (see Tim H.) 7:30	Discussion on "Steppenwolf" 1:00 Staff meeting 4:00 Mexican trip remembering The Laurel House 7:30	More movies after lunch Improvisational workshop 1:30

Governance

The participatory freedom that free schools emphasize by the ways in which learning situations are organized also characterizes the process of governance. From the comments of students about why they wanted to get out of public schools, it is clear that much of the alienation they express is due to their sense of powerlessness, of being regimented and ordered about, of not having any control over the conditions under which a major part of their lives is lived. All free schools have true student participation. A. S. Neill's Summerhill, the "grand-daddy" of free schools, set the all-school meetings at the center of the school experience; and Neill insisted on the point that even a six-year-old had a vote that counted as much as the headmaster's. Not all free schools would go this far; but it is the case, as the descriptions illustrate, that a serious effort is always made to involve even the young children in decision-making. In the high schools, students often take over most of the decision-making power, to the extent that in some student-organized schools like the Elizabeth Cleaners Street School in New York, *all* power is in the students' hands. They fire and hire staff, choose the building, set the schedule, formulate the philosophy, etc. In fact, it might be considered an irony, considering the intense concern with discipline and administrative control characteristic of most public schools, that some free school people find it a serious problem that students don't assume *more* control, that they sometimes seem to be rather passive, relying on the staff to make the decisions.

In elementary free schools, although students are involved, actual governance rests with the adults, usually the staff, or the staff and the parents together; there is by law, however, always a board of directors, whose role varies from school to school.

From the Community School description:

The school was run by the teachers, all decisions being made by consensus. There was no director. Because of the experience of the previous year (most of the staff was not rehired on the decision of the board) the second year's staff was anxious to define clearly the role of the Board of Directors. The board declared that it was their wish that the staff assume full responsibility for all decisions, including hiring and firing; and the new group began the year with the assurance that the experience of the previous year would not be repeated.

The staff met regularly, once a week. At an early meeting a list of "shared assumptions" was drawn up which related primarily to procedural matters, such as that all decisions should be made by consensus and that if any staff member was the cause of serious dissension that fact in itself would be an indication that he or she should not stay in the school. There was no clear articulation, however, of the educational philosophy which should direct the school or what the goals of the school were to be. This was probably because the experience of teaching in this kind of school was new to most of the teachers (the experience of teaching at all was new to a few); they did not know, therefore, what to expect or even what to hope for and tended to regard the venture as an experiment. Problems were discussed in these meetings as they came up and communication was considerably better than it had been the previous year (the school's first), although, in retrospect, it is clear that on a day-to-day basis the teachers generally acted independently with only a minimum of consultation or coordination of efforts. This was especially true in the academic areas. The topics of discussion at staff meetings were the tone of the school, problems with specific children, field trips, school rules, and structural questions such as whether the children should make out daily schedules (it was decided midway in the year that they should); curriculum, academic goals, and teaching methods were almost never discussed. These questions were left up to the discretion of each individual teacher. Nor was there much done in the way of evaluation. The teachers were generally wary of being critical of each other and thus problems were not discussed until they reached critical proportions. As for evaluations of individual students' progress, there were, for the parents who requested them, parent-staff conferences, but these were less than helpful all around, mostly because the staff tended to feel defensive about what they were doing and entered into these sessions determined to prove to the parents what a good job the school was doing with their children rather than to honestly evaluate the child's progress.

The New School has officially been a "parent cooperative" from its inception over five years ago, but the meaning of this in practice is not constant over time.

The amount of actual work (teaching, driving, cleaning, paper work) done by parents has remained fairly constant since the founding of the school. About one-third of the parents are actively involved, about one-third of the work is done by parents. Most of these parents are women, though there are always significant exceptions. The building and repair projects, which have gone on each summer to a greater or lesser extent, have given fathers in the group an opportunity to contribute time and labor and have served as a way for families to come to know each other.

Parent participation in the decision-making and policy setting processes has varied over the years. During the first three years, the parents met together constantly (at least weekly) and tried to decide everything—not just broad policy, but also its application. There was a great deal of anxiety, a lot of yelling at teachers, hostility between parents, and lots of genuine involvement with the daily lives of the children. The strain of that level of involvement got to be too wearing for most parents and was a great burden on the teachers. After the third year, the parents backed off a bit and left the day-to-day running of the school to a parent director and the teachers and children. After a year and a half of relative uninvolvement, the parents started again participating more actively, this time with less anxiety and less hostility. The parents now meet regularly on a monthly basis, but there are several committee meetings in between regular parents' meetings and various other activities which involve parents, teachers, and children. Weekly staff meetings, of course, involve several parents; one of the parents is teaching a ceramics course to all the New School staff; parents, staff, and children get together to order materials and equipment; staff and parents work together with children on the hot lunch program. Some of the parents, and even some of the teachers who would have been thought to suffer most from it, feel that the involvement of the parents in the school is the best thing about it, even when it's a negative involvement. They see the early years as the most vital. Others feel that the constant discussions of educational philosophy, teaching style, curriculum, etc., which consumed so much time during the early years were wasteful of energy and destructive of creative effort.

The Second Foundation School's description gives an indication of how important these democratic school meetings are, not just as an effective decision-making process, but also as an important experience in itself, where attitudes change and democratic and cooperative modes of interrelating are learned.

Questioned about student involvement in governance, Judy Vincent, one of the founding teachers of the K-12 free school in Minneapolis, said:

Now we have meetings once a week at 12:30 on Friday. All the discussion in terms of problems which have come up during the week, such as new students who want to come to the school, who broke the cat box, who's going to take the gerbils home over vacation, happens at the meetings. Everyone who's interested in coming to the meeting can come, and then we talk about these things. Sometimes votes are taken on things and sometimes not. There is a definite lack of procedure, and how well the meetings do generally depends on how well the chairman can control things, make people stick to the issues and so forth.

We started at the beginning of the year having a meeting every day at 3:30, and what happened was that just the staff showed up. Once in a great while some students might come. So we changed it to 12:30 during the regular school day to try to encourage more people to come. In that sense it's really worked out well. Almost all the people of, say, ten and eleven years and up come, particularly since they feel it is more their school, and they're making more of the decisions.

Previous to that change, the staff would end up making almost all of the decisions. Part of that was because we were afraid to let students make decisions because we didn't know how they would go. And some of it was also because the students felt that it was our [staff's] school, and that the problems were staff problems, and that staff should figure them out. Most of those attitudes have been very largely changed.

We used to have a system whereby a couple of the high-school students who couldn't pay tuition cleaned.

And that didn't work at all because everyone would just leave messes all over. So now, at the school meetings, we've decided everybody should help clean up. And that works fairly well, as long as there's an older person in charge.

Meetings have really changed attitudes. People feel more like it's everybody's school.

The participation question is of great concern to all free schools. The development just described—the emergence of trust in the students on the part of the adult staff (which is to say, actually living up to their claimed ideals) and the growth of a true sense of the school being "our place" on the part of the students—is a goal aimed at, but not always reached.

Many free schools are very informal about decision-making, depending on trust and good will while letting things develop and change as they go. But in the schools that are not middle-class in consituency, there seems to be a greater pressure to have some clear method of decision-making, some way of avoiding the looseness and casualness which to progressive middle-class people seems all right, but to other groups, more turned off to education in general and less experienced in active participation in the running of institutions, can seem like chaos, irresponsibility, or lack of seriousness. In the community schools that serve the black community or attempt to integrate diverse groups in the community, or in the schools attempting to serve working-class youth, a serious effort is made to set up clear and useful structures of governance in order to anticipate and avoid conditions of casualness which are tolerable in middle-class based schools, but can be very discouraging or even fatal in other circumstances. (Such a situation was noted in the account from the New Community School in Oakland, quoted earlier. It was felt that a building and a sense of solidity were necessary in order to earn the participation of poor black families, whereas for hip white middle-class youth and parents, this was not nearly so important.)

Staff

The descriptions quoted here have indicated the importance of warm and close relations betwen staff and students and of the kind of intense staff involvement that free schools demand. Deeply held values are invariably engaged and the necessarily high degree of participation in all phases of life of the school make for very great pressures on interpersonal relations, often resulting in a high incidence of serious conflict. "Freedom" also means freedom to have the opportunities for many kinds of conflict and confrontation which formal bureaucratic organizations systematically avoid by their definition of particular role and responsibility areas (at a high price, to be sure). Given the extremely low salaries that most free schools pay and the very large time input required (free school teaching is seldom 8:30–3:30, five days a week; most teachers are active on many evenings, weekends, and even holidays), it is obvious that the commitment of the staff is much more than in most jobs in this society, and this situation intensifies the conflicts that inevitably arise.

The descriptions from the various schools can give some sense of the staff questions—the attrition, the problems of developing a staff that can share ideals and be personally compatible. Also, it should be noted that free schools ideologically ignore official teacher credentialing; although, since the ranks of potential and actual free school teachers are continually swelled by "drop-outs" from public school teaching, a large number of free school teachers have credentials and public school experience. For example, it was public school teachers who started the Second Foundation

School. There is even a "Teacher Drop-Out Center" in Amherst, Massachusetts, whose sole purpose is to help disgruntled public school teachers find teaching jobs in free-type schools.

The question of qualifications is an interesting one. The variety of people who come into free schools to teach, either paid or volunteer, is very wide, due in part to the fact that there is no filtering process such as required education courses or state credentialing. Often, the people are qualified and active practitioners of what they offer to teach, rather than teacher college trained teachers of the subject. For example, last year the Group School in Cambridge, Massachusetts, a working-class based high school, had no science teacher on its full-time staff. Science and math programs were taught by two young men volunteers: one received his Ph.D. in microbiology from MIT last year, the other graduated *summa cum laude* from MIT in 1970, with a major in physics and a minor in mathematics. Having done original work in plasma physics research (the study of thermonuclear phenomena), this young man decided to refuse a three-year graduate fellowship to MIT, and instead spent a year teaching science and creative writing at the elementary Community School in Santa Barbara. He is now working in Cambridge, and volunteering his time as a science and math tutor at the Group School. This same Group School had an active drama workshop taught not by a credentialed English teacher who is interested in drama but by a professional actress-director from the well-known and respected Theater Company of Boston. This person also arranged a special project of the Theater Company which enabled Group School students to work along with an Equity repertory company as apprentices.

People like this frequently get involved in free schools. This fact in itself doesn't guarantee good teaching, but neither does a state certificate. However, having actual doers of the subject being studied is certainly significant. (An example of one such program in public schools is the Teachers and Writers Collaborative in New York.) Certainly, having a Ph.D. does not assure effective teaching, as anyone who has gone to college realizes. Still it is a vital aspect of free schools that such highly qualified people can easily become involved in the education of the young. Neither of the scientists mentioned above would be "qualified" for jobs as science teachers in most public high schools in this country, although it would be fair to say that in any test designed to show depth of knowledge of their fields of biology and physics it would be inordinately difficult to find a credentialed high-school teacher who could come near to matching them.

The New School describes its staff situation in the following way:

The ratio of paid staff to students is about 1:15. The ratio of adults to children at any given time is about 1:5. The staff is chosen by parents and children with fairly equal weight given to the opinions of all. Hiring is one area in which the students are willing to participate actively and the adults know how to involve students and help them participate. Most teachers have stayed for two years and there has always been a man and a woman on the paid staff. Salaries have varied widely and have been determined by a combination of the needs of the teachers and the income of the school.

Either a parent or one of the teachers has always acted as director or administrator. During the first three years of the school there were problems involving responsibility and authority. Twice there were severe philosophical and personality conflicts between teachers, each time resulting in the resignation of one of the staff members. The first time this happened the school was in its third year and the parents were actively and painfully involved in trying to solve the problems. (The problems were solved, but somehow to nobody's satisfaction.) The second time was this past year, the school's sixth, and the staff problems, of a very similar nature, were solved by the staff before most of the parents were even aware of their existence.

Between six and ten practice teachers usually work at the school, most of them Goddard students. At first, perhaps two or three were effective. This term five out of the six students made a real contribution. This is due to greatly increased cooperation on the part of the faculty at the college, to the school's staff developing ability to use student help effectively, and to the increasing sophistication on the part of the college students regarding education and the lives of children generally.

This past year is the first time the school has had staff with experience in other free schools. Up to now, the New School was the first unstructured experience any of the teachers had had and it generally took several months for most of them to find their feet. This process has been abbreviated this year, past experience probably accounting for the smoother start. The relentless "involvement," often simply meddling and heckling of the staff, which was an ingredient of the first three years of the school has subsided, partly because the parents learned better and partly because most of their fears about academic achievement have been allayed.

The opinion of many of the adults is that the children actually determine what goes on in the school (not through formal structures but through *de facto* control) and that it doesn't change all that much from one year to the next as far as its essentials are concerned. In other words, it seems possible that the New School is less dependent on staff members than many other schools.

The Community School (elementary) has gone through

several staff changes, and has hoped to encourage increasing involvement of parents. The fact of how, even with little money available, teachers continue to work with joy, dedication, and satisfaction is brought out in the descriptions. It should be noted how the staff relations change from one year of operation to the next. (These excerpts describe the second and third years of the school's existence.)

The staff this year is somewhat smaller than last year and the paid, full-time staff is considerably smaller. However parents have been participating in the school in ever increasing numbers and thus we have been able to maintain a high teacher-to-student ratio. The full-time staff is six people: two women and four men. Of these two are paid enough to support themselves (from $150 to $300 a month), two are paid less than $50 a month, and two take no salary at all. Three of these have had previous teaching experience in public school, one has a California teaching credential; three had taught previously in the Free School. Three of us have graduated from college and one of us is in college now. (Actually this fact is interesting only in regard to its irrelevance to our relative abilities to work well in the school.) One of us is a parent with children in the school. All of these teachers, with the exception of the college student who is actually only going to be with the school until Christmas, taught in the school last year. All of us are white and under thirty. Two of our teachers have specialties: the science teacher, who has done graduate work in biology and worked professionally in the field, and our art teacher who has a teaching credential in art and is a successful commercial potter.

The teachers meet together an average of once every two weeks for staff meetings. We discuss various kids and how they are doing. We go over the immediate past, discuss how our plans worked out, what need for improvement we have noticed, and we make plans for the immediate future—what trips we want to take and what crafts activities we want to plan for. This year, since we have been working more closely together in the academic areas, we have begun to also discuss the academic curriculum and teaching methods.

The New Community School in Oakland describes its staff situation as follows:

There are six full-time core staff at the school, and nine part-time teachers. Both teachers and core staff share in classes and administrative work. When hiring, the school is as interested in a person's organizing experience and background in community work as their experience in education. In a real sense, teachers are organizers at New Community School. Teacher turnover has been slight, which has been crucial in the development of an ongoing program. The fears and feelings of the teachers are often similar. Low pay, little job security, and no benefits are problems on the employment side of things. The main problems voiced at staff meetings include attendance and motivation of students. The staff is highly qualified, very enthusiastic, and probably is the most influential power group in the school.

These excerpts are intended to give some concrete sense of the staff situation in free schools. This is arguably the most crucial area to observe in attempting to understand the free schools, their present and future developments, and their chances for survival and success.

Using Space

As with most other aspects of free school philosophy, ideas on the right sorts of buildings and space usage are quite consciously protests against the normal practice in public schools. (For an insightful account of the "theoretical architecture" of free schools, see Robert Goodman, "The Liberated Zone—An Evolving Learning Space," in the *Harvard Education Review* special issue, "Architecture and Education," 1969. The article describes the process gone through by a group of high-school students who wanted to start their own free school and who worked along with Goodman's architectural design class at M.I.T. in evolving their own ideas of what they wanted for a school building.) The key to space use in free schools is improvisation and ingenuity. Although free school people know what they don't like—large stone and brick buildings with many corridors and many identical classrooms containing many identical desks, bolted to the floor or, in the more modern schools, movable—they are very open-minded and experimental in trying to find what they do like. But the constraint of very little money means that often a free school has to make the best of far-from-ideal physical situations. As in curriculum and governance, participation is an important factor. Often, the setting up and transformation of the physical space is one of the major tasks of the staff, students, and parents; and doing this work is considered an important part of the educational process itself and a good way of getting clear on the operational meaning of free school concepts. Also, the experience provides an opportunity for a participatory project that brings the whole school together in cooperative physical work, a good way for community spirit to be nurtured, especially in the early months of a school's existence.

The description of the Santa Barbara Community School, which found itself without an available building as the school year opened last September and then established itself in a park, with subsidiary "sites" in different parents' homes, is an extreme example of the capacity for experimentation. The success of the "park school" and the insights about various aspects of the educational process that this experiment-by-necessity gave the staff are also worth noting in respect to the meaning of space use in free schools.

The variety of spaces used by free schools is very great. Churches are an important source of space, since they often have schoolrooms that are already properly zoned and are up to school building and fire codes. Also, some sympathetic churches will even donate the space or charge very low rent. Remodeled residential houses, garages, former Hebrew schools, warehouses, Salvation Army buildings, YMCAs, former army barracks are the kinds of places that have become free school sites.

Relations of Free Schools to the Larger Community

The use of space is related to a very serious problem free schools sometimes face, namely, hostility from various groups in the community, especially the local and state authorities and public school officials.

As mentioned earlier, commitment to free school ideas is often correlated with liberal or radical political and social values. However, most people involved in free schools do not present their schools in openly political terms, though in the eyes of many officials and people in the community, free schools are havens for hippies, protesters, radicals, open users of drugs, "obscene" language, and sex.

It is impossible to deny, no matter how neutrally the school presents itself or how much it emphasizes that it is simply a kind of educational option that some parents and students are choosing, that free schools are in fact a living critique of the kind of education offered in most public schools. It is to be expected then that there would be individuals and groups in the community, especially within the public school system, that might feel threatened by free schools. The threat is not in terms of competition for students, but in the more-or-less explicit message of free schools that most public schools are *bad* for young people.

This hostility can become significant to free school existence when it takes the form of harassment. And it is often in the form of hassles about buildings and space that this harassment is expressed. Free schools are seriously challenging the dominant public school conception of what a *school* is, and the conception of what is good and proper as a physical environment is an important manifestation of this questioning.

The story of the building code problems encountered by the Second Foundation School reveals the kind of difficulties that free schools frequently run into.

Q: Did anyone give you trouble when you first opened the school?

JV: Once we opened we ran into trouble. What it seems happened last spring was that some officials of the Minneapolis public schools decided that the public schools had a *moral* responsibility for children attending free schools in the Twin Cities area. There was some debate between local officials and the State Board as to who had authority over free schools. It was decided that the local school district did. Since all the free schools in the Twin Cities are located in Minneapolis, it was the Minneapolis public schools.

School officials then became worried not about the kind of education students were getting in free schools, but in regard to fire and health standards. So one day, out of the blue, the health marshal arrived and took bacteria counts on our cupboards and he told us our refrigerator was sixty-eight degrees (which it was because it was broken at the time). He suggested we get a fan over the stove and an extra fire extinguisher and left. Then we got a phone call a week later from City School. They said that the fire marshal was on his way over to our school.

Now the first time they came over, there was the state fire marshal and the city assistant fire marshal. They came and they looked around and made a lot of critical remarks. The state fire marshal filled out a form on the school in which he approved the school. He suggested, however, to the assistant Minneapolis fire inspector that there were some things that were questionable, which the city ought to look into.

About two weeks after that we got a phone call from Phoenix School saying that the fire marshal had been there, had told them they were going to get an eviction notice because they were in an unsafe building, and that they (the fire marshals) had been to City School previously, and that they told City School the same thing—that they were going to get evicted.

The reason for the eviction was that there was a city ordinance saying that children in the third grade or below could not be above or below ground level. Phoenix and City Schools were both on second floors, and we're in the basement.

So they showed up. It was the director of safety for the Minneapolis public schools, the city fire marshal, the assistant city fire marshal, and someone who we never found out who he was. They marched in. They were all very big. One had a uniform on. Everybody got very excited. The four of them walked through the building saying things like, "How can you be teaching anything when you don't have blackboards?" and "How can you be learning anything when it's so loud and noisy?" We told them that they were the ones who had created that situation, marching in with their uniforms. Anyway, they indicated to us that we would be getting an eviction notice.

We called our lawyer who looked into the city codes. He found that the code they were referring to did *not* say "below ground level," only that children third grade or under could not be "above" ground level. He said he doubted they were going to get us on that.

Well, it turned out that they really turned their attention, after that, on Phoenix and City Schools. Both were evicted. Eventually Phoenix School folded because they couldn't find another place, and City School eventually found a church.

We didn't hear anymore after that from the city fire marshal until last July 16. On that day the city fire marshal and his assistant came down and informed us that our construction did not meet building codes.

They wanted us to tear down all of our walls, including the wall on the stage—and that wall was already Sheetrocked on both sides and surrounded by concrete. What they were concerned about was that the two by fours inside were not fire resistant. They said that we had to tear it all down and put in fire resistant wood.

We called our lawyer and he went down to see the city fire marshal and convinced the city fire marshal that it wasn't their responsibility to put free schools out of business.

Evidently the fire marshal had felt, from his instructions from school officials to investigate the free schools as to their safety, that that was rather an order to close them.

The upshot was that we could keep the wall that was sheetrocked on both sides. We did have to replace the other walls with two by fours and sheetrock on both sides.

The New School recently encountered similar difficulties, in its sixth year of existence.

> This year, the sixth of the school's existence, the State has refused to certify the school. This is not, according to the commissioner, a matter of policy, but rather of chance. That is, it's an accident that after five years the ceilings aren't high enough, the ventilation isn't adequate, the fire alarm system faulty, the shelf space short. Again, the physical aspects of the school are the easiest to attack. The lack of certification has kept the school from buying the buildings which house it from the parent who still, reluctantly, owns them, because no bank will lend money to an uncertified school.
>
> Although the official reasons for the school not yet being certified are health and safety factors, it is evident from the inspection reports that there are other motives. They seem to be upset also by the educational philosophy and methods and are distressed by such things as appearances of disorder, the language used by the children, and the life drawing classes. As of this date, the State has refused even to send their fire and environmental inspector to look at the facilities and we are still trying to obtain specifics about what we must do for certification.

The staff of the New School, like the staff of the Second Foundation, feels it has good grounds for thinking that hostility to the school is an important element in the "building" troubles, that it is their philosophy and life styles, as much as the actual physical conditions, that bring the unsympathetic attention of state officials down on them.

Sometimes the harrassment is based directly on educational "rules," as when the state officials refuse certification on the grounds that educational standards concerning courses, equipment, certified teachers, etc., are not being met. It is obvious that the ways in which these rules are formulated and interpreted are based on the view that a *proper* school must be like the traditional public or private schools, and so it is to be expected that the radically different free school approaches to education will not easily meet these requirements.

The question of relation to public schools is a complex one within the new schools movement. Some schools are isolationist, in the sense that their attention is almost completely inward: they feel that all their energies are well spent in making their own school work, and what they hope is that the various school and state bureaucracies will just leave them be. Other schools, especially community schools, feel that an important part of their purpose is to help effect changes within the public schools, and they relate their work to reform developments within the public schools. This doesn't mean that the relationships with public school officialdom are cooperative, except in very rare situations, but that these new schools consciously take account of the fact that most young people are still in public schools, and that free schools could be part of a broad based reform effort to change existing schools as well as generate new experimental places. (This subject will be discussed extensively in Chapter 5.)

In Santa Barbara, the Community High School was formed by students, some of whom had been "troublemakers" in the public high school, including the president of the student body who was one of the few vocal "student radicals" in a rather conservative community. Hostility between public school personnel and people from the Community School arose early on and has continued, though the Community School people have tried to work with sympathetic teachers within the public schools. Participants in the school see this hostility manifested in various ways—remarks of teachers and administrators and administrative "reprisals" against Community School students who transfer back into public high school, for example.

A former Community School coordinator gives the following account of relations with the public schools:

> The impact on the public school establishment of the founding of the Community High School was expected but revealing. Some of the participants in the Community High School were active in various protests at Santa Barbara High School and of course the directors of the project were vocal in their critique of the authoritarianism of the public school system. One of the directors was invited to speak to the high school assembly on alternative schools. In describing the reason for the need for such schools he delivered a severe and unflattering critique of Santa Barbara's high schools. The three hundred or so students seemed to be interested in the analysis and many gathered around the director at the end for more talk. The large number of teachers who had been present were nowhere to be seen, however, and one of the after-school students later reported that her teacher had argued in class that "those people should not be allowed to come into a school and say that" (i.e., to criticize the methods of the schools).

The following story (true) demonstrates how and why the Community School, as a real existing alternative, was a great source of concern to the public school administrators. The scene is a public high-school classroom:

TEACHER: That's a rather silly answer, John.
STUDENT: Well, I thought that the question was silly, *Tom.*

Sent to the office, the student was asked by the assistant principal how he would like to be served with five demerits for insubordination. (The demerit system is a punitive measure. If a student collects too many demerits he or she may be kept from graduation.) The student replied that he had no interest in the matter one way or the other.

Sent to the principal, the student was asked if it mattered to him that he was going to be suspended or even, perhaps, expelled.

The student replied that it did not matter. If they expelled him he would enroll in the Community School, which he did.

The story demonstrates how the existence of alternatives can undermine the absolute power and authority which schools have over students.

Toward the end of May, a couple of open-minded public school teachers who came by to see the school reported that at a meeting of the principals of all the high schools and junior high schools in the city, the Community School had been discussed at great length. The teachers said that their principal had reported back to the faculty that the "object of the school was to destroy the public school system and democracy as we know it."

On another occasion, at lunch with a public school teacher from the local Continuation School, the directors were told that it was a well-known fact that they (the directors) had been sent to Santa Barbara by John Holt, and were backed by that well-known communist front, the Carnegie Foundation.

Rather than viewing return to public school by students as an indication of a failure to be a "better" school, the staff encourages those students who feel ready to go back to do so. They feel that a year off for students is an important function of the free school, and that it is important to realize the limitations of a small school.

Some interviews with students who are now back in public school:

J: What did you learn at the Community School?

W: Well, I learned about the Community School, what

it was like. I think that it was good that I went there for a year because it's easier to go back to public school . . . well in a way it was easier and in a way harder, but I had a rest from public school which is what I needed, because I would have . . . I don't know what I would have done.

J: What do you mean in some ways harder and some easier?

W: In a way it's easier because I had a rest from it, and harder because all the rules are ridiculous.

J: What made you decide to go back to public school?

D: It was a lot of things. I wanted to get to know the people in public schools more. I didn't want to be isolated from people my age. I was worried about going to college. I didn't think that if I went to the Community School for a long time I would be able to go on to college because of credits. Another major part was that I knew my parents wouldn't let me go to the school for another year.

J: When you went back to public school did it seem different?

D: Not in the way it was structured or anything, except that I think maybe some of the teachers are a little more open in discipline ways. There are also a couple of better classes available, but other than that *I* was really different. Emotionally. And so public school seemed a lot different. . . . I'm more aware of things that are happening, of what people are doing, of what trips teachers are putting on over students, more able to talk to people and find out what they are thinking. I'm better able to discuss things with teachers.

Generally the city schools will test students for placement. So far, of all those who have gone back, all but one have been placed in their proper grade age level. The following experiences seem fairly representative of those who go back into public school:

J: So you were in the eighth grade when you first started coming to the Community School?

L: Yes.

J: You are in the tenth grade in public school now. Do you feel the Community School helped you?

L: I learned a lot. It's like a stopping place. In public school you don't really have time for yourself. I grew more emotionally there than I had in all my other school years, because I had time to do it in.

J: Do you feel you've been left behind academically? In going back to public school do you feel there is a lot you don't know?

L: No. As a matter of fact. . . . I haven't been to public school for almost two years and I took this SCAT, or SKIT or SIT or something test and I rated 78 or 79 in math and reading through my eleventh grade year . . . that's how I got my credits . . . I took the test and they said I'm smart enough. But really I don't know what they can learn in public school. It seems the majority of the people there don't have the time to stop and grow emotionally. It seems they won't learn academically.

I go to Dos Pueblos and that's the most liberal school in the public school system here. It's certainly a change from the other city schools . . . but if I went to [one of the other schools] and took the SKAT or whatever, they would just ignore it. They wouldn't give me the credits and I'd have to stay back a year, or else have seven periods. People who went to High from the

Community School, like Debby, they wouldn't do that for her.

J: Are the courses you're taking college preparatory?

L: I don't know.

J: Have you looked into this matter at all?

L: No. . . . I'm trying to get pass-fail in all my classes because its really just a mind fuck thinking about grades. At the Community School I didn't have that pressure. Now that I've got straight A's if I get anything lower I'll probably feel bad. I don't want to feel bad.

The idea that being in a free high school can be a rewarding stage in life for high-school people, that a year or two of this experience will be valuable for them if and when they return to public school, and that this process will be important in public school reform has been perceived by the people in the Community School.

The New Community School in Oakland has developed a formal program to involve students who are in the public high school:

Another major thrust of the school in the last year and a half has been the development of programs which would publicize the school, and inform the public—particularly high-school students—about alternative forms of education. Since many public school students, for various reasons from parents to finances, cannot attend an alternative school full-time, New Community School decided to offer after-school and summer school programs. These programs are attempts to meet the expressed needs of high-school students. To as great a degree as possible, school organizers try to develop programs from the ground up. This means asking students what they want from the programs, taking care to develop student leadership, and generally being responsive to the needs of students and the community.

Our first after-school program was conducted with students from Skyline High School in Oakland. The school is generally middle and upper class white. The pilot class in the humanities ran in the fall of 1970 with fourteen students. This class exposed the students to the curriculum and teaching styles of an alternative school. The next spring, a psychology class with two sections was offered, and twenty-eight students enrolled. Two churches in the Montclair area of Oakland donated space, and a good relationship was maintained with the Oakland Public Schools. This fall (1971) psychology and sociology were offered, but the feeling of the school now is that the courses should be developed for lower income white and Black students of the high schools in the immediate vicinity of New Community School. The school is presently trying to rent a large vacant lot across the street for afterschool recreation and other neighborhood activities.

In order to extend the school's program to even more students, increase publicity, and raise funds, a summer school plan was drawn up early in the year. While the enrollment was not as large as we had hoped, the publicity drew the attention of many public school students and staff to New Community School. Ten courses were offered. The enthusiasm was high, and almost all of the fifty students paid the nominal tuition fee (most people in the school feel it is important that every student pay something to attend, and we have found that in almost all cases this is possible without working extreme hardship). Most encouraging was the equally divided Black and white enrollment. The relaxed nature of the program and school created an interracial learning situation which was healthy for everyone, and which few of the students had ever experienced before. Considering the unusually poor education in the public schools in Oakland (Oakland test results are almost the lowest in California), it seems imperative that new ways be found to encourage learning in Oakland. New Community School has tried only a few forms, and plans to experiment with many more.

The next chapter takes up the problems of evaluating the activities and accomplishments of the free schools. The free school people whose accounts have provided the material for this chapter gave some brief evaluations on the basis of their own experiences. The staff and a parent (former staff member) of the New School, looking back on more than five years of operation, write:

Generally speaking, the school has remained well left of center in the spectrum of American education. Even the children feel they're fairly well in control of their own daily lives insofar as that's possible in this culture. There are an absolute minimum of adult-generated rules at the school (a few are that you can't play on the roof, go in the pond without an adult present, or leave the school without permission from either a parent or a teacher); the curriculum depends on what the children and adults involved are interested in learning and teaching, rather than on some preconceived notions of what should be taught in school; there are no grades (in either sense); children participate in the hiring of staff and are welcome to participate in budget decisions, but decline the responsibility.

Some parents have found the lack of structure disturbing and have withdrawn their children. Some children have withdrawn themselves. One was asked to leave by the staff and others would be directed to a more structured situation if one existed outside of the rigid public schools. As it is, there are constant small crises and problems but the school is generally acceptable to most of the parents and most of the current participation is supportive, most criticism constructive.

The new teachers at the school were previously active in another free school, and their view of the situation is as follows:

Having just left a similar school in Milwaukee, we (this year's full-time teachers) found many similar ideas, values, problems, etc. Both schools were established by white, middle-class, college-associated people disenchanted with public schools. Both schools had early problems with building codes, differences in philosophy of parents, noise, cleanliness, etc. But what may be significant is that both schools are somewhat more structured than they were last year. It seems that parents' expectations of children's abilities and desires to run their own lives and to want to learn spontaneously (what we *want* them to learn) may be too high. We are presently working toward a more structured curriculum, still with many alternatives, no grades, child-centered, but giving a child the right to some privacy and quiet. A child who doesn't feel like doing anything but being disruptive is free to go home (if he has his parent's permission). This change seems to be in line with what the children want. They have individually asked for more classes, more quiet time, more order, but collectively they are unwilling to provide it themselves.

Therefore we feel that it is our responsibility to provide alternatives and an environment conducive to learning.

As noted before, some new schools people, especially those dealing with constituencies other than the liberal, progressive section of the middle class, are aware of this question before they start their schools and try to avoid the problems.

The parent-cooperative model of the New School and, to an increasing degree, the Community School (elementary) appears to be quite feasible, and the number of such schools is increasing rapidly on the elementary level.

A Community School teacher evaluates its future developments:

We have tried to encourage parent involvement in the school because it is clear that the long-term survival of the school will depend on this. We do not have the budget to support the large staff that is necessary for the kind of educational environment we are trying to create. And while people can always be found who are willing and able to contribute a large amount of time and energy for little remuneration for a short time (a semester or perhaps a year) it is to the parents that you have to look for the kind of long-term commitment that will give the school the necessary continuity.

Furthermore it is my belief that the kind of education we are trying to create is most successful if parents are involved. Although certain children do exhibit regressive behavior in the presence of their parents (usually their mother), I think that on the whole the children relate better to the school if at least one of their parents is in some way a part of it (either as a part-time teacher, as a person who scrounges up materials, a person who makes up work sheets, the person who collects the tuitions, a person who comes and sings with us once a week, the person who answers the phone, or the person who drives everyone to the roller skating rink). And I think the parents relate better to the education of their children when they are able to work with experienced teachers. They get an idea of how reading can be taught, how math can be taught, etc. They take these ideas home and work with the children there in the evenings (the very best way, I think, for a child to learn how to read); then they develop new ideas of their own and bring these to school. As they develop a better understanding of the process of learning, they become less anxious about the *appearance* of learning, i.e., sitting at a desk all day doing endless papers.

So it is my hope that the school is moving in the direction of becoming a parent-cooperative. I would like to see parents taking major responsibility for running the school, hiring and firing the paid staff (which should number perhaps two or, at the most, three), and with that staff making all the major decisions regarding the daily operation of the school. Of course this would be predicated on at least a core group of parents working at least three days a week in the school. And, gradually, this has been happening. More parents have been teaching at the school and consequently more parents have been consulted, either personally or at parents meetings, in making both major and minor decisions. It was the parents, for instance, who decided on the dates and duration of the Christmas vacation. And recently when a couple of our parents proposed that if the school lend them, interest free, the money to make the down payment on a house they wanted to buy they would make a guest house portion of the building available to the school for either full-time or rainy day use, the idea was brought up at a parents meeting and decided on by the whole group. Also the parents have become involved for the first time in discussing questions such as whether the school should take back a retarded and emotionally disturbed boy who attended for a few months last year.

Meetings are one of the ways we have tried to involve parents in the school. Perhaps our parties have been more responsible, however, for any success we have had in this department—our parties, our camping trips, and our own personal relations with the parents. Greater participation in the school and at parents meetings has generally come after closer relationships, better communication, and mutual trust have developed between the staff and the parents on these more informal occasions.

It is difficult for us to evaluate ourselves in an over-all way. We consider that we are successful if we survive from year to year and if the same parents continue to believe in the school. We consider that we are successful on a day-to-day basis if we see the children happy and learning and if we ourselves are having a good time working at the school. My own feeling is that we will be successful, in the long range, whether the school survives four years or ten years or more, if it does in fact move in the direction of becoming a parent cooperative. If there is any idea that holds us together it is that it is the right and duty of parents to provide for their children the kind of education that they believe in. Not everyone believes in our kind of education. I am glad to see more and more public schools offering experimental programs, similar to our program, because I believe that this type of education is best for many, possibly most, children and I think that as more people are exposed to the ideas behind this kind of schooling more and more will come around to believing as we do in the free and open, nonauthoritarian educational environment. As I say, I am pleased to see more public schools offering this type of schooling at least as a choice for the children and parents in their district. However, I am even more pleased to see the parents take the initiative in this direction and take upon themselves the responsibility for creating an institution to suit their needs.

Steve Fisher of the New Community School evaluates the school's current situation as follows:

We are now at the point where we can begin to isolate conclusions and the difficult problems. For a small school, it seems to us that there must be some sort of focus and limitation. While the school's program should be as comprehensive as possible, it is not possible to admit every single student who applies; occasionally, it may even be necessary to drop a student or staff member. There is a great need for publicity in an alternative school. We need to know the community better, know how to serve it better; we need to direct ourselves outward continually. There is a great need to train teachers as organizers, and this is a continual task at the school. There is a need for a good approach to conflict, however it may arise. We need more clarity about policies, and at the same time better counseling and more attention to individuals—often difficult in the rush of community school organizing. Somehow, the administration of the school must become more a part of the life of the school. Finally, we need new sources of funding. At New Community School almost half of our $50,000 yearly budget is foundation supported, and the grant will expire in a couple of years. All these conclusions and needs are crucial to the survival of the school and, interestingly enough, many of them are in conflict with the prevailing notion of what an alternative or "free" school should be.

Evaluation of the school is difficult. Tests are inadequate and personal opinions vary too much to make much sense. Perhaps the greatest growth of the students is in areas of maturity, taking on responsibility, emotional understanding, and confidence of self-expression. The students (and staff) grow as the school grows—and, of course, always outside the school there is growth—and classroom-bound academic tests can never tell the story. It is difficult to see how the variety and richness of the learning experiences in a community school like this could ever be surpassed.

At this time the school is planning many things—land

development, a publicity drive in the local community, more after-school courses, preliminary accreditation—and though much has been accomplished leading towards stability, even after two years it seems as if the school is just beginning.

These descriptions give some sense of the variety of free schools. It's difficult to say what a typical school is, but these schools are representative in their concerns, transformations, hopes, and recognition of problems. There is one type of free school not described in these samples, and ironically it is perhaps the most widely held image of the free school. This is the Summerhill-type school, the full-time, live-in community for young people of all ages.

Although perhaps the purest form of free school, these schools are not the type of school that is most characteristic of the recent wave of new schools. As with Summerhill, their constituency is extremely narrow, almost exclusively white and middle-class, affluent enough to pay rates characteristic of boarding schools, and accepting of the Summerhill philosophy. Also, again like Summerhill, there tends to be a conscious isolation from the surrounding community. There is the desire to create an almost totally inward-looking intimate community of like-minded people. The basis for this ideal is the sense of creating a complex, sustaining, even therapeutic group; the kind of supportive group that can sustain self-expression, personal growth, working through of complex problems, experimentation with new life styles—all in an atmosphere of security and support. The idea is that this can best be accomplished by releasing young people from the normal day-to-day pressures of social life—the family, the public school, the impersonal city.

Summerhill Ranch School in Mendocino, California, describes itself in the following way:

Educationally, this school can be described as twenty-four-hour life tutorial, where students and staff learn in accordance with their own interests . . . our emotional developments remain primary. Self-awareness, individuality, and personal responsibility to oneself and to others here are most important. We have not the rewards and punishments nor the competitiveness of public schools. Many of us regain self-confidence and awareness here, both of which aid us in dealing with the impersonal real world.

In 1971 the school's twenty-three students and eight staff members all lived on a five-acre farm surrounded by many more acres of uninhabited land. The school supported itself on the $240 per month per student it asked for tuition. Allowance is made in quite a few cases for families that can't pay the full amount, and the state pays $375 a month for wards of the court placed there by the Probation Department. Salaries are very low, but room and board are provided.

There are horses and chickens, a vegetable garden and a green house. Classes are scheduled and meet irregularly in subjects like Yoga, drama, French, Spanish, and history, but the real education as seen by the participants comes from the experience of living together. Many normal distinctions between teachers and students are absent. The staff is young, and a visitor would have difficulty separating staff from students. As with Summerhill, self-government by the entire community is a high priority, and this can require some deliberate work on the part of the staff to get the students to take on more responsibility for running the school. At Summerhill Ranch, the staff once went on strike, stating that they were tired of having no authority, yet having all the responsibility to parents, state authorities, etc. The response of the students was to make rules for themselves (about hitch-hiking, upkeep of the school, etc.) that the staff felt they themselves could never have imposed on the students. Decisions like hiring new teachers, admitting students, or allocating money for various projects, as well as day-to-day decisions about the running of the farm are made collectively; and the work of buying and cooking food, maintaining the buildings, and the like is also shared among all members of the community. The emphasis is on creating a warm feeling of family. For many of the students who have broken contact with or, in effect, been abandoned by their own families, the school takes on this function completely.

The students are allowed to leave the school to travel, if they tell a staff member where they are going. Those students who take advantage of this opportunity probably expose themselves to a wider range of experiences than is usual for a white middle-class young person who lives at home and attends the local suburban high school. However, besides individual traveling, there is little communication with the "impersonal real world" and little evidence that the school will do anything to make an impact on any outside community. As Neill insisted for Summerhill, the purpose of the school community is to develop happy, integrated young people who will be happy adults, and the more happy people, the less social evil. This is essentially the "politics" of several of the schools of this type. (Interestingly, two years ago there was a split in the Summerhill Society in New York, with a politically radical Summerhill Collective being formed, in opposition to the more traditional Summerhill view. The Summerhill Collective defines itself, in *Vocations for Social Change*, as "a collective of five adults, serving as ex-cons to free the millions of kids imprisoned in schools and determined to get down to the real business of identifying those things in ourselves which cause us to oppress children.")

The ideal description of Summerhill schools is, of course, contained in Neill's own book, discussed in Chapter 1. The descriptions in this chapter are in part an attempt to correct the domination of the Summerhill image of free schools. It is interesting to note that in the choice of names "community school" has gained in popularity while "free school," which dominated the first years of the new schools development, has declined. Some new school people are quite articulate in denying that they are a "free school," in order to rebut the assumption that they are like Summerhill, which is the most widespread association with the phrase. (Jonathan Kozol's recent book *Free Schools* is very much to the point on this and related questions.)

The key issue—and one that underlies much of the analysis in this book—is that of the differing social and political perspectives (or lack thereof) that inform educational reform activity. In the kind of school just described, there is a dream of total self-sufficiency, a dissatisfaction with the limitations of the "part-time" nature of a school and the impositions of the "outside" world. An articulate expression of this feeling is given by Jerry Friedberg, formerly on the faculty of the recently shut-down Bensalem College, the experimental project of Fordham, and a founding director of Lorillard Children's School in the Bronx. In an article titled "Beyond Free Schools: Community," he expresses the dissatisfaction with the limitations of free schools just mentioned.

> . . . for myself and increasing numbers of others, the limits of free schools have become increasingly and painfully clear. Schools as such are a poor substitute for rich family and community life, both for children and for staff. . . . Beyond schools then, lie other alternatives worth exploring. The one I am most interested in is fairly new (and old) to me and my culture: small-scale, self-selecting, organic communities in which children and adults live, work, play, experiment, hassle, learn, and grow together. (Quoted in *Rasberry Exercises*, pp. 93–94.

In an interview, a teacher-founder of a small free school in Phoenix echoed this hope.

I would like to have a community, something like Jerry Friedberg has in New York state. He's the guy who had Lorillard Children's School, and left to start a community where everyone is just part of the community. There isn't any school, because the kids just learn from living in the community and doing things with people they like to do things with. There isn't any formal effort made to teach anything. And that's the way I feel things should really be. That anytime you try to get kids to learn something, you try to teach them something, that they haven't asked to learn themselves, you're weakening them in some way.

A parallel articulation of the opposing tendency, the conception of new schools as active and conscious agents of educational change in the larger community, is represented by another "non-school," the Central School in Cambridge, Massachusetts. Central School is a preschool and kindergarten, quite consciously aiming at changing the public schools. This commitment is so strong that the school, founded in 1969, refuses to become an above-kindergarten free school, though many people would like this to happen. The purposes of this institution are complex. Pedagogically, it is a free school for very young children, and the staff wants to show how well free education ideas can work and how much even very young children can learn, in all ways. But it is important that this be done with a completely integrated group, integrated across race and class lines. Also, it is vital that the parents be deeply involved in the school, that they hold the power and govern the school. (The parents have to formally rehire the entire staff each year, including the founding director.) In the course of their participation, the parents confront themselves and each other over hard questions of racism, sexual stereotypes, educational philosophy, and related issues. One basic aim of the school is to develop in the parents the will and capacity to act together to change the public schools. To this end the school offers itself as a community resource in education. There is a full-time parent coordinator who deals with community affairs. The teachers give a weekly workshop on "open classroom" techniques. The workshop is officially accredited by local schools of education and by the Cambridge School Board. The staff offered its building and its expertise to a group of Cambridge parents who formed a Committee for an Alternative Public School, an attempt to get an "open structure" elementary school within the public system.

The ideals of the school are impressive. Instead of being a self-selected white middle-class group, all of whom share the ideals of libertarian education and a common culture, thus making for a relatively comfortable situation, Central School has consciously gathered an integrated group of parents—black workers, MIT professors, *Boston Globe* editorial columnists, welfare mothers. There is no common culture, and often serious difficulties arise from the integration. (Part of the political insight of the school is that education is one of the few areas in which this kind of integration can take place, that people from diverse social groups can get together over improving education, and that this can spill over into other areas of social action.) The parents learn much about themselves, their own fears and prejudices, the politics of education, the meaning of racism and poverty. The operation of a preschool program for thirty youngsters might not seem to call forth such an array of complex, heavy issues, but at Central School this happens.

To say that the ideals are high does not mean that they are all reached (or that they are in fact reachable). Wilma Diskin, a former Central School parent whose daughter is now in the local public school, supports strongly the aim of training parents to become active agents of reform in the public schools. But she sees an irony in the fact that some of the middle-class parents, when the time comes for their children to go into first grade in the public schools, don't follow through with the principles of Central School, but instead send their children to one of the several expensive progressive private schools in the Boston area. (This problem is discussed in more detail in the last chapter.)

This parent also points out that what becomes painfully clear to the participants is how extraordinarily difficult and complex the problems really are. With all the good will and commitment to confronting deep-seated attitudes, the problems of racism and class stereotypes are not easily articulated and satisfactorily faced. Whatever judgments of success might be made, Central School clearly provides a very important experience to all those involved. And it is an experience that would not happen naturally in this society. There are more comfortable ways to have a high quality preschool.

That Central School is a fine place for the children is not in doubt to anyone who has spent time there. But evaluating the chances of long-range success for the larger goals of the school is a difficult task. If it is the only place of its kind in Cambridge, then how much can the very small number of parents involved accomplish? What about the dilemma of the middle-class parents who accept the ideas, participate in the school along with poor and minority-group parents, and then, when public school looms ahead, decide that they can't let their child suffer the damage they see the public school doing? They then find a good progressive or "free" private school, usually attended almost exclusively by other middle-class people. Meanwhile the poor parents, whatever their perception of the possible damage the public schools might do, find themselves with no choice.

These are agonizing questions about which it is hard to be clear and consistent. They arise because of the commitment of the institution to effecting serious change in the larger society, to improving the situation of people whose conditions are less favorable than one's own.

The tensions represented by these contradictory tendencies exist on all levels, from the most personal to the institutional. Staffs are split on this issue, individuals are at odds within themselves, people and schools agonize and vacillate over the relation to the larger community and the implications of this relation. What hopes one has for the new schools development and what evaluations one makes of present tendencies are bound up with this question.

In the next chapters, there will be some detailed analysis of the way these tensions appear in the new schools and what the potential developments are for this current movement of radical school reform.

NOTES

1 The source of the figures in this chapter comes from data gathered by the New Schools Directory Project which I directed in 1971. This project consisted of a group of free school people who received a grant from the Department of Health, Education, and Welfare to put together a directory of and report on existing free schools in the United States. A description of the directory and the project can be found in *The New Schools Exchange Newsletter,* No. 70, January 1972.

The descriptions of the schools used in this chapter came from the staff and students of five schools. The schools and the writers are:

The New School, Plainfield, Vermont (Liz and Stu Rosenfeld, Anita Landa)

The Community School, Santa Barbara: Elementary (Christopher Anne Boldt)

The Community High School, Santa Barbara (Tim Affleck, Ken Cruze, Jeremy Kramer)

The New Community School, Oakland (Steve Fisher)

Second Foundation, Minneapolis (Judy Vincent)

In addition, the material and background on Independence High School in Newark, comes from Carol Glassman, Alison Raphael, Steve Block, Norm Fruchter, and Bob Vailla.

3 · TOO GREAT EXPECTATIONS?
Achievements and Disappointments

Understanding the relation of theory and practice means evaluation. This is very forbidding territory, and I realize how hesitant and tentative any kind of evaluation must be. But given the great expectations and the dedication and energy invested in new schools, it seems worthwhile even at this point in their development to give a sense of the kinds of failures and disappointments that are already evident, as well as to note the way in which the high hopes are sometimes fulfilled.

The brochures and the self-descriptions quoted mixed theory, hopes, expectations, goals, and methods. In going more deeply into the problem of evaluation, it seems appropriate to begin somewhat critically, with an emphasis on the sorts of disappointments and failures that I and others have seen and experienced.

My interpretative evaluations will unavoidably be subjective, very much influenced by the political perspective I have been expressing from the beginning of the book, as well as by my own experience and observation. My sense of failure or success will often not agree with the evaluation of other participants or observers. Matching vague theoretical descriptions with concrete day-to-day happenings is very difficult. For example, what one person sees as honest self-expression another sees as neurotic "acting out." As in any attempt to interpret complex human actions and interactions, agreement on even a simple description is enormously hard to achieve. To try to move to deeper levels of interpretation and evaluation necessarily entails a mixing of bias, intuition, wishful thinking, self-criticism, and incomplete theoretical inclination.

Looking back to the free school literature I discussed in Chapter 1, one should notice that not much of it deals with the actual doing of a free school. There has been little systematic observation and chronicling of experience, for several reasons. Most of the schools are very young, and very few have existed long enough to have acquired extensive experience and the time to reflect on and evaluate this experience. The numbers of students involved are very small, and it is a problem to formulate and justify generalizations. Most important, there is an ideological and emotional prejudice against anything that smacks of objective evaluation and judgment. Part of this feeling comes from a reaction to the approach to education as quantitatively measurable and testable, since this view so directly violates the crucial free education emphasis on the elusive and difficult-to-define notions of self-development, autonomy, joy of discovery, getting to know oneself. Also, there is the intensity of commitment of the people involved. Far more than being a place for teachers to teach certain well-defined subject matters to an assigned group of students, the free school is an almost totally involving community, and this makes cool (objective) evaluation somewhat scary. This is especially true if it appears that the core assumptions, which are based on deeply held moral beliefs and commitments, might have to be modified.

Whatever the reasons, there has been little attempt at

systematic evaluation. What are available are mainly anecdotal accounts and personal experiences. But, as I said, interpretation of these is difficult. The observer's own biases and hopes permeate such accounts. In public schools, where evaluation usually means numerical scores on standardized tests, such biases are not so relevant. (Of course, this so-called "objective" kind of evaluation has many problems of its own.)

I intend here to draw out, however tentatively, some patterns and trends, and to discuss the meanings of these for the expectations of people committed to radical change in education. Given the very optimistic image of children and schools that underlies many of the reform conceptions, the high incidence of disappointment and even painful failure is not surprising. What the implications of failure are *in theory* is not clear, however sharp the disappointment in fact.

A distressing account by Jane Goldman, a free school teacher, appeared a while ago in *No More Teachers' Dirty Looks,* a journal published by a collective of radical public school teachers in the San Francisco area. The article, entitled "Summerhill, Some are Hell . . . ," described the beginning of a free school in Portland for five- and six-year-olds. The rhetoric of freedom was general among the adults.

> We were going to provide an atmosphere where our children could explore the world as their needs and desires dictated; we were going to remain subtly in the background while our children played and learned in patterns created by their own natural rhythms; we were going to contribute to the revolution in the schools by providing alternative modes of humane education. We decided to begin with no rules or structure; these were to emerge, organically, if and when they were needed.[1]

This description is very much in the spirit of the brochure descriptions and the school accounts of the preceding chapter. In this case, things didn't work out quite so well. The writer describes a situation characterized by much chaos, destruction, and even physical injury. Moreover, she had a radical political point of view and was quite aware of long-term goals of reversing the dominant socialization process of American society.

> We had hoped to change basic attitudes in our school simply by allowing children to interact in a free environment. Yet racism and sexism were as rampant in our school as in any public school. At our Halloween party, we had four brides, six nurses, one bunny rabbit, and two stewardesses among our girls; the boys were adorned in monster, doctor, astronaut, and scientist costumes. The boys still did wood-working, while our girls did mosaics or played in the Wendy corner. . . .[2]

Such issues are very difficult for dedicated teachers and parents to deal with, since it is hard to avoid generating guilt and creating a situation where accusations (sometimes self-accusations) about inadequate skill or lack of faith in the good ways of freedom or personal hang-ups come thick and fast. This teacher notes, with respect to confronting such problems, that

> when someone suggested we search out minority children to enroll, it was described as tokenism or as unfair to discriminate by color. When someone suggested the need for rules about the legitimacy of destroying a scientific instrument (our microscope), another person would scream, "Stop! That would be laying a trip on our children. If they're catching cooties all day or breaking equipment, it's because we failed. The children are bored. We don't have enough for them to do here." And so we would all rush out and bring in bigger and better projects, all the while feeling guilty that we weren't John Holt or Herb Kohl.[3]

Jane Goldman's sense of what went wrong is that by simply reacting against the old, the free school was prevented from developing good structures and procedures that would not be oppressive, as the authoritarian structures of the public school were. Also, she touches on a critical issue when she questions the theoretical virtues of simply "freeing" the children.

> They [free school people] need to band together not only because of the things they hate, but because they share certain values. This means knowing what sorts of human beings they want to create. It also means giving up the notion that children will just naturally change for the better. Children come to the free school with capitalism's values in their heads; they've learned sexism, racism, extreme competitiveness, obedience to authority, etc. from TV, from their storybooks, from the kids down the street, not to mention from their schools. My school failed because it left its children structureless and unguided, thus ensuring the retention of their old consciousness.[4]

I will be taking up the general political issues posed by an analysis like this in the next two chapters. What is most relevant here is that the school appeared to be a failure in the view of one of the people directly involved in it. Undoubtedly there were other people in the school who would have described the situation in different, more favorable terms, and who would not analyze the failures in such an explicitly political perspective.

The way in which this teacher perceived the failure touches the most common kinds of disappointed expectations. In the previous chapter, there were detailed descriptions of the types of new schools and their philosophies and goals. As might be expected, the disappointments are directly related to the kinds of hopes and dreams that are central to the new schools idea.

The question of structure was crucial in the description just quoted, and this word contains a host of dilemmas that are constantly debated within free schools. The dimensions of the debate are set by the basic opposition of the libertarian to the structures of conventional schools, the key objective being to abolish constricting and authoritarian philosophies. In theory, what will emerge when these are abolished is an organic flow of energies, a natural ordering of events and relationships which will grow from honest needs and desires. The abolition of coercion and its institutionalized structures will bring about the disappearance of all the undesirable forms of behavior caused by repression. (Note Neill's analysis in *Summerhill,* discussed in Chapter 1.[5])

Drawing lessons from his experience at the First Street School, George Dennison wrote:

> If compulsion is damaging and unwise, its antithesis—a vacuum of free choice—is unreal. And in fact we cannot deal with the problem in these terms, for the real question is not, What shall we do about classes? but What shall we do about our relationships with the young? How shall we deepen them, enliven them, make them freer, more amiable, and at the same time more serious? How shall we broaden the area of mutual experience?[6]

These are obviously very difficult questions, and good answers in practice are in short supply (in rhetoric, it's not so hard). The "vacuum of free choice" that Dennison mentions is to some degree an almost universal experience for free schools. One implication of this is that the theory is too simplistic and does not take sufficient account of the meaning of Dennison's questions. A definite tendency of most free schools that last is toward more structure as the school gets older. One form this tendency takes is trying out different modes of organization. For younger children, there might be a meeting where the various events, activities, classes, and trips available that day are described, and then the students fill in their own schedules. These schedules guide the teachers and students for that day. Another scheme, used especially in high school groups, is some form of contract system, where the students and the teacher formally agree upon the terms of the project, how long they will work on it, what the criteria for completion will be, what the expectations are, and so on. Another approach is to require participation in a certain number of courses or projects, leaving the choices up to the students.

Whatever the arrangements, the students themselves almost always participate in the discussion and decisions involving the various reorganizations. This isn't to say that there is universal agreement, either among the staff or the students. But there is a need to experiment with "structures for freedom," and very often the push for structure comes more from the students than from the more ideological staff.

What is usually clear is that something isn't working, that too many classes and projects aren't going well, that there is a good deal of apathy, boredom, anxiety about the learning of skills and knowledge, and sometimes even the kind of destructive chaos that the teacher from Portland described. What isn't clear is how to explain these conditions, and what, if anything, can be done to avoid or remedy them.

The kind of difficulties I have been discussing here focus on what traditionally has been considered the central explicit purpose of schools, namely, learning and teaching skills and knowledge. One very important element in free school approaches is an emphasis on what seems to be denied, neglected, or distorted by the traditional view, what is sometimes called the "affective" aspects of learning. As was noted in the school descriptions, free school people are deeply committed to removing the harmful effects of coercion, manipulation, enforced competition. Almost all free school people would agree with John Holt about the way they evaluate their own experience in school and what they hope to protect young people from. He wrote:

We destroy the disinterested (I do *not* mean *un*interested) love of learning in children, which is so strong when they are small, by encouraging and compelling them to work for petty and contemptible rewards—gold stars, or papers marked 100 and tacked to the wall, or A's on report cards, or honor rolls, or dean's lists, or Phi Beta Kappa keys—in short, for the ignoble satisfaction of feeling that they are better than someone else. We encourage them to feel that the end and aim of all they do in school is nothing more than to get a good mark on a test, or to impress someone with what they seem to know.[7]

Changing this situation seems a necessary condition for the warm and trusting relationships between student and teacher and student and student which the free school philosophy claims are in themselves a vitally important part of a good educational process and are a basis for good learning even of the traditional sort. That is, the idea of emotional growth and maturity receives great emphasis, and the quality of the relationships that make up the school community are perceived as the most vital element in this kind of education, as Dennison's questions suggest.

It follows from this emphasis that school activities that are closely connected to the emotional life will be very important. This means in practice that "creative" subjects (like writing), crafts (like pottery, weaving, leather work, and photography), sensitivity workshops, yoga, and meditation will be highly valued. In fact they are very popular in free schools, and are often very successful in obvious ways. In crafts, the work produced is frequently quite fine. The rich flow of creative energies would be evident to any observer who could see students staying into the late afternoon or returning to school in the evenings and on weekends to work on a lovely pot or a beautiful rug modeled after a Navaho pattern in a book or to develop hundreds of pictures in the darkroom. The students are clearly working joyously, without compulsion, for intrinsic satisfactions. There are no prizes, no grades, no extra-credit points to raise one's average, no anxieties that someone else's work might get him a little ahead in the race for high honors and the scholarship to Yale. They are learning skills and getting the satisfaction of developing real competencies. In the sensitivity or encounter groups, there is often opportunity for articulating and dealing with fears, anxieties, confusions, and self-doubts with adult teachers as well as fellow students involved in a way that is practically impossible to conceive of in the institutional and interpersonal arrangements of the traditional school community.

In activities like arts and crafts projects, free education methods frequently seem to blossom with wonderful results. The pleasures of voluntary, happy activity, of intense and rewarding application of energies; the satisfaction of a tangible product; the honest relation of teacher-craftsman and student-apprentice—all these are often marvelously realized. Moreover, the incidental learning so prized by free learning theory can happen quite strikingly in such projects. Often real craftsmen come into the school as volunteers, and projects develop from their own vivid working examples. Other times, the needs of the crafts projects stimulate the desire to learn math or history or other formal academic subjects, which often seem so distasteful to young people when rammed down their throats. The young person finds himself committed to work he personally wants to do, and he finds that he needs to read better or to look up historical descriptions or to learn how to do various calculations or work with a balance in order to do this work. So he goes out and learns, or he asks a teacher or older student to help him, or he joins a class on the subject. The process, at its best, is—to use a favorite free school word—organic. The organism seeks out learning relevant to coping with a personal world. This learning is the result of the encounter of personal needs, desires, intentions, and hopes with the recalcitrance of the external universe in its various manifestations. This is very different and, I affirm, much better learning than that which comes from a rigid, graded curriculum that never addresses the individual student in his personal rhythms, letting his honest, personal concerns generate the energies for activity, but that instead bases itself on energy forced out or cajoled by threat, punishment, and the sort of invidious reward accurately described by Holt.

George Dennison gives an excellent example of this process at work in a letter dealing with the issue of structure.

> It's not really hard to structure things according to present needs and talents, especially if you take community problems seriously and get involved in them. A really beautiful model can be seen in work that Timothy Affleck (later at the Santa Barbara Community School) did with black kids in Roxbury, Mass. He had been directing plays with the Theatre Company of Boston, and decided to do some plays with black teenagers, but starting from scratch, i.e., working up their own material from authors like Richard Wright and Claude Brown. The kids were electrified by the idea (he worked with large numbers of them); and when it became clear that they were actually forming theater companies, and would show their work through their own community, they became real zealots. Tim had no idea of *teaching* them anything—he was their resource in the problem of putting on their own plays. They turned to him because he was a pro, not a teacher. Among these kids were several teenage illiterates. In order to do this work which so excited them, they taught themselves to read—and they did it in two months, using Claude Brown's *Manchild in the Promised Land* as a text.[8]

Another good instance of this process, occurring inside a free school, was related to me by a friend who is herself an experienced free school teacher. The school is the Children's Community Workshop School in Manhattan, founded and directed for three years by a wonderful, energetic woman named Anita Moses. It is a marvelous model of an integrated, parent-controlled community school for young children. It has been featured in articles on free schools in *Life, Saturday Review,* and *Evergreen Review,* as well as in books by Holt and Dennison. The description:

> The top floor of the school building is divided into a number of ceramics studios. In contrast to the atmosphere in the rest of the building, the atmosphere here is peaceful. The studios on the top floor seem to provide a kind of retreat for students and teachers. They are sparsely populated, as few students are welcome upstairs at the same time. The people there are attentive, often serious, quiet. Several months ago there was no ceramics studio. Then, one day, two neighborhood women walked into the school, introduced themselves as potters. They asked if they could use space in the building to set up studios, complete with a kiln and two wheels. In exchange they offered to teach ceramics for a number of hours per week. Both women ended up teaching way beyond their expectations. The woman I talked with had been filled with wonder as she had watched the children grow in their work with clay. One child, she said, had a block against writing. He had not written anything all year in the classroom. Recently, he had been spending time in the ceramics studio. One day she discovered that he had written a word in the clay, and later that week, an entire sentence. Another child also began to spend time at the ceramics studio. This child rarely completed projects in the classroom, as his attention span lasted five minutes. One afternoon he watched quietly as one of the teachers threw a pot. The next day he came in and made an entire pot. He had learned the whole process by watching, and then spent one half-hour in concentrated work.[9]

Another paradigm of ideal free school education can be seen in a project that developed at Bay High, a free high school in Berkeley now in its fifth year of existence. One of the full-time teachers was particularly gifted both in science and in practical crafts like carpentry. He had set up a carpentry shop and two printing presses with the students. At one point he and some students became interested in designing cabinets for speakers that could be used with electric guitars and other electrified instruments. They worked hard, developed their own design, and built a set of cabinets on a commission from one of the country's top rock groups. The teacher and some of the students worked for months, often late into the evenings, on weekends, and on school vacations. In the course of the project, students learned about acoustics and electronics, as well as the carpentry skills of cabinetmaking. When the system was finally perfected and built, the students (many of whom played instruments) gave an informal concert in a neighborhood sports field. They blasted the neighborhood with the great quantity (and quality) of their sound, proving the worth of their design and construction in a vivid and satisfying way. This was a fitting climax to months of hard work, and the two thousand badly needed dollars that they were paid was very important to the school. Since then, the school has received several other orders for cabinets. The school had developed a good source of supplementary income and the students had gone through a beautiful learning experience, incidentally acquiring knowledge and useful skills.

Success stories like these can be heard from almost all of the schools; but then, so can stories of failure which are not so easily talked about. I noted that the successes seemed especially vivid in the affective realm, and that much attention and energy were directed there. But it would be only fair to discuss the kinds of failure that occur in this most favored area of free school life.

It's hard to specify failures as clearly as successes. Almost everyone can agree on successes like the ones I just described. And there are many incidents of behavior problems that responded beautifully to freedom in ways described vividly by Dennison in *The Lives of Children,* and by A. S. Neill in *Summerhill.* But, as I noted about the account of the chaotic free school in Portland, there are often differing interpretations of situations that might plausibly be seen as failures. The young people who continue to be destructive or hostile; the student who was bored and apathetic in public high school and continues to be bored and apathetic at the free school; the student who used a lot of drugs and cut school while at public school and who continues to do this while at the free school, ending up at the age of fifteen with convulsions and collapsed veins from shooting "speed"—such cases didn't seem to respond as hoped. Does this imply failure? If so, by whom and of what sort?

In terms of the institution itself, we could consider as possible loci of failure the theory, the practice, or the people. One problem is that there is no satisfactory way of separating these factors. A person could continue to maintain the truth of free school theory in the face of the most obvious disaster of a school, insisting that the application of the theory had been faulty, or that the particular people involved hadn't been sensitive enough or honest enough or direct enough or loving enough or something.

But it seems to me that this response is inadequate. My own idea, as expressed in Chapter 1, is that the theory itself depends too much on a rhetoric that projects unrealistic expectations. The social and psychological penetration of the theory is often shallow. What I mean is that, as with the spirit of educational reform thinking in general, there is an overemphasis on the school, whether good or bad, as a shaper of attitudes and behavior. Because the free school puts so much emphasis on its effects upon the young person in all aspects of his psyche and on the importance of the involvement of the students and staff on the most personal levels, there naturally develops an expectation of commensurately great changes in the people. The free school is seen not only as a better learning environment for young people, but as a "brave new world" from which a wonderful new culture and wonderful new people will emerge.

In *Rasberry Exercises,* the most detailed description of free schools written from an explicitly counter-cultural position, the authors state:

> It is a revolutionary act to be involved in a free school. Saying "no" to the heart of a culture—their schools—and establishing an alternative system for learning is an explicit rejection of a *set* of beliefs, and the web of promises, myths, rituals—the underlying faith—that goes with a set of beliefs.[10]

The authors go on to note that attempts at innovation within the existing system of education only increase the power of the system—"in the 'innovative public school' the *children* get to develop their own alienation freely and individualistically!" But for free schools, "the *joy* of *doing it* will be from energies flowing out of centered, authentic lives, and not from the wearisome hassling emanating from lives splintered between cultures.

"How long has it been since you taught a culture you believed . . . since you felt education simply to be sharing what you most deeply enjoy with those whom you love?"[11]

The image here is that free schools are *new cultures* in themselves; they involve people in a culture they believe in where there is a sharing of what one most deeply enjoys with those whom one loves. This is an enormous claim. The implication of the criticism of innovative schools "inside the system" where the children are free only to develop their own alienation is that inside the free school alienation will disappear and people will grow organically in a network of wholeness, becoming, loving, and sharing while creating a culture they can believe in. I haven't found this to be true. Alienation is a societal creation and can't be escaped in free schools, communes, or Gestalt therapy sessions.

If one starts with expectations of this dimension, it's no wonder that there is often serious disappointment and self-doubt. A perspective like this can generate a mood which can be seriously misleading. It misconceives the nature of culture by implying that a new one can be willed into existence by a small, well-meaning group of good people; it misconceives the nature of learning and education by implying that these are activities that demand as an ideal loving everyone one teaches or learns from. (Remember Dennison's comments on the ethic of love, quoted on page 30.)

With such a vision, the demands for results are virtually unlimited. If, as often happens, the students don't experience marvelous transformations, if they don't quickly become loving, open, spontaneous, sharing, active, and self-directed, then isn't the enterprise failing? Isn't the staff doing something wrong? Aren't the people too constrained, too up-tight, too unliberated from the old ways?

Well, maybe and maybe not. The truth is that the school isn't a world or a culture, and neither is the counter-culture. The demand seems to be that a school community accomplish the salvation of the children—and indirectly, of the parents and staff and, as a far ideal, of the whole oppressive society, which will be transformed from its "heart" by more and more tiny blossoms of freedom and joy. The image may not usually be expressed quite this explicitly, though in passages like the one quoted from *Rasberry Exercises* the rhetoric is close to that.

This vision builds in an almost certain disappointment. Free school theory says in opposition to the traditional emphasis on formal schooling that we learn everywhere and all the time, and in some sense this is true. We learn from the surrounding culture in all its manifestations— good and bad. We learn from TV, from books, from travel, from family, from neighbors, from work, from play. So even if the people involved in the school consciously attempt to create an atmosphere of loving cooperation, joyous self-discovery, and all other good things, they cannot filter out the culture around them or eliminate the forces of past experience and present circumstances. The controlled environment of the school is only one part of the total environment of the participants, and, as the teacher's account from the free school in Portland illustrated, it is not as easy an environment to control as the sunny rhetoric makes out.

My own experience is that in general the alienation of young people doesn't disappear in free schools; that the utopian images projected in school brochures and in books like *Rasberry Exercises* are seldom approached. Not because of some easily identifiable failure such as incompetent staff or unimaginative projects or lack of loving commitment, but rather because of a misunderstanding of the limitations of what realistically can be done. It would certainly be more pleasant to believe that a band of enlightened comrades can create a new culture and a new world which can—in a relatively short time—eliminate and transform the bad effects of the old world. But such expectations seem to me to lead to disappointment, to frustration, and to damaging self-doubt. Also they can lead to a devaluing of what actually can be achieved.

I noted that the specific failures in the affective area are harder to identify than the spectacular individual success stories which are eagerly recounted. There is a high rate of turnover of people in free schools, and not always because of wrongheaded anxieties on the part of parents (e.g., they aren't learning well—as if they would be in the average local public school). Under the rhetoric and unbounded expectation, there are all the confusions and ills of the dominant culture which is being fled and supposedly transcended, and the resulting institution can be the sad expression of these problems.

What makes identification of failure difficult is the exaggerated hope and the quest for personal salvation that I touched on. Given the intensity of the commitment and the scope of the expectations, it is very difficult to admit that, in fact, what was aimed at was beyond one's power, because to achieve all the goals for the school and the children and the adults would entail radical transformations in other areas of social life. Social and personal transformations of great scope can never be the responsibility of a single institution like the school. The badness of the methods and spirit of the traditional schools are not the main cause of the problems of children and young people, and placing them along with sympathetic teachers in a hopeful and theoretically beautiful environment, with, as Rasberry and Greenway say, "energies flowing out of centered, authentic lives," will not cure everything.

One big problem is that it is much easier to call oneself "centered and authentic" and to learn to manipulate the symbols of counter-cultural grooviness than it is to actually be new people in this hopeful sense. In free schools the self-description is the same for good situations and for bad. Since the unrealistically high expectations raise the ante considerably, bad situations can lead to sharp personal recriminations, to accusations of up-tightness, lack of openness, not being "authentic and centered people."

The small size and intense commitment of energy that are characteristic of free schools, combined with a philosophy that conceives of the school as a close community of people relating to each other on all levels, give schools the opportunity to work the wonderful emotional results that provide the great success stories. But these conditions also provide the power to amplify the troubles that can arise. This means that there are actively bad places living under the rhetoric of free schools. It means more than that there are free school situations that are failures, in the sense that the largest goals of the "new education" mood are not met (for example, the constant ecstasy projected in George Leonard's popular *Education and Ecstasy*). For, in many of these situations, given a more moderate expectation, what occurs can be seen as quite impressive. There may not be a new world, with a new culture and new people, living, sharing, and learning in totally new, radical, and joyous ways; but there will often be a more restrained improvement—more freedom, less fear and anxiety, a better chance for young people to deal with the confusing contemporary environment, more honest, less institutionally determined interaction with adults. These can and do have a real effect which sometimes is remarkable.

But when there are bad conditions, the results can be very depressing. Some critics of new schools point to the significant number of schools that close after a year or two as evidence of some general failure. But the meaning of this situation is ambiguous. Certainly schools that fold up after one or two or three years are not great successes in that they haven't built up enough support, dedication, commitment, or whatever to assure even a shaky existence. But some of these failures were quite successful in various ways while they lasted. Often many of the things that happened during their couple of years of existence were very good. But lack of money, hassles about buildings and health codes, the inability of key staff people to work practically for free for more than a year or two can wear down the energies and commitment below some critical level, and the school will stop operation. But not tragically or harmfully; in fact, the experience is often very valuable for staff, students, and parents, whether they go back to public schools or on to other attempts at starting new schools.

However, some failures are not so ambiguous. An account of one free school I had extensive contact with should provide a cautionary tale of how wrong things can get. (This is *not* in any way a *typical* account, though it is sobering.)

The school was enthusiastically founded by parents and teachers in 1967, very early in the current wave of free schools, and it folded with much unpleasantness in 1970, not because of dire poverty but because of deep internal failings.

The original founding director of the school set forward what he conceived of as a strong Summerhillian line, and this approach seemed very congenial to the staff he built up. However, his personality and way of operating antagonized enough people that after a year and a half he was asked to leave by the majority of the staff and the board of directors. The school then became a staff-administered institution, although there was still the all-school meeting as the official policy-making body.

These were the early days of the "flower child–love generation" spirit and this school (which was in California) was almost completely dominated by this tone. Accordingly, the activities consisted mainly of crafts, field trips, and sitting around "rapping." There was nothing that could honestly be called a curriculum, and this was very much the way both staff and students preferred it. There were few classes, and the courses that did get started generally petered out, with little work going into them when they did exist. Astrology and the spiritual were very popular, and one member of the staff was a professional astrologer (he read charts for money). One of the few conscientious teachers, who had done extensive academic work in biology, took students on fossil-collecting field trips and set up a hothouse where he conducted several interesting experiments in cross-pollination, grafting, and plant identification. There was also a popular class on sensitivity training where, according to one of the students who looked at the school with a wry and perceptive eye, an older "swinger" from the community could "grab-ass" the young girls under the guise of the very "in" group-therapy spirit. With few exceptions (a prominent one was the very able and tough-minded woman who worked with the youngest children), the staff was of the persuasion that everyone should "do his own thing," that legitimate authority did not exist, that anything was as worth learning as anything else. One teacher commented, "I seem to be growing anti-intellectual. I've come to the point where I really believe that knowledge as knowledge is basically worthless, even though it is many times fun."

There was no real organization for running the school, setting and carrying out policy, or settling disputes; setting up structures for accomplishing these institutional tasks seemed anathema to the people involved. For example, there was one teacher whom the rest of the staff agreed had to be fired, as he was simply unable to function (partly because of personal troubles). But several months later, during the interminable meetings that marked the death throes of the school, he was still there as a staff member. No one on the staff had told him of the decision that he had to go, no one felt such a task was his responsibility, and no mechanism existed for dealing intelligently with such problems.

While teachers went on with their own activities, they generally failed to convey enthusiasms effectively to the students, who (along with many of the staff) lounged around the yard and building, read comics, strummed guitars, and used a lot of dope. Most of the older students interviewed complained that there wasn't much to do, although the facilities and the library were quite respectable. One interview:

Q: What do you want to do? What are your interests?
STUDENT: Oh, I dunno, something man. Go up north.

(*Pause*) Get this truck I know, work on it. (*Pause*) Get stoned. Ball. I'm sort of getting into religion and it's really far out.

Q: Do you think you are learning the things you want to learn here?

STUDENT: Well, there isn't much happening. I'm . . . there are some far-out people here . . . but I'm not *learning* anything . . . but . . .

Q: How about going back to public school?

STUDENT: Oh, man, that's fucked.

Q: What do you think you'd like to do in the future?

STUDENT: I dunno. I'd like to get into leather. I could, like you know, do a thing [class] here at the free school. That'd be really far out.

Asked whether he felt the school was working for the older students, one teacher replied:

I don't want to lay my trip on any of these kids. If they really want to learn something, they'll come to me and say, "Look, man, I want to get into this, can you help me?" If they say that to me, then that's cool. If not, I'm not going to force them. That's a public school trip. What they're really into is finding out who they are, and they're *doing* it. That's really far out.

Drugs were a problem among the older students, for some a very serious problem. More accurately, there were deep personal troubles that manifested themselves in self-destructive drug use, but neither the deep problems nor the drug-abuse symptoms were honestly admitted and confronted.

Some of the staff broke off from the school to start their own free school, despairing of any real changes. Of the staff remaining, a minority protested the lack of any order, the physical conditions, and the drugs on campus (if only for the simple reason that they made the school liable to being busted by the police at any time). The teacher in charge of the younger children was competent and active, but she finally left after pleading with the rest of the staff to occupy the older students at least enough so that they wouldn't interfere with her work with the small children. Parental alarm at the general deterioration of conditions led the board of directors to call a meeting to see what actions were needed.

The meeting itself expressed the inability of the staff to agree on any issue, and worse, they seemed to be incapable of formulating any workable plan. Some of the parents supported various suggestions by board members, such as having some structured program, banning drugs in the school, and arranging therapy of one kind or another for students who were in serious need of it. The school bank account at this time contained several thousand dollars. One faction, loosely in accord, suggested that a couple of the staff and some of the older students take some of the money to finance a dome-building commune further north. Many of the parents felt that the suggestion was unreasonable since the money had been collected from tuitions from all the parents over the three years of the school's existence; that it should not be squandered on one part of the school. More discussion. As the hour grew late and wine bottles empty, issues became fuzzier if not lost altogether. Some people, parents especially, became silent after hours of inconsequential haggling without reaching consensus on any issue. Many still felt the school was basically all right and were defending that position.

One serious staff member, a shy and unassuming young man who was a dedicated teacher, spoke up toward the end. He suggested that the school be absorbed into another school with which he was also connected, and which was operating within the same city. He said that by combining enrollments, the younger children (who had recently been sadly neglected because of their teacher's leaving) would not have to go back to public school, older students could join or not as they pleased, and the remaining funds could be disbursed among departing parents who had already paid. There would be one consolidated free school. If the parents of the older students wanted them to go north to the proposed commune, they could use their reimbursements directly for this.

There was a pause. Finally the staff member who was the leader of the commune faction spoke up. He said he sensed negative vibrations, and that the disagreements could probably be ironed out if the maker of the proposal would come over to his place to have his astrological chart read.

Further meetings solved nothing and the depressing end of the school came soon. One group of staff and older students used some of the money for the trip to the commune in northern California. No one had found a replacement for the school building whose lease was up, and so school for the younger children ended. The remaining group of staff and older students, at the suggestion of the former director, convinced the board to accept the plan of bringing in a well-known radical former priest who wanted to do education things (he had no experience in schools). He came with his family, made big plans, and projected forthcoming financial support from rich liberals and foundations who knew him from his radical-priest activities. (This had been one of the big points in convincing the board to entrust the last few thousand dollars to him.)

In fact, the new director came with little knowledge of the actual situation. His summer program foundered partly because of his lack of experience, but mainly because of lack of support from the people who had convinced him to come. When fall came, there was no school, no funds, much ill-will and resentment, and a bad image of free schools for many people in town, part of which was ignorant prejudice, but much of which was felt by people who had a pretty accurate idea of what was going on.

As for the effects on the young people involved, it is hard to make definite judgments. Certain bad things seemed clear to me. When there is a lot of dishonesty and hypocrisy, the self-congratulatory rhetoric of the counter-culture helps to prevent confrontation with the deep problems of young people. When the school is so deeply involved in fulfilling the needs of staff people whose problems are perhaps even harder to deal with than those of the students, the school becomes a place to avoid facing these problems, and then the influence on the students cannot help but be negative. I'm not talking at all about the limited sphere of intellectual knowledge and competence, where the experience was really terrible for the students, many of whom had been seriously hurt in this area in the normal public and private schools they had attended. The isolation of the school and inward-looking "aren't we cool" tone seemed sometimes to become a kind of arrogance and contempt toward "straights" and "squares" —many of the young people in the public high schools, for example. Also reinforced by many of the staff was the spirit of counter-cultural apoliticality which was a part of the fearful disdain of the outside world that was so pervasive in the atmosphere of the school.

This particular path of failure was uniquely bad, and is certainly not representative. However, it is useful to see it as a vivid but very exaggerated version of the kinds of troubles that can occur in free schools. The more usual paths of failure are of the sorts I alluded to earlier in the chapter. The expectations are very high; the rhetoric is powerful but not very helpful on the specifics of day-to-day realities. Everyone knows more what not to do and how not to do it than what *to* do. Feelings of dissatisfaction and anxiety grow. Parents and students complain. Teachers also become anxious and guilty, thinking—as the teacher from the Portland school noted—that if only they were as sensitive and original as John Holt or Herb Kohl, everything would go well. How to interest the students without pressuring them; whether to push the little kids to learn how to read, as some parents wish—questions like these are discussed obsessively, without satisfactory answers. After the first few months, when the glow of the excitement of beginning wears off, this kind of question becomes a protracted discussion of structure. Various new ways of organizing the school are tried. Bad feelings arise among staff people as views about what should be done bring into conflict very deep beliefs and hopes. Sometimes there are splits; teachers or even directors are fired or pressured to resign. Parents withdraw their children under a barrage of recriminations. Financial difficulties pile up. Low tuition on a sliding pay-what-you-can scale doesn't bring in enough money to pay even the pitifully low salaries most free schools offer. Raising tuition would betray the intention of the school not to be another rich private school. So, valuable energy goes into fund-raising—writing futile proposals to foundations, approaching rich liberals in the community, putting on rummage and bake sales, and so forth. Then, some disaster like a building inspector demanding some expensive modification of the building, or some expected large gift not materializing, can plunge the school into a crisis which can result in even the dedicated core group giving up the struggle.

In such circumstances, there is often a mixture of good and disappointing. And in fact, far fewer schools have closed than might have been expected. Since the great majority of free schools are still in their first, second, or third year, it would be hard to calculate a meaningful figure, but considering schools founded two years ago, I think it reasonable to estimate that at the very most one out of five has closed, and probably not more than one out of ten. Many schools have the sorts of troubles I described, but most of them seem to be holding on more or less satisfactorily. Given the difficulties, both material and spiritual, this is impressive and conveys some measure of the energy and dedication generated by new schools. (For some time now, the figure of eighteen months as the average life span of a free school has been widely quoted. The figure was given by the founder of the *New Schools Exchange Newsletter,* but, from my own work at the Exchange, I know that this was a guess based on very little data.)

I mentioned earlier some examples of the vivid successes which free school people like to tell about. There is a more general sort of achievement which deserves more discussion. With a modest perspective on expectations, the general effect of the free atmosphere on personality and attitudes can often be seen as remarkably positive. In the areas of cooperativeness and relations toward adults with or without authority, for example, free school atmosphere does very good things. Even unsympathetic or neutral observers have noted the openness and lack of fear and anxiety that many free school children display in their encounters with adults, even strangers. Also, the opportunities for self-initiated individual and group activities, without the built-in competitiveness with peers and constant need to deal with the power-sanctioned approval and disapproval of particular adults, provide many experiences that are almost never possible in authoritarian public schools.

As a result, there is a solid basis in experience for a comment A. S. Neill made in a recent article. He was writing about *The Lord of the Flies,* which people have cited to me, when discussing free school ideas, as *proof* that young people cannot be granted the kinds of freedom I was advocating. (Their comments showed a great deal about the success of the authoritarian conditioning they had received as well as an absence of firsthand experience with young people.) Neill wrote:

> William Golding's tendentious novel, *Lord of the Flies,* is frequently cited by those who believe that human nature is inherently evil and that children must be made good by discipline, but to me the book is an excellent unintentional thesis on the wrong education. Make children afraid and make them follow what H. G. Wells call "God, the great absentee" and beat them up, and then put them on a desert island, and of course they will be full of hate and start killing each other. But if a planeload of Summerhill children were stranded on a desert island it would be very different. First there would be girls among them, which is an important difference. They would all have a council meeting to decide what to do. There would be no question of leadership, no forming of gangs. They would simply try to find food and other necessities together.[12]

This is somewhat simplified and idealized, but, I think, basically accurate. From my experience with free school kids, the problem could be that there would be too many meetings, too much group rapping, and too much fear that someone was trying to be a leader, "on an ego trip."

As Neill and others always point out, it is the *process* of freedom that works the good effect. Young people in this society have almost no chance to get the kind of experience provided in the new schools—not at home in their families, not in their neighborhood play activities, not in the Boy and Girl Scouts, not in the Little League, and especially not in their usual school situations which take up such a large and important segment of their lives.

This process is very important to understand. Free school experience shows how difficult it is for many young people to make the transition from highly structured situations completely controlled by adults to the open and relatively unstructured free school. (Of course, this applies mainly to students who have gotten used to the authoritarian, controlled environment of the normal public school.) As we know from history, "escaping from freedom" is not so rare a human response to freedom and responsibility, and free school experience reflects this. Often students need a good deal of help and support in making this transition, and some people come to the decision that they don't want it, that they are more comfortable with imposed order and external direction.

Discussing this process of transition during the first year of a "street high school" in a poor white neighborhood in a Midwestern city, a teacher-organizer said:

There was a whole time in the beginning when the students were very docile and accepted things. They didn't know what freedom or self-motivation meant and what responsibility meant. Then they discovered it. As soon as they discovered it there was an area where they discovered it and tried it out and some of them didn't come to classes, some of them dropped out. They were playing with that. Then at the end of the year it came down to some kids realizing they had to start exercising responsibility, form groups and start to do something. Another group was still playing with, taking advantage, exploiting their freedom to play around, doing nothing. Some people are still learning what it means to be completely responsible for your own education. A couple of people have expressed a desire to go back to public school because they want more structure, which is very interesting. That happens sometimes when you take away that need they have to be told what to do. One kid I know might go in the Army because he wants that kind of authority, and another kid, his friend, might go back to the South because he wants to be forced, he wants his parents contacted, all these things that he tried to get away from, not realizing that was what he really wants. But that's good. At least they're aware of what their needs are. Our school doesn't provide that kind of form. Our school is an alternative to that kind of punishment and reward system.

Whether the free schools are successful in meeting the needs of young people is a murky subject, since the concept of need is not at all clear. The problem of how to meet these needs has been indirectly touched on. One important need seems to be for a real connection to social and cultural reality. This need appears in various ways, and is not always seen as such. It is a fact that children and young people are in a stage of development; that their physical, emotional, intellectual, and cultural identities are essentially transitional. Not *only* transitional, of course, but to ignore the fact of transition under the guise of accepting the young as people in their own right distorts the relations of adults to children and of school to society. The problem, as noted in Chapter 1 where I outlined the normal educational function of socialization, is that the transition is very difficult and troubled today because the dominant culture is viewed so negatively by many people, young and old. The period of youth, however troubled, seems preferable to a mature adulthood whose attraction is severely limited. Maturity is ideally associated with full productive membership in a coherent and meaningful social community, but what seems to lie ahead for many young people doesn't look like this at all. So school (or whatever other learning networks and communities are available) becomes a very problematical institution. One trend that I have noted is for participants to think of their free schools as self-sufficient communities, for both the adults and the students. This is a popular image of the "new culture." The tendency of free schools with this perspective, as I described, is to move as far as possible from the larger world, psychically, culturally, and, where possible, physically.

Whatever the results of this kind of community in terms of the ideal goals—establishing identity, gaining the psychic health to go out into the world, finding a new and better way of living—there remains the problem of transition to the larger culture and society. There are no obvious answers, since, as was emphasized, this is a societal problem, not a simply pedagogical one. But there is a tendency to avoid confronting the issue. For example, in an attractive picture-essay entitled *Summerhill, USA*, there are quotes from various free school participants. The director of the Los Angeles Free School, talking about how young people do not seem to be following traditional paths of growing up, said:

> Most of them are not going right into college, not because they couldn't but because they don't choose to go. Most of them are so vitally alive that they're starting to create all kinds of new ways of living . . . new concepts of what you can do with your life to make it worthwhile. One girl who graduated here when she was sixteen has decided that she wants to travel through Europe for a few years and then start a school of her own.[13]

My sense of this situation is not nearly so rosy. Larger numbers of young people, even from top academic public schools and prep schools, are declining to jump right into college, and some are even seriously considering not going to college at all. The reasons for such decisions are fairly obvious and valid. For free school kids, this decision is not startling; in many free schools, the decision to go to college is the deviant one. It is true that they don't lack ability. Free school students are intelligent enough; and any middle-class young person with some money can go to a college, or, as in California, there are often large state higher-education systems that are almost free. It is not so clear that many free school students could easily get into the most prestigious colleges, but this is not at all a condemnation of the free schools or a sign of the high standards of college admissions officials.

But the claim that most of the students are "so vitally alive that they're starting to create all kinds of new ways of living" seems to me to be bravado and dangerously false optimism. I have seen free schools all over the country and have come into contact with many young people. Most of these young people have the same confusions about meaningful ways to live that any sensitive and perceptive young person would have today. The dream that the youth will find all sorts of new ways of life that we older people can't conceive of is one of the symptoms of our current cultural malaise. The young people are scared, and they mostly do not see themselves as exuberantly finding whole new ways of living. They are at least as confused as the rest of us. That the culture provides so few meaningful ways of living is a condition we are all suffering from, the young people most of all. The drug scene, the faddism of the youth culture, the quick movement from revolutionary politics to Eastern mysticism to organic gardening and the occult and so on, are signs of this sad condition, not joyful expressions of the finding of satisfying new ways. It is marvelously revealing that the one example of a new way cited is that of a girl who will travel in Europe for a few years (a traditional escape for well-off, middle-class, artistic young people who can afford it) and then will set up her own free school.

Exactly. I saw this happen too often. For example, when one young person I knew at a very hip free school got rather old to be a student, but did not want to leave the community and ambience of the school, he decided to learn glass-blowing as an apprentice and then come back to teach it at the free school. Often the ideal of free school people is to start another free school. But this is not a whole new way of living; it is in part a sign that one can't think of a new way and is falling back on the familiar.

I will discuss this cultural question in more detail in the next chapter. The point I am making here is that the problem of growing up and being in the world as mature adults is a very serious one for free schools. They have rejected much of what is accepted, but there is not yet a satisfactory replacement (and, in a sense, there couldn't be). This complex problem gets manifested in many ways.

It is a mistake to think that free schools can be a new culture or that the people there are finding many new ways of living or even of making a living. This last phrase is of course very troublesome. Adult life, for most people, still has as an essential aspect gaining the wherewithal to live and to support others. This means getting jobs or entering professions or having a farm or learning crafts or something. And nothing leads to connection with reality as surely as making a living. The heralded new ways of living have not been too successful in this area; again, this is no surprise, since the possibility of meaningful vocations is the kind of social question that can be solved individually by very few. The demand for sandal shops, groovy candles, organic food stores, and free school teachers and founders is limited.

So we are back to the question of the purpose for schools. Parents are often very anxious about the various futures that lie ahead: for young children, what they will do when they go back into public schools, as many do; for adolescents, how they will be able to cope with the world, to make a living. The hip counter-cultural schools try to avoid these problems with a happy rhetoric that says there won't be any problems because the kids will be better at everything.

But raising the question of *purpose* in this context forces attention on crucial aspects of what would count as *success* for new schools, especially ones that articulately oppose the generally accepted standards of the society. One perspective is to see free school communities of the inward-looking sort as refuges, warm and therapeutic communities that provide space and help during a very troubled time. Or they might be seen as stopping-off points, a year or two of "getting one's head together," while expecting to be back in the larger world soon. (The descriptions from the Santa Barbara Community High School in the previous chapter noted this way of seeing the free school experience.) But such ways of looking at the school are very different from the visions described earlier. I feel that the free school communities described in their counter-culture isolation are simply not rich enough places to do what the vision claims—are not truly enriching worlds in which to mature.

A relevant letter recently appeared in *Outside the Net,* a radical education publication. It is from the current director of Pacific High, one of the oldest and best-known of the counter-culture free schools. (Two years ago, announcements from Pacific appeared in various journals, inviting students who could pay $3,500 to join Pacific High's "Journey to the East," a year of touring ashrams in India with the staff and students of Pacific High. The journey finally didn't happen.) The letter gives an idealized history of the school (I have heard less self-satisfied descriptions from other people with experience at the school). It then gives a brief sense of where the school thinks it is now. The relation to the issues I have just raised is obvious, though it is not obvious that the letter points to a solution. (It should be noted that Pacific High is located on a beautiful piece of open land on the highest ridge of the Santa Cruz Mountains near Palo Alto.)

Dear Friends:

Pacific High School was founded in the fall of 1961 as an innovative non-authoritarian high school and has been evolving ever since. In 1967 Peter Marin became director and radicalized the school. In the spring of 1969 after two years as a radical day school, we found that the school, no matter how radical, groovy, or psychedelic, was much too limiting to fulfill the needs of either students or staff. In the fall of 1969 we became a live-in school and community of something over 60 people, 50 of them being adolescents.

We have been a live-in, democratic community high school for two years. We have built 18 geodesic domes, and put in many other improvements (kitchen, bath, dome, etc.) to change Pacific from a day school to a home.

The past two years have been beautiful, but now we find that it is time to change again. After two years as a live-in community school, we find that a community whose sole means of support is parents' tuition, no matter how comfortable, joyous, or supportive, is too unreal and too unconnected with the real world to survive. We therefore want to have more adults come to the community—adults who are working on valuable projects and want to continue doing so in a community together with adolescents. We also want more adolescents to join the community— not adolescents who want to "be at a free school," but adolescents who want to work and learn by being involved in real projects that have import and value beyond the bounds of Pacific High School.

We are changing. We need help, energy, and feedback. Let us hear from you.

Peace,
Michael Kaye,
Pacific High School,
12100 Skyline Blvd.,
Los Gatos, CA 95030.

In my view, the principled withdrawal from social and cultural reality is a critical point. To really help young people means not only to create a present atmosphere of freedom within the little world of the free school, but to be able to help their future growth, and this means, for almost all of them, their futures within *this* society. For little kids this problem isn't so great, for basic skills and a sense of emotional well-being are a good minimal goal, and these can be provided without too much worry about connection with the big world. There are, however, serious questions of how to deal with the socializing that is happening to the children, willy-nilly, as the account of the Portland school earlier in the chapter illustrates.

But when the children are a little older, and especially high-school age, the problems of relation to a larger social reality are central. Paul Goodman in the past, and now Ivan Illich and others, have argued against the existence of high schools in any form (except as therapeutic communities for the seriously disturbed) on the grounds that high schools, including free high schools, isolate young people from responsibility for their own development and opportunity to grow by honest work and learning in the context of the adult world. (More on Illich in the last chapter.) Moreover, the adults who are used to being with young people only in schools don't bring in enough of the outside world, especially if they have involved themselves in free schools in order to escape the larger world and so project their own fantasies and hopes onto the little world of the school.

Very few who have worked in a working-class or black school or project could accept the counter-cultural escape image contained in passages like these from *Rasberry Exercises* on what the dream of free schools as a new world and culture is:

> We will not be limited from dealing with our social rage if we must, perhaps more freed to work on "wholes" rather than "problems." We will visit the Pentagon, be in the stink of cities, know the limits with the rednecks in the country, know the dehumanization of those in the factories, the diploma mills, the nurturing places for specialists, the army warehouses, the endless corridors of the bureaucracies. Together, we and our children must know what we're leaving so that the new ways will be more than pale reflections. . . .[14]

The implicit elitism and contempt for the "unenlightened masses" expressed in such a passage is disturbing and all too typical of that part of the free school spirit of which *Rasberry Exercises* is such an accurate expression. The "if we must" is very serious, and my experience is that most of those involved don't feel they must. And so far as knowing the limits with the rednecks or the dehumanization in the factories, that is just talk. The being in the stink of the cities will be as brief as possible, if necessary on a trip up to Big Sur or out into Sonoma County. The key point is that these are things that might be known about only because *we* are leaving them to go on our new ways. But there are many people in those stinking cities and factories who don't have much of a choice about leaving them, who are trying to fight the dehumanization where it is and not lulling themselves into thinking they can flee it. It is only those with some means who can afford this illusion. More expressive of the core of the escape vision than "knowing the endless corridors of bureaucracy" are the final passages on the final page of text listing some of the things "we" will do:

> Perhaps there is an abandoned lookout high in the North Cascades.
> Maybe we can build a balloon and go high over an ocean. As a family, we can go to an African village and live without pretense, to barter as equals.
> All this is starting now.
> Tune in Sunday Evenings. (Bring the kids.) We'll share what we share. There are no limits. We'll make lots of books and change lives—and our children will have *lives* instead of schools. . . .[15]

But there are limits. Those limits are in the social conditions and in us. And it won't be that easy to change lives. Very few of us can fit in a balloon, and even fewer have the money and leisure to try it. What I am insisting on here, as I have before, is that schools are limited institutions, that the social reality cannot so easily be avoided, and that free schools can't help but fail if they base themselves on a counter-cultural spiritual bravado and a self-serving vision of beautiful escape to new consciousness.

In fact, most young people don't finally go off to start new communities. They don't just "know" the society in order to escape; they eventually go to those "diploma mills," work in those bureaucracies, live in those cities. Not in order to know what not to be when they escape to the brave new world, but, we hope, in order to change them, and finally the whole society.

My own bias toward educational reform with a political perspective should be quite clear by now. The importance of involvement in the larger world seems to me crucial. It may well be that schools as we know them are too constricting, even good free schools. But schools are not *necessarily* constricting institutions, if by schools we mean places where young people can be together and where adults who enjoy working along with them can get together. Young people need places that are their own, away from their homes, and unfortunately, traditional schools have not been this. Free schools have sometimes attempted to do this, but their efforts are only a beginning and are not the solution to educational problems or to the cultural and personal confusions that affect young people so strongly in our culture.

If we think only of the being together, the emotional, therapeutic aspect of a youth-oriented community, then—although these in themselves are good things—we haven't begun to answer the more mundane *school* questions about learning and knowledge and skills and intellectual understanding (which are certainly not everything but are also not simply a bad "head trip," as the spirit of the counter-culture seems sometimes to imply). If we think beyond the self-contained school community and the meaning of the immediate experience of the group to the problems of the future for young people, their ability to make their way to a meaningful maturity in this society, then we have to address directly that classic core of schooling, namely, what is to be learned and how; and we have to ask how the free schools as institutions can relate to the broad political and social realities of America today, what their potential effects can be as part of a development of serious educational reform, which, finally, must mean radical social change.

The second question will be dealt with at length in the final chapter. The first question, the problem of what can and ought to be learned in school, involves all the confusion of purpose just discussed. In the analysis of radical school-reform theory in Chapter 1, I argued that this question was not satisfactorily dealt with. The uncertainties emerge constantly in the actual practice of the schools, as the descriptions and analyses in the past chapters have shown. The confusions on this point can be illustrated by another quote from *Rasberry Exercises*, where the authors are giving practical advice on how to do a free school. Noting the problems of teachers in knowing what to do, they state what they think is obvious: "Everyone rejecting the bad things like *knowledge, authority,* and *structure;* and accepting the good things like *freedom, sharing,* and *creativity.*"[16]

Not only is this not obvious, it isn't even true. It is a little weird to think that words like "knowledge," "authority," and "structure" should become abstractly *bad.* Not because they are often misused to cover phony erudition, authoritarianism, or repressive organization in traditional schools just as other good words have been misused to cover many bad happenings in free schools, but simply in themselves. But this kind of approach completely avoids that dilemma about what is worth learning that exists for free schools as it does for anyone else who looks realistically at the deterioration of the quality of life in this most advanced country in the history of humankind. The rhetoric does not solve it. Neither can I, but in the next chapter I will try to say something about it, at least to peel off the rhetoric so that the problem can shine through clear and depressing.

NOTES

1 JANE GOLDMAN, "Summerhill, Some Are Hell . . . ," from *No More Teachers' Dirty Looks,* Vol. 2, no. 1; reprinted in *Socialist Revolution,* No. 8 (Vol. 2, No. 2) (March–April 1972), p. 115.

2 Ibid., p. 116.

3 Ibid., pp. 116–17.

4 Ibid., pp. 117–18.

5 For a recent reassessment and reaffirmation of Neills' beliefs, see his essay "Freedom Works," in Paul Adams et al., *Children's Rights: Toward the Liberation of the Child* (New York: Praeger Publishers, 1971).

6 GEORGE DENNISON, *The Lives of Children* (New York: Random House, 1969), p. 110.

7 JOHN HOLT, *How Children Fail* (New York: Dell Publishing Co., 1970), pp. 208–9.

8 GEORGE DENNISON, letter printed in the *New Schools Exchange Newsletter,* No. 40 (May 1970), p. 2.

9 These notes were given me by Barbara Gates, now teaching at the Group School in Cambridge. For a marvelous account of a new school which discusses the kinds of learning related to crafts and creative art work, see Elwyn Richardson's *In the Early World* (New York: Pantheon Books, 1969).

10 ROBERT GREENWAY and SALLI RASBERRY, *Rasberry Exercises* (Sebastopol, Calif.: Freestone Publishing Co., 1971), p. 37.

11 Ibid., p. 37.

12 NEILL, "Freedom Works," in *Children's Rights* (New York: Praeger Publishers, 1971), p. 141.

13 RICHARD BULL, *Summerhill, USA,* Penguin Education Special (Baltimore: Penguin Books, 1971), no page numbers.

14 GREENWAY and RASBERRY, *Rasberry Exercises,* p. 87.

15 Ibid., p. 89.

16 Ibid., p. 41.

4 · TEACH YOUR CHILDREN WELL
The Dilemma of Curriculum

Having looked in detail at the kinds of new schools and having attempted to evaluate some of their achievements and failures, I want to concentrate in this chapter on the central pedagogical issue of curriculum. This sticky question is essentially related to the problem of method which receives the main attention in free school theory. The ubiquitous "structure vs. nonstructure" discussions that go on almost continuously in practically every free school express the unresolvable uncertainties about the concrete meaning of the philosophy of freedom for both the proper content and the method of education.

As was noted in the first chapter, the free school wave of reform echoes the struggles of the progressive education movement, especially as regards the more strictly pedagogical concerns. The basic structure of the discussion was well stated by John Dewey in a short essay entitled "The Child and the Curriculum," written seventy years ago. Dewey notes the differences between the organization of subjects as they are taught and the child's own experience:

. . . first, the narrow but personal world of the child against the impersonal but infinitely extended world of space and time; second, the unity, the single wholehearted-ness of the child's life, and the specializations and divisions of the curriculum; third, an abstract principle of logical classification and arrangement, and the practical and emo-tional bonds of child life.

Dewey sees the old education as concentrating on the

importance of the subject-matter of the curriculum as compared with the contents of the child's own experience. It is as if they said: Is life petty, narrow, and crude? Then studies reveal the great, wide universe with all its fullness and complexity of meaning. Is the life of the child egoistic, self-centered, impulsive? Then in these studies is found an objective universe of truth, law and order. Is his experi-ence confused, vague, uncertain, at the mercy of the mo-ment's caprice and circumstance? Then studies introduce a world arranged on the basis of eternal and general truth; a world where all is measured and defined. . . . Subdivide each topic into studies; each study into lessons; each lesson into specific facts and formulae. . . . Thus emphasis is put upon the logical subdivisions and consecutions of the subject-matter. . . . Subject-matter furnishes the end, and it determines method. The child is simply the im-mature being who is to be matured. . . .[1]

Dewey sets this view against its polar opposite. For the "child-centered" sect, he says,

the child is the starting point, the center, and the end. . . . His development, his growth is the ideal. . . . To the growth of the child all studies are subservient. . . . Per-sonality, character, is more than subject-matter. Not knowl-edge or information, but self-realization, is the goal. . . . Literally, we must take our stand with the child and our departure from him. It is he and not the subject-matter which determines both quality and quantity of learning.[2]

The watchwords that Dewey ascribes to the opposing

camps have a familiar ring: for the "conservatives," discipline, adequate training and scholarship, guidance and control, law; for the "new education," interest, freedom and initiative, spontaneity. One side charges "chaos and anarchism" and the neglect of the sacred authority of duty, the other charges "inertness and routine" and "suppression of individuality through tyrannical despotism."

Dewey sees both of these positions as extreme, and his own position was always an attempt to avoid the errors of the extreme. More accurately, he was always an adamant critic of the traditional view; for him the real task was to prevent distortions of the progressive view. More than thirty-five years after "The Child and the Curriculum," in the lectures published as *Experience and Education* when the influence of the movement he had inspired was at its height, Dewey summarized the traditional position as follows:

> The subject-matter of education consists of bodies of information and of skills that have been worked out in the past; therefore, the chief business of the school is to transmit them to the new generation. In the past, there have also been developed standards and rules of conduct. Moral training consists in forming habits of action in conformity with these rules and standards.
>
> The main purpose or objective is to prepare the young for future responsibilities and for success in life, by means of acquisition of the organized bodies of information and prepared forms of skill, which comprehend the material of instruction. Since the subject-matter as well as standards of proper conduct are handed down from the past, the attitude of pupils must, upon the whole, be one of docility, receptivity, and obedience. Books, especially textbooks, are the chief representatives of the lore and wisdom of the past, while teachers are the organs through which pupils are brought into effective connection with the material. Teachers are the agents through which knowl-

edge and skills are communicated and rules of conduct enforced.[3]

Throughout this book, the characterizations of the public school and its methods and effects have come from people who strongly oppose the system. This, admittedly, leaves me open to the criticism of not giving the opposition a fair hearing. Even Dewey's formulations of the traditional view are somewhat tainted by the fact that he is trying to describe what his opponents believe. In fact, most people in this country, including educated people, do not claim to be radically dissatisfied with the dominant educational system.

Before going into the curriculum discussion specifically, I want to analyze extended descriptions of the public school and its goals and methods presented by two respected social scientists who have specialized in education. Their positions are clearly different from those of radical critics like Goodman, Friedenberg, Kohl, Kozol, or Herndon. These social scientists, far from condemning the system, express a qualified approval without pretending that it is perfect. They are conscious of flaws, but they accept that the schools have societal functions to perform and that, in general, they do this passably well. My own comments on these descriptions are meant to pose the critique of public schools, not against the fatuous rhetoric of school officials or school board chairmen, but against a much more realistic analysis. The descriptions touch both on the methods of teaching and organization and on the "hidden curriculum," that is, the way the methods and organization socialize young people by conveying attitudes and values.

The first work is a small book on child psychology intended for use by teachers, written by a professor of social relations at Harvard University. In *Understanding Children: Behavior, Motives, and Thought,* Jerome Kagan discusses the schools primarily in terms of how psychology and the understanding it provides can help the teacher in the task of teaching skills, especially academic skills. One of his main concerns is motivation. Much of the text is simplified "scientific psychology" (to express my own prejudice, it is mainly heavy-handed jargon used to restate common sense, often dubious or debatable). But, for my purposes, what is important is his clear acceptance of the schools' function in the Durkheimian terms described at the beginning of the first chapter. The author's concern is not the hidden curriculum, but the ostensible academic and skill-teaching function. Kagan raises doubts about the most puritan or coercive methods of enforcing society's discipline, but he assumes the reasonableness of the demands. He notes the kind of school failures everyone admits and offers his "scientific" understanding of motivation as an aid in avoiding such failures and improving the operation of the system.

Professor Kagan seems to be sensitive to the disaffection of many young people, to their indifference to traditional goals, to their denial of the legitimacy of standard motivations like good grades, and the problems this causes for the schools' objectives. But he never notices any deep structural causes, only disillusionments with technology and a misplaced sense that doing well in school means not concerning oneself with the moral crises of the time. This is nonsense, and Mr. Kagan gives no evidence of where he got his experience with high-school students or whether his experience is confirmed by other people who spend a lot of time with young people. For example, he doesn't deal at all with the question of the superior academic achievement of many of the students who participated in radical political activities and demonstrations. Anyone interested in this issue should read a recent monograph by Richard Flacks, *Youth and Social Change,* for a very different and, to me, much more convincing account of the sources and significance of the student revolt of the 1960s.

But his real point is that teachers should use good techniques to enable the school to fulfill the aims of the society. For example, he says that mild uncertainty is useful in spurring action, since it supposedly "vitalizes the latent need to know the self better." Kagan finds nothing wrong with the practice of grading bright children lower than they deserve "to prevent overconfidence and subsequent apathy."[4]

Let me translate and extend the meaning of this. First, compel all children to go to school; set the goals and the curriculum; subject them to the total power of the teacher in the classroom (he should use it judiciously, of course—no whippings); then evaluate and grade often, placing great emphasis on how important grades are—for the child to know how good he is, how worthy of approval; make sure the parents are allies in this (they should know that the famous school record goes along with the child, and how important it is if he is to do well, even get into Mr. Kagan's Harvard); then, when the child is properly "motivated"—good and anxious that his grades are high—then, for his own good, lest the real situation not generate enough interest to involve him in his work, lie to him a little. That is, grade him lower than he deserves by the teacher's *own standard*—scare him a little, for his own good, of course. This is Kagan's "maintaining of mild uncertainty."

This translation might sound rather harsh, considering that Kagan and people of his persuasion want to "humanize" the schools. But it is obvious that this kind of reform still accepts the basic values of the system. For example, Kagan supports decentralization of schools, not for the reasons Goodman and Dennison give (see Goodman's *Compulsory Mis-education* and Dennison's *The Lives of Children*)—the intimacy and elimination of bureaucracy, which small size makes possible—but in order to provide the opportunity for more valedictorians, more prize-winning poems. For Kagan, "the more the child actively shares in the prizes that the community values, the more salient his motive for mastery and the healthier the school atmosphere." Well, one person's health is another person's creation of winners and losers, tracking to maintain the class structure, instilling of an ethic that will make for better pilots to bomb Laotian peasants and better salesmen of unnecessary and ecologically damaging products to maintain high profits for large corporations.

Of course Kagan does not raise questions like these. This would be difficult for any defender of the public schools. According to Kagan, what the teacher should do is find the goals the child somehow has acquired and attach academic mastery to these. Kagan's examples of "secondary motives" taught by society reveal a moral and political obtuseness which is depressing but appropriate to the position he represents. He says, "The ten-year-old, middle-class child in Evanston, Illinois, is motivated to attain 'good grades' "—no mention of why, at what cost, the reasons he will more likely attain them and be rewarded for them than the working-class black child a few miles away on Chicago's West Side. He continues, "The ten-year-old child in Guatemala wants to be a better coffee cutter."[5] Although he leaves out a class description in this instance, Kagan does not mean a child of the small elite who own the coffee plantations or manage them for United Fruit Company. He clearly means a child of oppressed coffee workers, being paid starvation wages. I doubt if ten-year-old Guatemalans are motivated this way. (Mr. Kagan, the "scientist," cites no empirical studies, so I assume we're trading speculations.) When they have to go to work, probably at that age or earlier, these children have no choice but to try to help the family earn enough to eat. They are motivated not to starve, or they are motivated by their parents' motivation not to starve.

Kagan is for self-motivation, of course. This means that

if the teacher can get the child to *believe* that doing what *the teacher wants* is his own decision, he will work harder. Kagan's illustration of how to persuade the child that learning skills will be valuable, so that he will undertake this by his own decision, I find very disturbing.

> For example, the primary grade teacher might persuade her students of the importance of learning to read by announcing that during one recess period, each day, no child will be allowed to play with another unless he can first read the child's printed name on the blackboard. The value of clear writing might be promoted by announcing one short period during the day when no child is allowed to speak and any communication to another must be done by written note.[6]

In other words, put away the rattan. No doubt avoidance of threatened physical pain can often motivate quite well, but it is too crude and has some undesirable side effects. A little sugar-coating will do. Make the deprivation subtle; use your power to make the threat real.

This view of children, schools, and motivation depends on an acceptance of the basic values and goals of the dominant culture. An illustration of this can be found in Kagan's comments on adolescence and its current "troubles." Again, it seems clear that Kagan speaks for many understanding and sympathetic people. It's not that today's young people are spoiled, rotten nihilists. It's just that the young person is puzzling about the integrity of his beliefs and is experiencing

> uncertainty over his ideology. Campus unrest, the damning of adult authority, and occasionally apathy, are the consequences of this moral void. These disquieting phenomena will continue until young adults find a code of values to which they are willing to give spiritual commitment.[7]

It never seems to have occurred to this nice, concerned

professor that "campus unrest" and all that goes into it are not the signs of a "moral void"; that the student protests on Vietnam (which are never mentioned), civil rights, draft resistance (one instance of damning adult authority) are all signs that many young adults have chosen, and are willing to fight and suffer for, moral values, values that are superior to those of many adults who, fortunately, were less than totally successful in socializing these young people. Far from being "disquieting," such activities have been among the few encouraging happenings in America (even taking into account excesses, self-serving participants, and all). Contrary to Kagan's hope for some nice quiet, self-motivated adherence to values that will prevent the "unrest" which he deplores—sympathetically, of course—I hope that these phenomena will grow in seriousness as more young people act on the spiritual commitments that give rise to them.

Referring specifically to schools, Kagan emphasizes the legitimacy of society's demands to determine what happens in school. Naturally he opposes the "romantic" theory, while admitting that the child feels generally negative about school and school-imposed tasks. He grants that the child wants to determine his own actions.

> If society had no special preferences as to the talents it wanted children to attain, children would obviously be more enthusiastic each morning. They would select tasks in accordance with the values of their peer group, the immediacy of feedback, the likelihood of success, and the degree to which sensory and motor delights were part of the learning experience. Spelling, arithmetic, history, and science would not rank high on their list of preferences. These academic skills were given priority by society, and the decision was partly rational. If we believe in this decision we must tolerate the dissonance generated by the possibility that the child will not agree; we must be less Pollyannaish about academic mastery. Speaking, running

and climbing are natural activities that the child wants to perfect; reading, writing, and arithmetic are not.[8]

On the basis of this point of view, Kagan attacks the "harsh and almost totally destructive criticisms" which "place the total responsibility for educational failures on the authoritarian and rigid structures and practices of the elementary school system and suggest—dangerously, we believe—that if the child were left completely free he would seek the proper intellectual diet." Naturally, Kagan disagrees with this, and he mentions that he has seen many unstructured classrooms where he was unimpressed with the motivation and the intellectual progress.

To get a description of the "hidden curriculum" aspect of school (the part that Kagan hardly touches at all) without the spirit of critique and condemnation that suffuses the works of the "radical reformers," I will consider Philip Jackson's *Life in the Classroom,* a social-psychological study of public school teaching. (Conveniently, almost everyone has gone through public school and can supply his own raw data.) Professor Jackson notes as some key elements in the standard classroom the role of teacher power, the training in "learning to live in a crowd," "to become used to living under the constant condition of having his words and deeds evaluated by others," to experience "a place in which the division between the weak and the powerful is clearly drawn."[9] He emphasizes what the school imposes as the price of being "successful" as a member of the institution and as a student. *Patience* is crucial.

> The quintessence of virtue in most institutions is contained in the single word, *patience.* Lacking that quality, life could be miserable for those who must spend their time in our prisons, our factories, our corporation offices, and our schools. In all of these settings the participants must "learn to labor and to wait." They must also, to

some extent, "learn to suffer in silence." They are expected to bear with equanimity, in other words, the continued delay, denial, and interruption of their personal wishes and desires.[10]

The society is represented by the teacher; and through constant evaluations, "in most classrooms students come to know when things are right and wrong, good or bad, pretty or ugly, largely as a result of what the teacher tells them." The evaluation—of both the academic mastery Kagan concentrates on and the even more important adjustment to the demands of the institution for the display of conforming behavior—is connected to success in school and, it is drummed in constantly, later on in life. As Jackson points out,

> most students soon learn that rewards are granted to those who lead a good life. And in school the good life consists, principally, of doing what the teacher says. Of course, the teacher says many things, and some of his directions are easier to follow than others, but for the most part his expectations are not seen as unreasonable, and the majority of students comply with them sufficiently well to ensure that their hours in the classroom are colored more by praise than by punishment.[11]

Jackson recognizes that whereas it might make sense to talk about intrinsic motivation as superior to extrinsic when applied to academic learning, it is hardly plausible concerning the behavior fostered by the hidden curriculum.

Another important aspect of the authority-and-reward condition is the "relative impersonality and narrowness of the teacher-student relationship" in the classroom.

> It is there that students must learn to take orders from adults who do not know them very well and whom they do not themselves know intimately. For the first time in the child's life, power that has personal consequences for the child himself is wielded by a relative stranger.[12]

The idea of work in the sense of "a purposeful activity that has been prescribed for us by someone else; an activity in which we would not at that moment be engaged if it were not for some system of authority relationships" is developed in school.[13]

Jackson emphasizes how adaptive school training is.

> In the best of all possible worlds it is expected that children will adapt to the teacher's authority by becoming "good workers" and "model students." And, by and large, this ideal comes close to being realized. Most students learn to look and to listen when told to and to keep their private fantasies in check when class is in session. Moreover, this skill in complying with educational authority is doubly important because the student will be called upon to put it to work in many out-of-school settings. The transition from classroom to factory or office is made easily by those who have developed "good work habits" in their early years. . . .
>
> Habits of obedience and docility engendered in the classroom have a high pay-off value in other settings. So far as their power structure is concerned, classrooms are not too dissimilar from factories or offices, those ubiquitous organizations in which so much of our adult life is spent. Thus, school might really be called a preparation for life, but not in the usual sense in which educators employ that slogan. Power may be abused in school as elsewhere, but its existence is a fact of life to which we must adapt.[14]

Jackson notes that there is a potential tension between the two curriculums, in the sense that the qualities that make for a creative and daring intellect might not be easily compatible with those inculcated by the hidden curriculum. But this is not a condemnation; it simply presents a problem to be dealt with. Given the necessity of education in the Durkheimian sense that was noted earlier, Kagan and Jackson defend *society's* right to educate. Kagan, speaking about the costs extracted by the kind of academic training he discusses, emphasizes that there *could* be more freedom, more enthusiasm, more joy—and presumably the good effects on personality and general well-being that such experience has. But he warns that "spelling, arithmetic, history, and science would not rank high." And he defends the rationality of the society in deciding to compel this open curriculum—along with the hidden curriculum that Jackson describes. Anyone who does not agree with the rationality of this course of action is "Pollyannaish."

This point is very important. Whatever the radical critics might say, Kagan would get support from most parents, teachers, and even children. The training in the hidden curriculum would also be approved, though Jackson's terms may be a little too stark; talking about these matters publicly usually requires a less unpleasant vocabulary than Jackson's. For example, a reasoned defense of the character training in schools would stress proper respect for authority, helping young people to adjust to the demands of making a living, and teaching them how to get along well in the real world, rather than conformity, passivity, powerlessness, resentment, learning how to fake so that one can handle one's powerlessness. (The temptation is great, in such discussions, to give anecdotes from one's own education—how to con teachers by playing on their vanity, how to cheat on tests, how to manage stomach-aches and anxiety attacks connected with the chance that a good friend got a higher grade in math.)

With respect to academic skills, Kagan's examples point up a good way to further develop the argument between radical reform theory and the system's liberal defenders. As described in Chapter 1, the claim of the so-called romantic theory is that many young people will, in proper time and out of their own questioning, become interested in all sorts of things. Spelling is no big deal, and if an oppressive use of power is necessary to compel spelling drill, then it isn't worth it. History is again naturally interesting

to many young people. It is a particularly bad example for
Kagan to use, since looking at junior high and high school
texts will show that the compelling of history as a subject,
especially American history, does not teach much real
history and certainly not a critical attitude. Mainly it drills
in a myth to support the political status quo in America,
and teachers can get into trouble if they do too much that
is politically dubious according to the local school board.
But this is another demand of society's that Mr. Kagan
might, to be consistent, find quite rational.

What radical reform theory would say is that forcing
everyone to go through the set curriculum does not
guarantee that everyone or even most students learn those
subjects—though the process is certainly part of transmitting the hidden curriculum. And if, in free schools, some
young people didn't learn those things, but became good
at making pottery or fixing cars, while remaining bad
spellers—well, so what? Given the record of the public
schools and given the cost in certain desirable intellectual
qualities that Jackson noted, can defenders of the public
school system claim scientific evidence that more people
going through the required curriculum have more knowledge of history or science than would happen under a
system not thoroughly compulsory, regimented, and authoritarian in character?

To be honest, a defense of the public schools, even their
ideal, would have to expand Kagan's support of society's
claim to compel attendance in a situation that grants certain state-approved officials the power to administer a state-
approved curriculum. Some further argument justifying
the hidden curriculum as observed by Jackson and others
would also be needed. In brief, a reasonable defender
could say that we live in a complex mass industrial society
dominated by various hierarchically and bureaucratically
organized institutions—corporations, the military, the government. In order to make a living, adults are required to

work in such organizations. Work is often not pleasant; one often has to do things that are boring, to take orders, to deal with many people in their roles rather than as whole people; one often has to bear down and work in a disciplined manner, even though it is unpleasant. In our society, the purpose of most work is not intrinsic satisfaction but monetary wage which will enable the earner to participate in the very high material standard of living which the system has produced, whatever else one may say about it. Whatever the problems, given the standard of human possibility and not some utopia, America is a pretty good society and worthy of support. It is reasonable to expect the public school to prepare people to participate loyally in this society, and it can be argued that the system does do this, as Jackson noted.

Many parents and many high-school students themselves accept this analysis. They know there are more "fun" ways of spending their time, even of learning. But when it comes to the serious business of education—to fit one to life, to prepare one for getting into a good college, for the kind of professional or business success that can provide a materially secure and comfortable life—then "fun" isn't so important. If one adds that schools have had to handle immense numbers of students from all sorts of cultural, ethnic, and class backgrounds, especially in the early immigration years of this century, then the defense of the method can be understood.

Of course, it is admitted that there is always room for some reform, for new techniques, for eliminating excess repressions (such as dress codes); but the point that the public schools are agents of the dominant societal values and institutions and should prepare young people to fit into the roles and needs of the society must remain fundamental.

Before going on to my main concern for the rest of this chapter—the problems of curriculum and method as they arise *inside* the radical reform perspective—I want to mention some specific reasons why I think the defenses of the traditional public school curriculum and methods are wrong. (My objections are not those of an objective observer. Having gone through a traditional public school education, including one of the most prestigious all-academic college-prep high schools in the country, I feel that my own experience informs all of the general remarks I make about public schools.)

First, in all descriptions of education and school in the abstract, there is no reference to age. That is, the spectrum between elementary ages and adolescence is not differentiated and given significance. But we all know that for very young children, it makes no sense to conceive that one is passing on to them the "massed wisdom of the ages," to use one of Max Rafferty's felicitous phrases. The school is baby-sitting (usually not very well), teaching some skills like reading and writing, doing some number work, and giving kids an opportunity to play together, broaden their opportunities for projects, games, developing "social skills." This is at best the way the public schools operate. The primary grades begin the disciplining and socialization to the forms of the school which will be used "educationally" later. That is, a child begins to learn how to respond to marks, to have workbooks, do homework, sit silent while in a group, compete in spelling bees. Very little "massed wisdom" here, or training in logic and clear thinking. Even some public school officials are coming to realize that it is possible to ease up in the early years. In Los Angeles, a ruling was made a couple of years ago *allowing* schools to drop graded report cards during the first three grades. (If you have kept your early grade report cards, look at them; they're revealing. The author can recall, as his only vivid school memory from second grade, coming home and weeping while being reassured by his mother after receiving an N—"no good"—in penmanship for the second period report. As Jules Henry so vividly describes in *Culture Against Man,* it is very important in this culture to get children to internalize the "essential nightmare." *"To be successful in our culture one must learn to dream of failure."* And the training should start young; but perhaps, it seems now, not quite from the very beginning.)

Any abstract conception emphasizing "wisdom" and "culture" needs must make its claims for the later years of schooling, basically what we, in America, call junior high, high school, and college. (There are certainly pedagogical issues about how skills may best be taught to young children, and what sorts of cultural preferences go into the choice of methods, but this is a different issue.)

Second, even when more narrowly applied to the high schools, the traditional description of education seems to me almost totally unreal. The study of social subjects like history, political science, economics, and civics is little more than an exercise in indoctrination and in the inculcation of just the wrong habits of thought for the forms of inquiry these parts of the curriculum ideally express. As noted before, history textbooks are memorized and "right" answers demanded on tests. Interpretations are taught as facts. This kind of criticism can be carried through in all the disciplines. (Only the most objective subjects—namely, mathematics and science—are sometimes well taught and well learned, within their narrow academic form.) Even defenders of the system will admit that most of those who attend school—especially junior high and high school—do not learn the "wisdom of the ages." Many students don't take the "academic" program. Many of those who do fare poorly, and fail even by the standards of the system. And most of the teachers are officially considered competent only to teach in high schools, and could in no way be regarded as examples of people who *do* the subject they are teaching or as being even near competent to explain and unfold the subject for anyone seriously concerned with it. (The almost universal academic contempt in which schools of education and the quality of their training are held by the academic parts of the university is only partly snobbery. Much of it is understandable. This point was raised in Chapter 2 in relation to the professional—as opposed to official pedagogical—qualifications of teachers in free schools.)

In all honesty, I find all this to be hardly debatable. That some people come through the customary process of schooling knowing important things and able to do creative intellectual work is an obvious truth whose implications for schooling and curriculum are not at all obvious. My experience is that *most* of the really good and creative students who emerge from traditional public schools do so *in spite of* the school and its curriculum, not because of it. What is usually the case is that interests, even passions, are acquired—from home, parents, books, friends, a rare inspiring teacher somewhere. Usually the development of interests is not at all coincident with the routine curriculum in school, which for these students is easily mastered, as part of the game of "doing well," for the obvious rewards. The individuality of the good student's development is not likely to match the term-by-term, lock-step curriculum, even assuming, contrary to fact, that there are significant numbers of intellectual teachers, good materials, and a free atmosphere of inquiry. Much of the intellectual achievement of the good students turns out to be incidental to the school process. This especially applies to creative fields like music, art, crafts, and poetry, where the standard public-school approach of grades and lessons and teacher-imposed standards is particularly deadly. But even in the most mainstream curriculum knowledge-fields—the standard curriculum, so to speak—this is the case.

Einstein expressed his own response to traditional school techniques quite eloquently:

It is in fact nothing short of a miracle that the modern methods of instruction have not yet entirely strangled the holy curiosity of inquiry, for this delicate little plant, aside from stimulation, stands mainly in need of freedom; without this it goes to wrack and ruin without fail. It is a very grave mistake to think that the enjoyment of seeing and searching can be promoted by means of coercion and a sense of duty. . . .[15]

As Dewey emphasized in his description, individual student choice and interest are discounted when weighed against the standard curriculum. The system of tests, grades, constant competition for external rewards provides the active motivation since the basic premise is that the society has decided what is worth learning, and that the uninformed and immature young certainly cannot be trusted to come to worthwhile decisions on their own or even to participate significantly in decisions. So, good students do well in school, and some coincidentally acquire education, though the relation between these two facts is often almost nonexistent.

I offer my own experience as a case in point. I was an exceedingly successful student in school from the beginning. Coming from an intensely intellectual family where there was a deep love for learning (my father was a teacher, and a marvelous one), I, like the rest of my family, read a great deal, developed an appreciation of music and an interest in history and politics—all totally independent of what was going on in school. When I was in the early years of my high-prestige high school, I was reading authors like Dostoyevsky, Tolstoy, and Conrad. But in English class, the reading assignment was *Johnny Tremain*. However, as a savvy student, I knew that English class was one thing and loving literature was something else. So I read the assigned book, studied it for the "book test," got my A; and then, on my own time, I read *Crime and*

Punishment, and *Lord Jim.* My teacher, of course, knew nothing about my interest in literature, and nothing in the way English class was conducted or the relationship of student and teacher made this fact relevant. Similarly, I had acquired a real interest in physics at the age of fourteen and had made a decision to be a physicist. So I read and studied physics on my own during the years of high school. Of course, as a senior, since physics was the required course for seniors taking science, I took physics. The fact that I had already learned far more than the poor and simplistic high-school text contained didn't matter. As was required, I did the homework and took the tests. Given my own knowledge, I could do all this redundant work quickly and still get my A (for honors, scholarships, prizes—the *real* rewards), and then, on my own time, continue on the path of learning physics (for its essential interest, my desire to understand, my aim of becoming a physicist: motives that had never entered into the school experience).

I think this is a fairly typical experience for the so-called "excellent" students. The bad students who fail and refuse to master even the standard curriculum as laid out obviously haven't acquired the massed wisdom of the ages. What the school has given to them, and to many good students as well, is a resistance to and fear of anything intellectual, so long as it reminds them of school.

During three years of teaching freshman humanities at M.I.T. I always asked my sections about their experience of the humanities in high school. The answers were revealing. Almost every student had been required to read a Shakespeare play; out of approximately 150 students polled —and these are some of the best students coming out of the high schools—not one had ever been tempted to read another Shakespeare play on his own. And when I asked a group of these students (almost all of whom were A students in English, as in everything else) why they had chosen this particular freshman humanities course (Contemporary Moral Issues) rather than the "great books" type, the answer most frequently given was, "It had less literature than the others, and I hate literature."

Of course, I recognize all the exceptions: the good teachers who convey both their honest love of the subject and respect for the students; the students who get turned on to Shakespeare or poetry, even by a clumsy required initiation; and so forth. My point is that these good events are the rare exceptions, that they are deviations from the norm, and that the bad norm is systematically created. And further, the central point is how wild the pious "wisdom of the ages" justification is for the curriculum, its structure, the inflicted-by-force character of its imposition, and the hidden curriculum that accompanies it. The fact that there may be a loosening up now—"curricular reforms"—can't negate the fact that the defense and justification were offered for what was *actually* going on, not for some better future now being suggested by some reformers. (All of my comments apply to the same public school system I hear being defended in works like Kagan's and Jackson's.)

I have noted all through this book how inextricably the methods of teaching and the organization of schools (justified ostensibly by their educational purposes) are connected with the hidden curriculum and the fulfilling of social and political functions. To sharpen the issue in pedagogical terms for the discussion inside the reform perspective, I want to narrow my concern to the questions of curriculum and learning and teaching methods as if they were independent of political and social problems (which they clearly are not). The question then becomes: If we abolish the disciplinary apparatus, the bureaucratically determined requirements, the lock-step age grading, the competitiveness based on promised future extrinsic rewards, then what can be said about culture, knowledge, the process of learning, the relation of the individual to the culture, that can lead to a reasoned position on the problems of curriculum and method?

One end of the progressive spectrum can be typified by the following passage from an issue of *The New Schools Exchange Newsletter*. Answering a query concerning the problem of curriculum for alternative schools, the editor, Harvey Haber, wrote:

> Dear Bob: If we consider that absolutely anything that happens, either spontaneously, or pre-planned, in a free school situation is curricular, then worried decision-making is greatly minimized. Generally, new schools provide core curriculum classes for their younger students—reading, writing, arithmetic—and let the rest occur organically. Remember, a walk on the beach is learning, cooking lunch is learning, talking with visitors is learning—and no one should attempt to pre-structure any of it.[16]

Now certainly, if everything is learning, and the specifically educational enterprise is about learning, then there are no problems. But the approach represented by the quoted passage is clearly silly and dogmatic. Its chief fault is its totally reactive (and unexperiential) quality. Obviously, it is a reaction against the view of education described above, the traditional view which is based on planning formal lessons, with little or no opportunity for spontaneous or student-initiated activity, and with an almost complete concentration on the narrowly academic as the only respectable learning, at least so far as the school is concerned. One simple way of reacting against this view is to negate every aspect of it. So, while a formulation as the one quoted above sounds positive—all too positive—it is essentially negative.

Such a view is comforting in its negativity. As stated, there is no need to worry, make decisions, argue values and priorities, try to relate the past, present, and future, because everything is cool—whatever is happening, that's learning. Looking closely at the philosophy of free education, of which such views are dogmatic, simple-minded, and self-serving caricatures, we can see what is really at issue. One important point is that many kinds of experiences that have traditionally been ignored in school situations *can* be quite fruitful and significant learning experiences. And it is also important to see how much significant learning arises from experiences that are unplanned and incidental. If we take the individual young person's concerns and interests seriously, then we will observe how much is learned—often unpredictably—in the course of being engaged in the world in an active way. This is contrary to the idea of having the teacher plan the goal and process of each learning experience, impose this on the whole class, test to see what percent of students learned what percent of the proffered "learning," and then give them their grades.

But the reaction is only the beginning of the task, not the end. The real negation of the denial of the worth of everything outside the traditional classroom is to emphasize the *possibilities* of all the ignored experiences, along with denying confidence in the worth of the traditional curriculum even in its own academic sphere. But caricature results from translating this vitally important affirmation of possibility into a dogma, that "everything is learning," with no room for judgments of relative worth, fertility, or usefulness and no scope for any "preplanning"—which is to say, hardly any active role for adults, except to watch all the "learning" and answer questions when asked.

Dewey, in *Experience and Education,* dealt with a similar polemical situation at the height of the progressive education movement. Dewey wanted to reaffirm his ideas of a reformed education while analyzing and explaining the excesses in theory and practice which he saw in the movement he had helped inspire. After noting the clash of abstract principles represented by the conflict of educational philosophies, he writes (referring to the new progressive ideas):

> A philosophy which proceeds on the basis of rejection, of sheer opposition . . . will tend to suppose that because the old education was based on ready-made organization, therefore it suffices to reject the principle of organization *in toto,* instead of striving to discover what it means and how it is to be attained on the basis of experience. We might go through all the points of difference between the new and the old education and reach similar conclusions. When external control is rejected, the problem becomes that of finding the factors of control that are inherent within experience. When external authority is rejected, it does not follow that all authority should be rejected, but that there is need to search for a more effective source of authority. Because the older education imposed the knowledge, methods, and the rules of conduct of the mature person upon the young, it does not follow, except upon the basis of the extreme *Either-Or* philosophy, that the knowledge and skill of the mature person has no directive value for the experience of the immature. . . .
>
> . . . the general principles of the new education do not of themselves solve any of the problems of the actual or practical conduct and management of progressive schools. Rather, they set new problems which have to be worked out on the basis of a new philosophy of experience. The problems are not even recognized, to say nothing of being solved, when it is assumed that it suffices to reject the ideas and practices of the old education and then go to the opposite extreme.[17]

I am sure that Dewey would reiterate these remarks today while still supporting the new attempt to transform the schools radically. It isn't Dewey's authority I want to call on; simply the reasonableness of his observations, referring as they do to a development he had been passionately committed to. The importance of the observations can be pointed up by noting that the "doing anything is learning" passage was an answer to a letter from someone starting a new school and expressing a real confusion over the question of curriculum. The answering by unhelpful citation of rather mindless slogans is unfortunately too common. Certainly, in practice, the question can't be answered in this way. Students and teachers and parents working in schools (especially high schools) are constantly troubled by this issue, and the more sensitive they are to the really knotty problems involved and the more experience they gain, the more hollow and mindless such sloganizing sounds. In free schools characterized by considerable apathy and boredom, with almost no academic endeavors, few other projects, much beginning of activities that rapidly peter out, adults sitting around passive lest they be accused of structuring or pressuring, "laying on their trip," or in some way not being free enough of the old ways, the emptiness of such confident pronouncements is vividly dramatized.

Under the pressure to be free of repressive ideas and modes of organization, free school people have sometimes fallen into the kinds of rhetorical excesses Dewey deplored, and these have also had their effect in practice. As in other parts of the movement for radical social change, people can too easily be trapped by "more-radical-than-thou" ploys. When one's own identity is involved, as it must be, it can seem the most serious of charges to be accused of not being radical enough, of not having exorcised one's hang-ups from the old culture. And since any kind of radical personal transformation cannot avoid the question of authenticity, in this sense, people undergoing such changes do honestly and appropriately suspect themselves quite often. So an accusation from others can make one quite defensive and prevent one from voicing ideas and beliefs that one really feels. The burden of proof seems to be on the person who is accused of not being radical enough (where "radical" is defined in terms of degree of negation of the old ways), no matter how far-fetched the claim of the "super-radical" is.

What is lost sight of is a simple and obvious point that Dewey expressed well.

> It is not too much to say that an educational philosophy which professes to be based on the idea of freedom may become as dogmatic as ever was the traditional education which is reacted against. For any theory and set of practices is dogmatic which is not based upon critical examination of its own underlying principles. Let us say that the new education emphasizes the freedom of the learner. Very well. A problem is now set. What does freedom mean and what are the conditions under which it is capable of realization? Let us say that the kind of external imposition which was so common in the traditional school limited rather than promoted the intellectual and moral development of the young. Again, very well. Recognition of this serious defect sets a problem. Just what is the role of the teacher and of books in promoting the educational development of the immature? Admit that traditional education employed as the subject-matter for study facts and ideas so bound up with past as to give little help in dealing with the issues of the present and future. Very well. Now we have the problem of discovering the connection which actually exists *within* experience between the achievements of the past and the issues of the present. . . .[18]

The problem as posed here is what any free school has to deal with in some way, though too often it is by rhetoric, avoidance, or the hope that, however troublesome the present may appear, freedom will work, at least in the long run. If we think of the "anything is learning, especially if it isn't planned" conception as an extreme point on the spectrum, we should, of course, look at more serious and complex and less extreme statements of the free learning approach to curriculum to see how the problems arise.

In Chapter 1, I discussed some of John Holt's observations on the theory of freedom. Here I want to look more closely at his remarks on curriculum, since his views are representative of a fairly widespread belief among educational reformers, radical or not. (As we shall see, Paul Goodman, who is radical and an inspiration to the new schools movement, expresses some quite different conceptions.) Holt notes the claim of the system that there is essential knowledge that everyone should be taught—the "massed wisdom of the ages"—and points out how little of what is taught is retained by most students. His real point, however, is not simply that because of the oppressive techniques used the goal is not reached, but that the whole curriculum conception is nonsense. "The notion of a curriculum, an essential body of knowledge, would be absurd even if children remembered everything we taught them."[19] Holt's basic argument against the idea of a curriculum, as he interprets it, is that knowledge itself changes, and that

> we cannot possibly judge what knowledge will be most needed forty, or twenty, or even ten years from now. . . . Since we can't know what knowledge will be most needed in the future, it is senseless to try to teach it in advance. Instead, we should try to turn out people who love learning so much and learn so well, that they will be able to learn whatever needs to be learned.[20]

Holt parallels these observations with the idea that "learning is not everything, and certainly one piece of learning is as good as another." However, this egalitarianism is contradicted in the next paragraph, where he states:

> It is not subject matter that makes some learning more valuable than others, but the spirit in which the work is done. . . . We cannot know, at any moment, what particular bit of knowledge or understanding a child needs most, will most strengthen and best fit his model of reality. Only

he can do this. He may not do it very well, but he can do it a hundred times better than we can. The most we can do is try to help, by letting him know roughly what is available and where he can look for it.[21]

I want here to summarize this widely shared perspective in order to emphasize some key points before raising critical questions. The leading assumption is that curriculum means that body of knowledge labeled "essential" and worthy of being transmitted by compulsion to the new generation. This knowledge is divided up into standardized subject matter organized in graded sequences (as described before). I want to ignore the compulsory aspect. The view is then that, compulsory or not, there is no sense in choosing any subject matter over any other in the scale of significance. Holt assumes that the criterion to be used is future usefulness of the knowledge, and that we cannot do a good job in predicting this, because knowledge and the world are changing so fast. What will be useful is the capacity "to learn how to learn." At the extreme, as in the passage from the *New Schools Exchange Newsletter,* the idea is that any experience is learning, so long as it is spontaneous—and nothing more need be said. Certainly there is no place at all for adults being active or doing any planning. Holt seems to imply something like this when he says that one piece of learning is as good as another, but the modification (or contradiction) that he himself makes represents the confused perceptions that seem to characterize many reform educators. Once we look at real children learning, we know that it's obviously false that "one piece of learning is as good as another." To learn how to play tic-tac-toe is not as good as to learn how to do arithmetic. And Holt's modification—that it is the spirit in which the learning is done that accounts for the difference in value—does not satisfactorily answer the objection.

Clearly, what is at the core of this new education position is the intense reaction against the traditional method, the traditional curriculum, and the stupidity and obtuseness of the justifications offered for these. Reformers point to the varieties of ways learning takes place in real experience and the value of enthusiastic learning endeavors that arise out of a young person's honestly engaged interest and concern in real situations, and compare these with the ubiquitous stupidity the same children often seem to display under normal school conditions. They also emphasize that what is of real value to a student can only be determined if the individual and his experience, interests and capacities are taken into account. Finally, they claim that the traditional curriculum coupled with the traditional methods does not take any of this into account.

All this can be agreed to, but as I noted, the apparently opposing positions—that everything is learning, or that any learning is as good as any other, or that it is only the spirit that determines the value of learning, or that the fact that we don't know what knowledge will be most useful in the future means we must avoid making judgments now about the relative value of what is learned—are very dubious. The principle of reaction that Dewey noted seems at work here. The questions involve the role of adults; the grounds of evaluating the significance of learnings; and the possibility of saying anything about subject matter, fields of study, and so forth (curriculum). I have noted how a position can be constructed by simply negating the obviously bad aspects of the traditional education. But the position is not satisfactory, clearly.

More can be said beyond the simple assertion that the student learned something, or even that he seemed to do it with a good and joyful spirit. We know that learning joyously is good because it means that the success and satisfaction will encourage more learning activity, and this is good. But we often can say something about the quality of the experience, about the fruitfulness of what is learned, about the way it opens up other valuable activities and ideas, about the capacity of the experience to generate skills and capabilities that will be important, and, so far as subject matter is concerned, we can consider the conceptual relations of a given subject matter to other valuable knowledge.

To go back to the tic-tac-toe example: What makes tic-tac-toe less valuable than arithmetic is that tic-tac-toe is essentially very limited. Not that it is nothing; one thing that can be learned is that the game can be played systematically so that the person who goes first never loses. But it clearly does not have the complexity of arithmetic, nor the place in a process of intellectual growth that leads outward into more and more complexity and significance. This kind of consideration can be applied to many of the activities of a learner. And the issue is not decided simply by interest or inclination; the students may be most inclined to play cards, read comic books, or run on the beach. This doesn't settle the question.

Clearly compulsion, a set curriculum, and ignoring the child's inclinations, interest, and experience are bad in many ways. Dewey pointed out seventy years ago that to simply accept the expression of interests and the activities coming from them, while standing aside, helping only when asked, in accordance with the idea that nature unfolds nicely in the child and he learns what he needs—so long as there is no interference—is a sentimental idealization and ignores the facts of process and growth (even while it seems to emphasize them).

> If we isolate the child's present inclinations, purposes, and experiences from the place they occupy, and the part they have to perform in a developing experience, all stand upon the same level; all alike are equally good and equally bad. . . . It is the danger of the "new education" that it regards the child's present powers and interests as something finally significant in themselves.[22]

More than thirty years later, worrying about the progressive schools, he noted:

> Over-emphasis upon activity as an end, instead of upon *intelligent* activity, leads to identification of freedom with immediate execution of impulses and desires.[23]

These considerations of value applied to learning cannot be separated from the issue of teaching and the roles of adults. For one thing, the teacher is often making a judgment of value simply by being himself and expressing his interests. This is a very important point, since the conception of staying out of the young person's way so that his natural development is not interfered with implies a conception of adult neutrality that is extremely misleading. Dewey himself was emphatic on the vital role of the adult, even within the child-centered educational environment. His tone differs sharply from Holt's "get out of the way" conception which is quite representative of the contemporary free school; though in practice the divisions would not be so great. Following from his theory of the importance of experience moving forward and into future things, Dewey affirms that

> the greater maturity of experience which should belong to the adult as educator puts him in a position to evaluate each experience of the young in a way in which the one having the less mature experience cannot do. It is then the business of the educator to see in what direction an experience is heading. There is no point in his being more mature if, instead of using his greater insight to help organize the conditions of the experience of the immature, he throws away his insight. . . . The mature person, to put it in moral terms, has no right to withhold from the young on given occasions whatever capacity for sympathetic understanding his own experience has given him.[24]

(Recall Dennison's story of José, from *The Lives of Children*, noted in Chapter 1.) The concept of teacher as leader in a group is repeatedly emphasized by Dewey in opposition to the tendency in the progressive education movement of his time (and perhaps even more today) to make an adult feel guilty for doing anything that the child or young person doesn't explicitly ask for. (This is less of a problem with small children, where the abstract idea is modified quickly when confronted by reality, but it is a crucial question with adolescents, who are the main subject anyway for problems involving the interaction of curriculum and methods.) Dewey writes:

> As the most mature member of the group he has a peculiar responsibility for the conduct of the interactions and intercommunications which are the very life of the group as a community. That children are individuals whose freedom should be respected while the more mature person should have no freedom as an individual is an idea too absurd to require refutation. The tendency to exclude the teacher from a positive and leading share in the direction of the activities of the community of which he is a member is another instance of reaction from one extreme to another.[25]

It seems fairly clear why the idea of neutrality is misleading. Young people come to the school from their own individual situations: some seem seriously hurt, like Dennison's José; others less so; some hardly at all. But they are all constantly being affected from all sorts of sources—parents, peers, the media. Their interests, their confusions, their hurts, their anxieties, their possibilities—all are partly the result of such "non-neutral" pressures. The child's present being is not simply the unfolding of ideal natural growth. So, the reaction against the authoritarianism of the public schools and the central role of the all-powerful teacher is certainly well-founded. But the abstract polar opposite of not imposing anything on the kids is delusion. By being there, by being honest about who he is and what he cares about, the adult cannot help "loading the environment," influencing the young people, no matter how much he is committed to not initiating, planning, or in any way interfering with the children's own doings. More than that, the laissez-faire mode of "being there" is often a very serious value decision, for which the adult must assume responsibility. It is not simply a "letting be"; it is a conscious avoidance of doing and saying things that could very well affect the young people involved. It also projects a definite feeling about relationships, what it is to care and to take responsibility. The idea that not asserting oneself, not intervening and initiating even when one feels it is appropriate, is truly not to affect the unfolding of the child's growth and education is ideological, in a bad sense, and an avoidance of necessary choice and commitment, an avoidance than is itself a choice with consequences. This does not mean that active adults will never make mistakes, never intervene when it is not appropriate, or misjudge the direction of the child's experience, or apply pressure in an unwarranted and even harmful way. Of course, we do the same with our own adult friends and risk making these mistakes.

But the philosophy of freedom applied in this area of curriculum and methods seems to have gotten somewhat confused, as Dewey noted. Reacting against authoritarianism and boring, sterile, simple-minded, and often propagandistic subject matter, some new schools people took their affirmation of freedom to imply never interfering with children, never asserting values and priorities with the knowledge that one was quite possibly influencing the young people, condemning the idea of authority and the idea of the significance of subject matter ("the process of learning is what counts.").

But this really is a confusion on basic principles. Where freedom comes in, as Dennison reiterates throughout his book, is primarily in the absence of *coercion*. José could have always finally said no: his autonomy was respected. But this did not preclude Dennison from pushing, insisting, doing everything he could to get José to have reading lessons. And it was Dennison's own *judgment* to try, a judgment that arose from real commitment and even friendship between two free people, one older and one young. It was not based on institutional power and powerlessness built into the impersonal roles of "teacher" and "pupil."

As was illustrated in Chapter 2, in free high schools, students in general come voluntarily. They invariably share in the power (decisions are often "one person–one vote," as in Summerhill); subjects, projects, and courses are chosen voluntarily; often the students themselves hire the teachers. Here the dangers of open authoritarianism are nonexistent—though not the possibility of manipulation. This danger is always present, however subtly, even in the most implacably noninterference situations. One way to deal with this problem is to have the issue out in the open all the time, rather than avoiding it by an impossible (and undesirable) conception of "no adult influence."

My own experiences in doing and observing free schools led me to a strong feeling on this point. One experience particularly seems revealing. Three years ago I was working in a new free school, the Community School in Santa Barbara, with students ranging in age from preschool through junior high. (This school was described in Chapter 2.) During the course of the year, public high-school students began dropping by our school. After a while they formed their own after-school classes, and in the spring, Tim Affleck and I opened up a full-time high-school part of the school. In the first weeks many classes started (most teachers were volunteer undergraduates and graduate students from the nearby state university campus). The first flush of freedom saw students signing up for too many classes of all sorts. The usual problems of sustaining interest were compounded by the fact that classes met in many different places. Students and teachers had trouble making efficient arrangements. Dissatisfaction led to an experiment with longer time blocks—a whole morning, for example. The Cambodia invasion and its aftermath interrupted a full trial of this experiment, but there were a couple of seminar attempts. I had offered to do a social studies seminar. On the evening before the scheduled seminar, some of the students had organized an open meeting on the Cambodian situation at the Community School building. They leafleted the high school; both public and free school people were there. A couple of public high-school students spoke up in favor of the American government's position. There was heated discussion, naturally. One point that I raised in the discussion was the issue of who was on whose side in wars like the one in Vietnam; for example, how few rich landowners or big businessmen were fighting with the NLF or were more sympathetic to the NLF than to the Thieu-Ky interests.

That night I was rereading some George Orwell essays and was struck by the appropriateness to the evening's discussion of Orwell's essay "Looking Back on the Spanish Civil War." One of Orwell's main points was how one could not look to the press in England for an honest account of what went on in the war—that left, right or center, they all lied, exaggerated, and distorted in the interests of their beliefs. But, though not able to be sure of particular facts, one could know which side was right, all things considered. Orwell described the vision and struggles of the oppressed people of Spain, the hopes and dreams of the anarchists and socialists, and compared these with the world that Franco, the generals, the fascists, the rich landowners and churchmen wanted; and he expressed his sense of why the Republican side, however betrayed by the Communists and however distorted some of its actions, was in the interests of the possibility of decent human lives for all people.

When the social studies group met the next morning, I referred to the discussion of the previous evening and brought up the accusation of one-sidedness which was often leveled at the Community School (only "radicals" teach there; they don't give both sides of the story.) I then proceeded to give a sophisticated defense of the United States involvement in Indochina. The problem about disputed facts, details, etc., came up, as well as more far-reaching questions of interpretation and conscious and unconscious bias.

I then brought out the Orwell essay and said I had something I wanted to read to the group. The students listened with great interest. At the end one asked if the essay had been written in the last couple of years; it had seemed so pertinent to the issues just raised in connection with the Vietnam war. People were really surprised to discover that it had been written almost three decades ago.

The discussion focused on the topic of what were the key factors in twentieth-century politics: what were the major revolutions and wars about; how could the contending interests and values be understood; and how could one raise considerations of morality. The teacher spoke for much of the time, giving historical background and helping to formulate the issues. Great interest was expressed, and it was decided to continue the general topic at the next social studies seminar.

For the next seminar, I chose reading material that would be useful in developing some of the themes raised at the first session. I xeroxed copies of Orwell's well-known essay "Politics and the English Language," some excerpts from Dwight Macdonald's essay "On the Responsibility of Peoples," written at the end of World War II, discussing the concentration camps of the Nazis, the saturation bomb-

ing and atomic bombings of the Allies and leading to reflections on contemporary state power and the question of
responsibility, and also a short article from a current issue
of *Trans-action* (now *Society*) magazine which discussed
the My Lai massacre and the responses of the American
people to the relevations. When the seminar met (on the
beach), these were passed out; about an hour was spent
reading, with people sharing copies; and then there was a
general discussion in which the teacher again had a prominent role, giving appropriate background knowledge and
leading the discussion.

The school year ended at this point, and so did the
seminar. But even this meager two-session "course" seemed
to point up in experience some of the ideas just described
theoretically. It was the teacher who shaped the experience
to a large extent. The students didn't ask for a course on
the "roots of twentieth-century politics" or "politics and
morality in the twentieth century," which was what was
developing. They expressed a vague interest in having
some course or seminar on "social studies." The adult-
teacher, on the basis of his own perception of the young
people, his own particular interests and commitments, and
the actual experience of an event outside the school—
namely, the evening discussion on the war—structured the
course. He found the reading material and brought it to
the group. It wouldn't have made sense to wait for the
students to ask to read Orwell or Macdonald or whomever
—they weren't even aware that those writings existed. Also,
reading them and the works that would have followed
had the class continued required the teacher's active
role of giving background and suggesting further reading.
Finally, the result of a whole course would have been not
only the gaining of some knowledge, opening up of new
areas of study, and aid in formulating and testing one's
own ideas that comes from good and intensive discussion,

but also a particular approach to the subjects coming from the teacher's own preferences and beliefs.

The students were, of course, free not to come or to make suggestions about reading and topics or to criticize the role of the teacher. They knew this and the teacher knew this, and the fact that they knew him as a person, and had done things with him outside of school, was the basis of their trust in his judgment, their willingness to accept the legitimacy of his concern with them as people, not just as pupils assigned by the school. The authority he had was not institutional power masked by an ideology that "your teacher knows best and has the right to force you," which adheres to adults in their institutional role of teacher in the public school. (No teacher in a public high school need earn respect or trust. From the first day in class, all students must obey him under threat, whether or not they eventually decide he merits authority.) In this case, the students respected the views and knowledge of this person because they knew him and had worked with him, and they had freely granted the authority he was exercising in choosing the reading, formulating the topics, leading the discussion.

So far as influencing young people toward a particular point of view, a teacher can only be as honest as possible: that is, he can be a good teacher, raise his own doubts, explain how he got to where he is, try to bring out the plausibility of differing views, but without expressing some phony methodological neutrality aimed at preventing the young people from figuring out what he really believes. (This, of course, makes it impossible to take account of the teacher's bias and leads them toward a false conception of objectivity.)

One final point concerning this example. I did not think the importance of the topic was a matter of taste, that anything in social studies would have been just as good since it is the process of learning and the method of inquiry that are really the vital items in education. It is true that these are vital, and should be crucial in any study, but it doesn't follow that the content is irrelevant. To understand what is happening in the society we live in is important for anyone. This value judgment doesn't lead to a set curriculum or to the idea that the particular way used to approach the issues is the best or only way or that everyone should have been required to take the seminar. But it does express the idea that certain general problems and issues are central in importance because we are in *this* world at *this* time, and that concern with these problems is not merely an expression of personal taste.

The question of whether anything can be called "essential" was raised by Holt in opposition to his interpretation of the justification for imposing the traditional curriculum. The issue seems to be quite confused. Obviously there is no school subject that is essential to individual survival. People survive and even flourish who have flunked out of school or have never gone to school. The idea of being essential must have reference to the individual in terms of some *value,* however vague—for instance, "essential to being a competent participant in a democratic system" or "essential to understanding the world one lives in." Another perspective on the "essential" relates to the survival of the group—like American society or the human race. Again, survival in ways one values rather than sheer physical survival is in question.

In a sense, this whole chapter is an attempt to deal with this question. It obviously is possible to say concrete things about what might be called "essential." (For example, see two recent books on reforming education in the public schools, Joseph Turner's *Making New Schools: The Liberation of Learning* and Arthur Pearl's *The Atrocity of Education.*) But such analyses seem to me finally to be at best useful suggestions to teachers about good approaches, possible ways of tying material together, not really addressing the basic question. What I mean is that on a general level one can say that the curriculum should be relevant to the great problems facing the human race today—but this doesn't say much. One could make a list of subjects like ecology, social studies, history, science and math, psychology, the arts and humanities, religion, and so forth; and then one could show how bad the traditional textbooks are and how much the traditional curriculum misses. (A very good analysis concerning this is Jules Henry's article "Education for Stupidity," *New York Review of Books,* May 1, 1968.) Or one could list all the traditional *names* of subjects, and say that all the relevant concerns could be subsumed under the old names, properly elaborated and done with interesting new methods. It could then be said that we need good learning of all of these things by as many people as possible, so that we can have citizens who can cope with the problems of running a democracy, saving the environment, preventing nuclear war, finding meaningful lives, coping with moral dilemmas in their own lives, and so forth.

And nothing would really be solved about curriculum, as I understand the issue. Practically, it would be valuable to describe new courses and projects that seem to address directly the deep problems of our day, just as it would be valuable to hear of new approaches to literature that have been met by good responses from students. The problem I am trying to get at here is not one of listing sort-of-essential subjects. It is the questioning of method and content together, in order to make problematic the point of view *behind* any discussion of curriculum and methods; the importance of engaging in a discussion of the purposes of education and curriculum in terms that go beyond what everyone admits is good. I would like the discussion to be more controversial, less pious. For example, the curriculum lists from the free high schools reproduced in Chapter 2, if expanded and justified, as the teacher from the Santa Barbara school did for his history course, would clearly lead to controversy. Saying that the curriculum should enable young people to break through the ideological conditioning that the dominant institutions of the society provide so that they will be able to see how radical changes in this society are necessary for group survival and a decent quality of life for the people of this and other countries would be unacceptable to many, though saying that teaching history and sociology well so that students can develop a critical spirit would be accepted.

My concern in this chapter has been to discuss the issue in the context of free school theory on method and curriculum. I am raising questions that have been continuously present throughout this book: the educational purpose of schools that choose to deviate from the purposes of state-run schools; the roles and responsibilities of adults in helping to shape the minds of young people; and the relation of a political understanding of the role of schools to what actually goes on inside the schools. I think that this discussion of curriculum has not been adequately engaged by radical reformers in education. I think that the dominant free-learning notions have been that nothing interesting can be said because there is no good basis for valuing one piece of learning above another; that each child is an individual and will naturally unfold his own interests and seek the learning he needs for these interests, and all that teachers need do is help in this, making sure not to intervene or exert influence except when directly asked; that this is right, and this is what young people truly want. I don't think these ideas are true, though I have found them tempting. (They can appear to get one off a lot of sharp hooks.)

My own experience in simply offering myself as a resource person brought me finally to realize that I was being too theoretical and ideological on this score. In fact, young people often want the adults who have committed themselves so far as to be teachers or organizers of schools and other learning places to really be there as adults, to take some responsibility, even to push young people into doing things (partly because if a project doesn't work out, it can be rightly seen as also an adult's mistake and not another totally self-initiated failure for the student).[26] Thinking back, I can remember students who wanted me as a teacher-friend to choose work for them and put pressure on them to do the work. I would lecture them on how this bad need came from their bad training in public school and that I wouldn't indulge them in this, but that when they had something they really wanted to do, I would be glad to help. It seems to me now that what I thought was only partly right. There is the bad training which has for most young people stifled their capacity to work on their own initiative. But beyond that, there is also a legitimate request for some cooperation.

This problem of what sorts of needs for adults young people have is important. (They don't need "pals" acting as if they don't know more than the young people, or as if their more extensive experience really didn't mean anything.) It very much affects how the idea of teacher is conceived, and what range this role has.

Dewey wrote, with reference to what he saw as mistakes in the application of progressive education ideas:

> In an *educational* scheme, the occurrence of a desire and impulse is not the final end. It is an occasion and a demand for the formation of a plan and a method of activity.
>
> The teacher's business is to see that the occasion is taken advantage of. Since freedom resides in the operations of intelligent observation and judgment by which a purpose is developed, guidance given by the teacher to the exercise of the pupils' intelligence is an aid to freedom, not a restriction upon it. . . . It is impossible to understand

why a suggestion from one who has a larger experience and a wider horizon should not be at least as valid as a suggestion arising from some more or less accidental source. . . . The teacher's suggestion is not a mold for a cast-iron result, but is a starting point to be developed into a plan through contributions from the experience of all engaged in the learning process.[27]

This notion of teaching deserves careful consideration. It goes counter to the traditional authoritarian approach practiced in the traditional school and to the conception of "training" by means of "operant conditioning" put forward by Skinner and his adherents. However, it also seems to oppose the dominant trend in new schools thought as I have explained it. Dennison, who is enthusiastic about Dewey's thought as an important basis for the work at the First Street School, calls the idea that learning is the result of teaching a myth. I have already discussed Holt's views; and Paul Goodman recently wrote, "My bias is that 'teaching' is largely a delusion."[28]

Actually, the opposition here is more apparent than real, though, as I tried to show in my interpretation of some of Holt's statements, the position can slide toward the extreme end of the spectrum. Both Dennison and Goodman affirm the serious and responsible role of adults (and both are somewhat testy critics of the youth culture and its fetishisms). They are really opposing the authoritarian and imposed character of normal teaching and its necessarily adjunct effects of conventional socialization. In the free school spirit, Dewey's idea would be confirmed in fact, except by extreme rhetorical "freedom-to-unfold" adherents, though in any particular instance there would be differences on how much guidance is appropriate (when it becomes teaching in the old bad sense).

Part of the difficulty in theory (or in rhetoric) has to do with people fixating on a particular paradigm, and then arguing as if this were definitive of "education" or "learning." Goodman's own bias has always been toward "incidental education"; that is, for high school and beyond, young people should learn by being out in the world, taking part in the doings of the society—as apprentices, helpers, watchers, whatever. Then adults would often "teach," but only by now and then paying attention to the young and explaining about what they were doing. As a model for a good deal of what can be learned, this seems fine; and it is a serious critique of our society to say that it is not open to young people in this way, and that it is impossible now for such a mode of education to become widespread. But this aside, it is not hard to think of kinds of learning, especially of the academic sort, that aren't obviously amenable to this sort of treatment. The image I get is of a carpenter working on a new house. The young people bring him materials when he asks, do simple jobs that he assigns them, watch him while he makes complicated joints and proudly explains the tricks he has learned to make really good ones, and so forth. But a mathematician doesn't use arithmetic-learning apprentices in this way, and neither does an economist or historian or psychotherapist or novelist.

For some things, then, the education will look more like teaching-learning—in a Deweyan sense, of course—than like incidental learning through apprenticing. But none of this is an argument for teaching exclusively in *schools* in the way schools do. The confinement to schools, even free schools, is damaging for young people and prevents them from developing their powers and capacities in real environments doing real things. (Paul Goodman is very eloquent in his "reformation" thinking, expressing a vision of incidental education and its potentially marvelous effects. See *New Reformation,* pp. 85–90.)

Both Goodman and Holt make a great deal of the model of the child learning his first language. (Goodman makes an admittedly inexact analogy to show how reading should *not* be taught.) The learning of the first language by a child is projected as the model of the best kind of natural incidental learning, the opposite of the teacher-dominated modes. What makes language learning such an ideal model, in view of the leanings of most free school people, is that it dispenses with teachers; teaching doesn't help significantly in learning language in spite of all the attention to "da-da" and "say 'ball' " that middle-class parents often indulge in. The achievement is quite staggering in its complexity. (For a discussion of the issue, see Noam Chomsky, *Language and Mind.*) It is done by all children (barring extraordinary circumstances such as deafness or brain damage); and they just pick it up, getting all sorts of useful inputs from older people speaking around them, though they are not teaching.

But just because we would so want it to be a model, we should be warned to raise doubts about its applicability to other situations. Noam Chomsky is the person who has gone most deeply into this question, and his ideas point in the direction of seeing language-learning ability as "innate" (in a precise sense that is controversial and needn't be gone into here). One implication of his work is that the way a child learns language might very possibly be particular and not an enlightening model for other sorts of learning that don't depend so directly on innate structuring. Just because it is so imposing an achievement and is done so easily, one might suspect that it is a dubious model for the natural way to learn everything. (The worship of the "natural" is present here again.) Chomsky has commented that language is so complex that an informed Martian who just looked at the structure of English and compared it with the structure of theory of contemporary physics would not guess that English is learned naturally by two- and three-year-olds, while physics takes years of study by very intelligent grownups. But sad to say, that's the way it is. We don't learn physics incidentally, by just being around—nor mathematics nor poetry nor even silk-screening. Instruction, concentration, and practice (even drill) are often necessary, however much we would prefer the "natural" way.

On the other hand, if opposition to the destructive authoritarianism which may characterize traditional schools tempts free education adherents to use language learning as a paradigm for the role of teaching and the best way of learning, their opponents often seem to fixate on a model like learning how to play the violin. In learning to play the violin, several factors stand out. Perhaps there are some natural musical geniuses who just pick it up incidentally, but I don't know any. Good violinists are taught quite strictly. The intensive attention of a well-trained professional is essential. The student must practice and drill regularly, and this activity is distinctly unpleasurable for a long time. Children are most often forced or cajoled into learning to play the violin; they almost never ask for it themselves. They have hardly a notion about why it is so important to undertake this difficult activity. Adults decide it for them, for the young person's own future good and pleasure (as judged by a concerned adult).

Given this image as paradigmatic of significant learning, it is clear how one would support something like traditional schooling, idealized, of course. The idea is that children's natural interests will not lead them to acquire the really important skills and knowledge that they will later value and that society needs. (I noted this view, expressed in a mild and liberal manner, in my analysis of the defense of the schools in the work of Harvard psychologist Jerome Kagan.) Accordingly, society must provide professional teachers by special training, pedagogy courses, and credentialing. They will then be given a suitable institutional setting—the school—and appropriate power so that they can teach important skills and knowledge. As with playing the violin, young people may not understand now, but they will be grateful later on in life when they can use their skills and knowledge for their own pleasure and profit. They will realize that all the discipline, the required subjects, the dominant position of the teacher and his power, the drill—all were to give them the capacities that they need when they mature. An error common to both views (which is, in fact, a quite common tendency in many arguments of this sort) is the fixation on one particular model for all instances of a general category. Which is to say, simply, that learning to play the violin does seem to go this way—that the child is pressured into it, however mildly—and that it sometimes turns out all right. But this doesn't mean everything is learned best or even well in this manner. Similarly, learning language does happen naturally, and how it happens is still unexplained. Anyway, drill, pressure, instruction, qualified trained teachers are all totally irrelevant. Reading is not quite like that, but, as both Goodman and Dennison argue (and also, by pointed anecdote, James Herndon in his marvelous *How to Survive in Your Native Land,* in the section where he tells of his adventures as a teacher in the land of remedial reading), it is more like that than it is like violin playing. A not very startling conclusion is that we know very little about how learning happens, in a scientific sense; our experience seems to be quite varied concerning both what is learned and the particular young person doing the learning. Some children do best with a great deal of help; others seem to need only to be left alone so that they can zoom ahead, asking a little advice now and then; and there are all shades in between.

This mild conclusion is not trivial. It refocuses attention on the dilemma of learning and teaching. It denies the claims of the traditional dominant pedagogy and raises deep doubts about the claim that what gets trained in teachers colleges is good teachers. It emphasizes that general claims about learning or nature obscure the complex and varied range of things that get taught and learned and the fact that we don't have solutions, even in theory. This means that, as Dewey noted, freedom only sets the problem, it doesn't solve it. This also means that the value of freedom shouldn't be used to hide the need of the adults involved to face the responsibility they have taken on by engaging themselves with young people in educational enterprises, and to accept the necessity of making value judgments and often making errors.

In the realm of curriculum proper, an analogous, unstartling conclusion seems in order, which can be derived from some rather general and pious-sounding remarks I made a few pages back about thinking seriously about curriculum and the relative importance of subjects and making judgments. The conclusion is that, as I just said about method, there is no simple solution; hiding behind a freedom ideology or the notion that anything anyone does is learning, and it is all cool, is a cop-out.

At the beginning of the first chapter, I mentioned Durkheim's sociological conception of the function of educational institutions. As a description of what functions such institutions characteristically serve, it is quite accurate. I noted that a new factor in modern society is the idea of self-conscious social change, especially radical social change. (I should add that the *secular* idea of the conscious personal transformation to new kinds of people is a similarly modern development.) I want to expand on this point here and try to relate this problem of cultural and social change to the dilemma of curriculum.

An important aspect in disputes over both method and curriculum is the current cultural situation. It is now a bit trite to talk about the "cultural crisis," but it does feel like one. In many cultures, the problem of what should be learned hardly arises, nor does the problem of method. Most learning has always been incidental; sometimes the family provides the main school, sometimes there are wise men. For example, Eskimo children learn how to survive in their very harsh environment; they learn necessary knowledge about food and dress, the habits of the animals they hunt, how to make the implements and tools, the religion and ritual, the customs of courtship and marriage. Neither content nor method is a problem. Nor is "learning how to learn." It would be silly to say that it would be fine if the child learned about lions and llamas, because he would get the process of learning, and then, when he was old enough, if he chose to live an Eskimo life, he would apply this process to seals and polar bears.

What is silly isn't the idea of learning as partly developing the capacity to deal with new situations. It is that in stable cultures like the traditional Eskimo culture, it makes no sense to separate content and method. It is clear what one has to know to survive and be a proper member of the tribe, and one learns it. In the process one also develops skills that will be of use in some new situations, though not if they are too new.

This conception has implications for the discussion on curriculum outlined before. The ideal defense of the traditional curriculum is not, as Holt tries to make out, simply that the particular knowledge chosen is essential, as if it were the Eskimo child learning how to hunt seals. The complexity and change characteristic of modern society could be acknowledged; then the idea that in learning the "massed wisdom" one learns the best way to learn while mastering the present state of knowledge of the disciplines and the process (history) of how the knowledge was accumulated. Of course, the state of chemical theory won't be the same in twenty years; it wouldn't be a live science if the situation were otherwise. But by studying and learning the chemistry of today, one enters into the world of science, one learns about the enterprise of science, and one becomes capable of understanding the future developments and changes of science, in particular, those changes that make obsolete what is being learned now. (Remember this is all ideal and isn't relevant to what the schools actually do.)

The cultural past of the society is not meant to be useful in any simple way in the young person's future activities, especially what is academically called "the arts and sciences." Of course, the public schools lay themselves open to charges of "irrelevance" because they themselves express an ideology of training and usefulness much more than they do the more classic idea of development of the understanding. They usually try to mix the two together, which results in contradiction and confusion, and the students pick up on this. They get neither the practical skills and techniques, best taught in the incidental apprenticeship manner Goodman espouses, nor a liberal, humane education of the spirit.

This last point about "liberal education" is a knotty one. The cry for relevance expresses a deep crisis in our culture. The word seems to have lost its essentially relational meaning—relevant *to* some valued activity or goal—and to be used as a quality in itself, like "yellow" or "sharp." This situation cuts across political lines. Alvin Toffler, author of the best-seller *Future Shock,* finds the entire curriculum of schools and colleges irrelevant. He proposes that all education should be based on "councils of the future," "teams of men and women devoted to probing the future in the interests of the present." He says, "The creation of future-oriented, future-shaping task forces in education, could revolutionize the revolution of the young. . . . The direction is super-industrialism. The starting point: the future."[29] He doesn't say the schools fail to teach English, economics, mathematics, or biology, but that it's irrelevant because such a curriculum is not designed to grasp the future. His idea is that this curriculum should be scrapped and "the future" made the curriculum. But the real cultural problem is that we don't know what is relevant to what or we are very confused, for deep reasons. Toffler suggests "courses in science fiction writing, literature about the future, because they can lead young minds through an imaginative exploration of the jungle of political, social, psychological and ethical issues which will confront these children as adults."[30]

Perhaps. My experience is that one problem in most science fiction is that, although some of the technological and scientific projections are fascinating, as literature it is extremely thin in its conception of *human* experience—ethical, social, psychological, and political; and for the foreseeable future, at least, we and our children will continue to be recognizable human beings. At the risk of sounding reactionary, I would suggest that the reading of traditional good literature will deepen one's sense of human possibility and of the experiences of love and loyalty, courage, passion, despair, and hope more than will science fiction; and what could be better training for whatever the future holds than a complex sense of human experience and character such as great literature helps provide? The same considerations apply to "old" philosophy and political theory.

To concentrate so exclusively on the present and the future is to misconceive "relevance," if we mean a complex relevance to truly *understanding* the present and future. Paul Goodman, the "Dutch uncle" of free schools and free universities, is deeply distressed on this score. He discusses the problem in a sometimes crotchety fashion in a recent book which I have referred to several times already. The problem I have been trying to get at here is the significance to education of the confusions of our culture, and the way these confusions get expressed in discussions of relevance and curriculum. Goodman feels that the crisis is much larger than that of schools. He attempts to express what the meaning (the "relevance") of the transmission of culture really is, and why we seem to have lost a sense of its worth—whence comes the attack on curriculum except as it immediately comes from the student's interest or as it is directly useful for the future. He writes:

> The young have strong feelings for frankness, loyalty, affection, freedom, and other virtues of generous natures. They quickly resent the hypocrisy of politicians, administrators, and parents, who mouth big abstractions and act badly or pettily. But in fact, they themselves—like most politicians and administrators and many parents—seem to have forgotten the concrete reality of ideals like magnanimity, compassion, honor, consistency, civil liberty, integrity, justice though the heavens fall, and unpalatable truth, all of which are not gut feelings and often not even pragmatic, but are maintained to create and re-create Mankind and the possibilities of the Second Coming.[31]

Goodman sees the impossibility of forcing this kind of cultural transmission.

> The bother with transmitting humane culture is that it must be re-created in spirit or it is a dead weight upon present spirit, and then it does produce timidity, pedantry, and hypocrisy. And then it is better forgotten. Certainly the attempt to teach it by courses in school, or by sermons like this, is a disaster. . . . apart from the spirit congealed in them, we do not really have our sciences and arts, professions and civic institutions. It is inauthentic merely to use the products and survivals, and I don't think we can, in fact, work Western civilization without its vivifying tradition. . . .
>
> I have previously mentioned a young hippie—it was at Esalen—singing a song attacking the technological way of life, but he was on lysergic acid and strumming an electric guitar plugged into the infrastructure of California. The poem was a pastiche of surrealism and E. E. Cummings, but the rhythm and harmony came right out of the Smoky Mountains. I couldn't make anybody see why this wouldn't do.
>
> I tried to make clear to a young lady at the Antioch-

Putney School of Education that a child has a historical right to know that there is a tie between Venus and the sun—I showed it to her—and thanks to Isaac Newton we know its equation, which is even more beautiful than the Evening Star itself. It is not a matter of choice whether he ought to know this or not. Yet she is right, for if it's not his thing, it's pointless to show it to him, as it was to her.

But it won't do. It won't do. Wilfully ignorant of the inspiration and grandeur of our civilization, though somewhat aware of its brutality and terror, the young are patsies for the "inevitabilities" of modern times. They no longer know what to claim as their own and what to attack as the enemy. Omitting Prometheus, Faraday, Edison, the longing of mankind for light and energy, they are left with Consolidated Edison owning the field, and themselves saying, "Shut it down." If they cannot take on our only world appreciatively and very critically, they can only confront her or be servile to her, and then she is too powerful for any of us.[32]

I think it right that Goodman have his say. It is important to confront these ideas, and even Goodman's slightly querulous tone, because the thoughts come from someone to whom the free school movement owes as much as to any other living American. Goodman emphasizes how much a proper understanding of our present situation is rooted in our understanding and participation in the past from which the present grew. But the present seems so confused, and understanding so hard to acquire. We seem to have lost what Goodman values so highly, the confidence in the vivifying capacity of "culture." Everything is grasped at, and many young people seem to be in the grip of salvational fashion—and damned be coherence and consistency. Some of the same people who damn the authority of teachers or the worth of Western culture accept completely the power of a guru fresh from the East—whether Baba Ram Dass or the Maharishi or Swami Satchidananda or whoever

—to bring salvation; and they will listen raptly and accept every word. New drugs, old yoga, Buckminster Fuller's technocratic projections, primal therapy, astrology, the return to handiwork, and living in the mountains—all these will be accepted by the same people, sometimes in sequence, sometimes simultaneously.

I have less excuse to sound crotchety than Goodman does. I do think that the confused grasping at ways of affirming significance and value in an environment that makes this so difficult comes out of real needs, and the arrogance and "we're so cool" tone which sometimes characterize the counter-culture often cloak a despair and terrible sense of being lost. But what does all this imply about education? Suppose we find ourselves extremely dissatisfied with the adult world and its culture and values (the "culture" obvious to young people is not Goodman's but what they see and hear around them, which rightly turns them off and blocks the view of Goodman's "humanistic culture"); and suppose we reject the ideals of a "good life" as determined by the dominant values of the culture; and suppose we reject the worth of continuing this culture, its forms of work, its established adult roles, its dominant conceptions of pleasure, achievement, integrity. Then obviously we don't want education to serve its traditional societal functions.

How then, do we find good purposes? What functions should our education serve? To say simply that we want to prepare young people to make their own decisions later doesn't solve much; it mainly expresses our sense of being at a loss to conceive the continuity of social existence and values clearly enough to provide content to the idea of transmitting a world to the young. How could our schools not reflect such a crisis? We find it difficult to educate, not because we can't imagine the kind of technological changes Toffler claims we have to prepare for, but because we are so unsure about what will be worthwhile and satisfying ways of life, in any technology, including the one we have now. There is a natural tendency to ignore the question of curriculum because we are so conflicted about what is worthwhile, in a human sense, not primarily because we aren't sure what will be useful. Unlike the Eskimos, we don't have culturally secure images of what adults should be like or what they might do that is fulfilling; to the extent that we don't really have a world, we have trouble thinking of a curriculum, even in the best, most open and nonauthoritarian sense.

As often happens in the new schools, people hope that absorption in the present, concentration on the *process,* on the vitality of the spontaneous interest, will serve to provide a sufficiently rich educational soil. The future is too scary to think about and offers no help since it doesn't seem to be the unfolding of a valued and understood present. The past seems to be irrelevant to grasping our present situation. At the worst extreme, in Goodman's words, we are "swamped by presentness. Since there is no background or structure, everything is equivalent and superficial."[33]

In a way, the drug experience, especially the psychedelic "trip," becomes the paradigm for the good learning experience. It is frequently talked about that way, with the subjects of the learning being the most subjective "self" on the one hand, and the most abstract "universe" or "nature of reality" on the other. The beauty of the drug-experience model is obvious, given the cultural situation just sketched. It is immediate and personal; it takes no preparation, hard work, cultural tradition, study, or knowledge; it seems cosmic in dimension, but it doesn't engage one in the mundane day-to-day processes of the social world. It is absorbing and seems to be self-justifying. And it doesn't implicate a future. I admit that this is a one-sided description; like the cultural situation, the drug experience is more open and complex than my purposely simplified description implies. For some people the drug experience is a path to breaking out of rigid and constricting personal structures; it sometimes radically alters the individual's perception of personal possibilities; and this can be seen in serious changes, personal and otherwise, undertaken after drug experiences, and even in the decision that no more such experiences are needed. But to push this strongly would be to err even more seriously on the optimistic side. Very often extensive drug use is a symptom of much deeper personal troubles, and these personal troubles of youth can't be understood apart from the more general cultural and social malaise.

Goodman says:

> The most hopeful way of looking at the problem, how to transmit humane culture, is as follows: If the institutions of society are made vital and functional and the young can take on those institutions as their own, identify with them, be free in them, participate in their management rather than as hired hands, then they will have the humane culture. . . . And the converse must be true. If the institutions are such that there is entry into them and freedom is possible in them, the young will pick up their principles. The humanities are not obvious in the environment, but they are the causes that make it a good environment. It is not that good institutions make possible a good educational system; they *are* the good educational system.[34]

This applies to more than the humanities. The meaning of these reflections for curriculum is clear. Since we don't have the kind of society and institutions that make this ideal possible, then all of the various ideal functions of education must be distorted. Vocational training can happen well only if we value the vocations open to us; liberal education, the passing on of the cultural tradition, helps form a good content of education inside and outside schools only if that cultural tradition is valued and sustaining to us. Without these conditions, especially beyond the early years when basic skills and play are what is wanted, what education proper—schools, in our case—can do is highly problematic. It is understandable that there be an overvaluation of the present educational experience in new schools, partly as a justified reaction to the terrible undervaluation characteristic of traditional views of youth and education, but more significantly because of the cultural crisis just discussed. Past and future seem increasingly difficult to connect to fruitfully.

One plausible implication of the conception of good education Goodman describes is the bringing into being of a world in which the good conditions—institutions and freedom—could help give content to a new curriculum. In the kinds of schools I have described, it is those that are informed by such sense of purpose—call it political or social or moral—that seem to be most coherent on the question of curriculum and method. Black schools, liberation schools, working-class schools, community schools whose students and adults are really involved in the life of the community find that they begin to generate a curriculum of sorts, and that the problems posed by their situation lead them to connect to the kind of historical culture whose apparent irrelevance Goodman regrets.

Prince Kropotkin, the great anarchist thinker whose works have recently been republished (a good sign), wrote, in "A Letter to the Young": "Ask what kind of world do you want to live in? What do you need to know? What are you good at and want to work at to build that world? Demand that your teachers teach you that." This seems to me the most satisfactory way of approaching the dilemma of curriculum. It doesn't solve it, but it sets the problem in a fruitful manner. With respect to this question, it is particularly useful to look at a book cited in the first chapter. It is a truly unique work called *Letter to a Teacher,* written by eight peasant boys, aged eleven to thirteen, in a new school in Italy. After having been flunked out of public school the boys, together with Father Milani, a radical parish priest, formed their own school. As a year-long project, they wrote an analysis of the Italian school system and how it helps to perpetuate a nonegalitarian and unjust society. The book is beautifully written and intensely moving. But many free school people in America would have trouble dealing with it, partly because the culture of the boys is so different from the hip counter-culture style of many free schools. There is no talk of ecstatic education. But the uneasiness would arise mainly because the boys see their school in terms of the struggle for a better, more just society; and they construct a curriculum to further this end. They work very hard; there is nothing "groovy" about their school. And they frankly and starkly state their political conception of schools, education, and culture.

> Nothing but politics can fill the life of a man of today. In Africa, in Asia, in Latin America, in southern Italy, in the hills, in the fields, even in the cities, millions of children are waiting to be made equal. Shy, like me; stupid, like Sandro; lazy like Gianni. The best of humanity.[35]

Their world is not obviously very close to that of most of the young who populate new schools—though the black schools and working-class schools would respond immediately to the spirit of the book. But considering what they say and what they did points to a fruitful path into the dilemma of curriculum, as does Kropotkin's advice. The boys say:

> We are searching for a goal. It must be an honest one. It must demand of a boy that he be nothing less than a human being—*that* would be acceptable both to believers and atheists. I know this goal. My teacher-priest has been impressing it on me since I was eleven years old, and I thank God for it. I have saved so much time. Minute by minute. I knew why I was studying. The right goal is to give oneself to others.

In this century, how can you show your love if not through politics, the unions, the *schools*? We are the sovereign people. The time for begging is gone; we must make choices—against class distinctions, against hunger, illiteracy, racism and colonial wars.[36]

This is said very simply, without sophistication, without qualifications. Perhaps to us life seems more complex, more murky. But their forthrightness cannot but move and challenge us. If you oppose the oppressions of the times, they say, if you are against the way the dominant institutions work, if you want social justice and a humane society, then you are political and your educational task is set.

This is an extremely distressing issue within the new schools. As in much of the counter-culture, politics is sometimes treated as a dirty word. But as the schoolboys of Barbiana note, if you are serious about your oppositional values, your hopes for a decent world for the young to be educated in, then the question of politics can't be avoided.

NOTES

1 JOHN DEWEY, *The Child and the Curriculum and The School and Society*, 2nd ed. (Chicago: University of Chicago Press, 1915), pp. 7–8.
2 Ibid., p. 9.
3 JOHN DEWEY, *Experience and Education* (New York: Macmillan Co., Collier Books, 1963), pp. 17–18.
4 JEROME KAGAN, *Understanding Children: Behavior, Motives, and Thought* (New York: Harcourt Brace Jovanovich, 1971), pp. 53–54.
5 Ibid., p. 78.
6 Ibid., p. 74.
7 Ibid., p. 66.
8 Ibid., p. 146.
9 PHILIP W. JACKSON, *Life in Classrooms* (New York: Holt, Rinehart & Winston, 1968), p. 10.
10 Ibid., p. 18.

11 Ibid., p. 26.

12 Ibid., p. 29.

13 Ibid., p. 31.

14 Ibid., pp. 32, 33.

15 Quoted by Paul Goodman, *Compulsory Mis-education* (New York: Vintage Books, 1964), p. y (from *Examining in Harvard College*).

16 *New Schools Exchange Newsletter*

17 DEWEY, *Education and Experience,* pp. 21–22.

18 Ibid., pp. 22–23.

19 JOHN HOLT, *How Children Fail* (New York: Dell Publishing Co., 1970) Dell, p. 217.

20 Ibid., p. 218.

21 Ibid., p. 220–21.

22 DEWEY, *The Child and the Curriculum,* pp. 14–15.

23 DEWEY, *Education and Experience,* p. 169.

24 Ibid., p. 38.

25 Ibid., pp. 58–59.

26 With relation to this question I suggest reading Philip Slater's provocative analysis of American culture and character, *The Pursuit of Loneliness* (Boston: Beacon Press, 1970). Slater feels that our culture thwarts what he sees as a valid human desire for "dependence"—"the wish to share responsibility for the control of one's impulses and the direction of one's life" (p. 5).

27 DEWEY, *Education and Experience,* pp. 71–72.

28 PAUL GOODMAN, *New Reformation: Notes of a Neolithic Conservative* (New York: Random House, 1970), p. 72.

29 ALVIN TOFFLER, *Future Shock* (New York: Bantam Books, 1971), pp. 404–5.

30 Ibid., p. 425.

31 GOODMAN, *New Reformation,* pp. 106–7.

32 Ibid., pp. 107–8.

33 Ibid., p. 109.

34 Ibid., pp. 109–10.

35 Schoolboys of Barbiana, *Letter to a Teacher* (New York: Random House, 1970), p. 73.

36 Ibid., pp. 88–89.

5 · THE PROSPECT
Educational Reform and Social Change

The young schoolboys of Barbiana viewed the school system in openly political terms. Their historical and political analysis of the function of the schools in Italy is crystal clear and easily applicable to any capitalist industrialized country. The system has helped maintain class power and privilege and has helped keep the poor in their place. Somehow the boys managed to see through myths (which are even stronger in American society than in Italian).

I touched on some of those myths in the various critiques of the public schools in Chapter 1. I want to expand on that here because it points directly at the political context of educational reform of any sort, including the establishment of free schools. This question of politics is a very touchy issue within the new schools movement. But it is the crucial question for trying to get a sense of how the movement might develop, what strategies for survival and growth are available, and what its possibilities and significance are.

The dominant political tradition in America is liberal.[1]

Whatever troubles liberalism has fallen upon since the Camelot days of the "new frontier," the ideas of progress and reform are still the mainstream political current. One aspect of the liberal approach to social action is to view social problems as solvable by application of new techniques, inputs of resources, and government expertise. More concretely, the progressive spirit does not challenge the basic social, political, economic, and ideological structures of the society, and definitely does not share the radical critique which relates various social problems, such as the war in Indochina, racism, slums, poverty, and alienation, inextricably to structural aspects of the social order —for example, to the distribution of wealth and income, the private ownership and profit system, and so forth.[2] The "inextricably" is what is critical. The real issue is whether one can conceive of solutions to social problems like those just mentioned without basic changes in the structure of society; that is, whether the problems can be isolated and treated as manageable malfunctions of a basically good system.

The sphere of education is especially important for the progressive spirit. This emphasis makes sense. Liberalism, like the Enlightenment from which it developed its modern form, views human history—or at least the relevant modern parts of it—as the story of human progress. The key to this progress is the increasing enlightenment of the human mind—which means to a large extent the growth of knowledge of man and society ("science") and the rational application of this knowledge to the improvement of the individual and his society.[3] Naturally this vision must put education at the center of its hopes. Universal education will enable all individuals to participate in the march of progress—as productive members of society, as the autonomous citizens who are the essential basis for our conception of liberal political democracy. Moreover, education will be the key to fulfilling basic humane and democratic values such as equality of opportunity. By providing each individual with knowledge, skills, rationality, and judgment, education makes possible the transcending of divisions of class and caste; it enables individuals to develop their own abilities, and to be rewarded for these, regardless of race, class, and ethnic or religious group, as the saying goes.

Education is at the core of the exhilarating and appealing liberal dream of progress. In the past, says liberalism, we see group hatred and oppression, prejudice, discrimination, poverty, despair, injustice, and tragically unfulfilled human potential. But education can enable human society to transcend these evils, to raise new generations of children who will not pick up the accumulated badness of the past, but will instead be part of an increasingly enlightened future when all individuals from all groups in society will have an equal opportunity to develop their abilities, express their individuality, and contribute to their own and the general good.

Within the profession of education, we have already seen this attitude in reformist works like those of George Leonard, Neil Postman and Charles Weingartner, and Charles Silberman. What is characteristic of this kind of progressive reform spirit is the optimistic expectation that the problems of education are solvable by changes strictly within the educational institutions, and moreover, that the solutions are quite feasible, involving the determined application of new techniques and technology—themselves the product of education and the progress of science.

Expectations about the effects of education are in this tradition almost unbounded. (Recall the discussions in Chapters 1 and 3 of the great hopes of free school theory and practices.) Socialization (developing commitment to the dominant values of society) is normally expected from a state-supported educational system, but for the liberal reformer, many other tasks are also assigned to the school: the "Americanization" of newcomers (whether immigrants or internal minority cultures); training in proper social morality; the development of individual skills; and a large part of the solution of social problems, particularly problems of equality of opportunity. If there seem to be large troubles in the schools, there is a corresponding pressure to believe that internal educational solutions are possible. Otherwise it would be difficult to maintain the belief that the schools will be successful instruments in eliminating social problems like racism, poverty, inequality of opportunity, and alienation of youth. One of the appeals of education as an instrument of change is that it can be viewed as relatively nonpartisan and nonpolitical. In fact, if good schools could nullify advantages of race, class, and wealth with regard to opportunity, then we would have achieved a fair meritocratic social order, just as the American myth says, without having to confront the divisive and highly partisan political questions of distribution of wealth, income, and power—for these are the ultimate questions around which historical social struggles have been intense, and often violent and protracted.

According to David Cohen and Marvin Lazerson, two social historians at the Harvard Graduate School of Education:

> Most reformers have accepted the principle of merit selection because they saw education as a vehicle for promoting social reform through individual mobility. The notion that education was a means for deferring direct (redistributive) social change by displacing it onto individual achievement has been a central element in modern American liberalism. It rests on a desire to promote social justice without attacking the distribution or ownership of property. The consequence for education has been curious—the more evidence has accumulated that school success depended upon inherited economic and social status, the more the liberal reformers insisted that the schools should compensate for environmental differences among children. Such

efforts have been tried increasingly over the past four or five decades, but there is scant evidence that they work any particular advantage for the children concerned. Nonetheless, every evidence of failure seems only to reinforce the idea that more compensation is required. Because of the liberal commitment to social reform through individual achievement, the development of school reform has been perversely related to the evidence: *the more it shows that school performance is profoundly conditioned by inherited status, the more insistent the demands for compensatory schooling have grown. There never has been much mention of directly reducing the underlying status inequalities.* It is a testimony to the power of liberal ideology and the class character of school reform efforts that evidence on the educational consequences of inequality produces efforts to improve the meritocracy, rather than efforts to reduce the inequality.[4]

The implications of such considerations for free school approaches are very important but not as directly obvious as they are for liberal reformers within the public school system. The reformist perspective, most popularly available in Silberman's *Crisis in the Classroom,* acknowledges many of the faults of the system, and in terms close to those used in past years by the radical reformers. (This was touched on in Chapter 1.) In fact, if one looks at the report of the National Education Association (NEA) *Schools for the 70's and Beyond: A Call to Action,* one finds a quite radical-sounding demand for great changes in the schools to transform them into "humanistic schools." Much of the radical reform critique is accepted and a kind of "alternatives in education" spirit permeates this document from the bastion of the teacher Establishment. The report says that

the schools must now go beyond their previous role of preparing children for social functions, whether these functions are traditional or in line with our changing society, to preparing children to become totally realized *individuals*—humane, self-renewing, self-directed individuals—who will not only *survive* in society, but will take conscious roles in *shaping* it for the better, as George Counts asked us to do years ago in *Dare the School Build a New Social Order?*[5]

The entire report echoes the "romantic" criticisms concerning the relevance of curriculum, authoritarianism, student choice, and grading. The staff that put the report together states:

Humane education, finally, insists that learning is one of the most exciting and deeply fulfilling human activities, and that something has gone haywire when the whole process has to be surrounded by a Gestapo-like environment that stresses order, discipline, neatness and SILENCE WHEN YOU ARE NOT RECITING, and hooks the whole business up to a system of emotional punishment.[6]

The report is very much in the line of Silberman's book, which is frequently quoted as support. Crucial to the liberal reformist conception is the sense that educators can bring about all of the desirable changes in the schools. For Silberman, the explanation of all the horrendous aspects of schools that he documents for hundreds of pages is simple: "mindlessness."

What makes change possible, moreover, is that what is mostly wrong with the public schools is due not to venality or indifference or stupidity, but to mindlessness. . . . This mindlessness—the failure or refusal to think seriously about educational purpose, the reluctance to question established practice—is not the monopoly of the public school; it is diffused remarkably evenly throughout the entire educational system, and indeed the entire society. . . . If mindlessness is the central problem, the solution must lie in infusing the various educating institutions with purpose, more important, with thought about purpose. . . .[7]

That's pretty much it, so far as explanation goes. Not a word about the distribution of wealth and income, of class power, of corporate interests. The Vietnam war is never mentioned in any of the references to student dissent. "Tracking" is never discussed as such. All of these neglects are important to the liberal reformist view. If the war is only the result of mindlessness, mistakes on the part of well-meaning people, perhaps too enthusiastic in supporting democracy around the world, then our foreign policy can be easily fixed. Just elect people not so different from the ones we have who will be more careful and avoid such mistakes. Then there will be no need to look into concepts like imperialism or the pattern of United States intervention in, say, Latin America over the past eighty years. And certainly it would be more comfortable not to recognize how much *mind* (rather than mindlessness) there was in the formation of these policies—as Daniel Ellsberg among others has been passionately trying to show over the past couple of years.

Similar considerations apply in educational reform. Liberal reforms like Silberman seem to assume that individual characteristics, dubiously extended to vaguely defined groups or even institutions, can explain important societal developments. So he tells us that "stupidity," "indifference," and "venality" do not explain the problems of the school. Having eliminated these, he apparently feels that "mindlessness" is the only explanation left.

But what should be considered is that none of those terms explains social phenomena. Only descriptively or analogically are institutions stupid or social groups venal. Nazi Germany did many horribly barbaric and sadistic things; but the explanation is not that the German people are horribly barbaric and sadistic. The Johnson Administration made many "mistakes" in Vietnam; the explanation is not that the Administration (or the individuals composing it) was stupid or mindless. The public school system is generally harmful and destructive, as Silberman says. But his analysis of causes—that people have forgotten to think about the purposes of education (apparently waiting for Charles Silberman, backed by $300,000 of Carnegie money, to remind them to think)—and his expectation—that it can all be fixed, by the same people, in the same society, with nothing else in the social order significantly changed—are totally inadequate. (In fact, Silberman, in line with the liberal spirit, thinks that changing the schools will be the big step in seriously altering the society.)

What this perspective cannot admit is that in important ways the school system is not a failure; that in the way it is working it serves very important functions for the system and that there are powerful social and economic reasons that help explain the very "mindless" features of the system that are now so deplored by many people.

For example, "tracking" is so prevalent a characteristic of the system that it might seem astonishing that Silberman does not choose to discuss its operation and economic functions.[8] But this omission is understandable because a discussion of tracking raises directly some very critical questions for reformers that can't be talked away with empty concepts like mindlessness. If, in fact, a social order distributes its wealth and income on the basis of private ownership (which is distributed enormously unequally), and if it ascribes success and failure to individuals largely in terms of income and wealth and the level of material consumption these make possible, and if a status system is built around this material achievement and conspicuous consumption, then young people should obviously be socialized to a competitive world where profit considerations are dominant in the structuring of work. In a society structured this way, there are only a relatively few high-status, high-salary positions in the professions, business, etc. This condition sets a very important problem for the socializing institutions. The obvious fact is that those with privilege will make every attempt to pass this privilege on to their offspring. The advantaged classes—in wealth, income, power, status—will use these resources to improve the chances of their own children against potential competitors in the supposedly fair and equal race. This will mean better schools (public or private), special tutoring, widened experience outside of school, advantages in getting jobs, getting into good colleges, and so forth.[9] Almost everyone will admit that the privileged pass on privilege. After all, it's not *wrong* for parents to do everything in their power to make their children happy—which, since the structure of this society necessitates winners and losers, involves making them "winners" as concerns material goods and status. Now, of course, America stands for equality of opportunity. In theory, although it is impossible to erase all the advantages that make this value less than 100 percent operative, still, the free public education system and the adherence to the principle of merit throughout the society will minimize the effects of unavoidable inequalities. Just as the immigrant groups came to America poor and saw some of their children make it, so the poor blacks and Puerto Ricans and Chicanos and white working class can do it today.

But a little simple thought can raise serious doubts about this rosy picture. If the economy isn't rapidly expanding and changing as it was in the early decades of the century, and if there are *too many* college graduates already for the number of appropriately good jobs, and if there are even science Ph.D.'s from M.I.T. who can't get proper work, and if this situation is becoming worse, then there will be increasing competition for the scarce good positions.[10] The school system isn't failing to produce the number of skilled, competent people needed by the economy—in the particular form of social organization that presently exists. In fact, if the schools did overcome—by some reformist miracle—all of the societal causes for the "deprivation," the "motivational problems," the "behavior disturbances," etc., ascribed to "disadvantaged" young people; if every young poor dropout heeded the warning about being called "boy"; if every young black was "Harlem Prepped" and became able to go to college—what would happen? Would they all get the good jobs that they are promised if only they would shape up? No way! Because prestige accompanies kinds of work and income in a society predicated on individuals (and corporations) doing the best for themselves, whatever the price to others or the environment or the human spirit or social justice or any other value you can think of, there have to be a lot of losers. Even if the poor young people believed the exhortations and worked like little beavers and listened to the teacher and tried to talk right and be nice, most of them still couldn't make it. The system has a few winners and a lot of losers, and the winners aren't about to let their children take their fair chance of becoming losers.

One of the important aspects of liberal progressive reform thought is that it ignores the important function the school system performs by separating the winners and losers and "cooling out" the ambitions of the lower class, as well as stigmatizing loser children and getting them to believe that their situation is somehow appropriate (after all, in America you have a fair chance, and anyone who really has the stuff and works hard can make good). The myth has real individual instances, obviously, but those poor young people who stick it out and get diplomas and even a college education, and then succeed in getting relatively decent jobs are able to do so only because so many of their brothers and sisters didn't stick it out and became the losers taking welfare, being janitors, cleaning streets, grinding on assembly lines, waitressing, and so forth.

The problems are basically rooted in the social conditions and not in the schools. The problems are manifested in the schools, but they aren't created there and they can't be solved there. The implications of this basic perception are that liberal reformist discussions of school problems are essentially too narrow and that hopes for solutions are fated to be disappointed if conceived of only in an educational and pedagogical perspective.

My firm view is that attempts at truly humanizing the public schools must run up against the fundamental social realities—the sickness of American society. The liberal dream of cure by means of education is misconceived. As I mentioned before, this realization is most directly relevant to public school reformers. It doesn't bother conservatives who value a hierarchical society and take a pessimistic view of the possibilities of individual and social perfectability. They never have wanted an egalitarian meritocratic society, and they have never asked the schools to accomplish this along with the cure of other social ills. It is the liberal who has placed this burden on the public educational institutions.

The implications for free school people are not so obvious, but examining the issue closely is vital to developing a long-term perspective on the new schools movement as radical reform. I have indicated before that the radical perspective on which this analysis is based is not very widely shared. This was evident in the discussion of the range of free school theory and in the actual practice and the philosophies expressed by the people who are doing free schools. Many free school people balk at the idea of what they call "politicizing."

George Leonard, Neil Postman and Charles Weingartner, and John Holt are and have been very popular with free school and public school reformers, just as they are now being cited more and praised by high government education people, Establishment writers like those of the NEA, for example. What makes this possible is the acceptability of the accompanying political analysis—or more accurately, the accompanying lack of political analysis. The

NEA *Schools for the 70's* documents and Silberman's book with its glowingly favorable reception in almost all quarters illustrate how successful—at least rhetorically and intellectually—the "romantic"-humanistic reformists have been.[11] One doesn't hear too much from the formerly highly vocal educational conservatives who want more strict discipline, hard work, concentration on academic skills. The forms of curriculum and school organization that have been dominant do not seem to be able to articulate a respectable self-justification, though a majority of parents and teachers would still say they were in favor of the status quo. But trends are what is important for developing an analysis that can aid us in understanding future developments. The situation as seen by Mario Fantini, a well-known school reformer with the Ford Foundation now at the State University of New York, is stated in his *The Reform of Urban Schools*, published in the NEA series.

> For while the standard public school system continues to be acceptable for the majority of its users, this majority has dwindled. In fact, we now have a critical mass of discontented educational consumers (students and parents) for whom the public schools are no longer a viable choice. They are demanding reform at a time when education is crucial to their own survival and to that of society. Unless reform is realized soon, the entire fabric of our real society will be in serious trouble. We are entering a new age of education but we have entered with an outmoded institution to meet its obligation to society, groups, and the individual.[12]

This constituency has generated the new schools movement. Fantini and some other educational liberals would agree with the general reform analysis, even with many of its "romantic"-humanistic aspects, but they want to incorporate the new schools into a revitalized public school system, which would be radically decentralized and responsive to parent and student needs and desires, and which would contain a wide spectrum of schools from the hippest Summerhillian community to a tough straightforward college preparatory school.

In common with the constituency he is referring to, Fantini does not politicize his analysis. As with liberalism, the public good is what the proposed reforms will achieve, and without the vast structural and ideological revisions that the radical perspective emphasizes. I have described the variety of new schools, and I have emphasized the political contexts and made evaluations from my own highly politicized outlook. (Even in curriculum, the analysis of the problems led to politics.) It will be useful in this final chapter to return specifically to the range of perspectives on the politics of educational reform expressed in the new schools movement.

The politicization issue is a complicated one. The free school spectrum is not a representative microcosm of the culture and politics of the country. The great majority of teachers, parents, and high-school students involved are quite self-conscious about their opposition not only to the public school form of education but to many other dominant institutions and values of contemporary America. That is, almost all of them would be considered very liberal or radical in their inclinations, whether they were consciously political or not. Many of them, especially the high-school students and the teachers, are devoted to many aspects of the counter-culture. On issues like sexual morality, the use of drugs, experimentation with life styles, deemphasis of social prestige and material success, free school people are very much part of the new oppositional minorities which have emerged over the past decades. It would be difficult if not impossible to find a free school person—student, teacher, or parent—who supports the American role in Vietnam or thinks that Richard Nixon is a fine president and Ronald Reagan an admirable governor or that users of marijuana should be put in jail or homosexuals arrested. It follows from this that free school people would want a society rather different from the dominant social and cultural order that exists today. In this sense, even though some new schools people are relatively straight and moderate and others are so involved in counter-cultural "spirituality" that they deny any relation to social movements, the great majority would be included in the vague and diverse constituency that wishes to transform the political culture of America. I have mentioned the growth of political insurgencies throughout most areas of institutionalized social life in America. New schools should be seen in this context, as I argued in the earlier chapters.

Most organized groups of the "movement"—the civil rights organizations or the radical professional groups in law, for example—are articulately political in their insurgency. One of the main efforts of the radical critique of the past years has been to expose the ideology of liberalism in order to show the political point beneath the surface rhetoric. In the professions and the university, especially, it was vital to show the bias toward supporting the status quo that was built into the operation of supposedly neutral ideas and activities.[13]

In education, this kind of analysis has been built up over the past few years. But the conception of education as ideally neutral still remains strong. In more concrete terms, there is a hope that schools could be places where each child could unfold his own individuality, while learning skills in a joyful, personal way, and so forth—the now familiar "romantic" conception. The complaint against the traditional schools is that their way of teaching is stifling, emotionally and intellectually. When politics does seep into the critique, as in opposition to the hidden curriculum, tracking, political pressure on teachers, censorship of reading materials, patriotic activities like army recruiters or State Department films on Vietnam, it is with a negative connotation. The onus of politicization is on the system; one of the aims of the free school idea was to free education from the political indoctrination expressed in the form, content, and organization of public schools.

On the basis of this perception it would seem right to conceive of good education in terms of learning places free from politics, where the child is encouraged to develop a critical, inquiring mind, where all points of view are examined but none is officially sanctioned. The ultimate hope is for all schools to become open and free in this way, for the sake of the public good. I have already analyzed this image of school reform as it appears in the works discussed earlier. Holt, Postman and Weingartner, Leonard, and Toffler concentrate their attention on education leading to good, skilled, inquiring, and critical people—a result that will be good for the nation and the world since such people will cope better with the rapidly changing technological society and will be better able to solve the terrible problems that plague us today.

In this way, the political and social values of progressive reformers will be furthered by their educational endeavors, but without the necessity of dealing with openly political questions. The educational activities are not to be contaminated by partisan politics or propaganda or indoctrination from any source, bad or good. The values directly encouraged are personal qualities that are unarguably good and uncontroversial, though rather unspecific in content. These values are the obvious ones, some of which were just mentioned. The brochures from most free schools relate these qualities to the ideally successful free methods.

What is the argument about politicization? As I have emphasized before, it is in the differing *perspectives* that the debate resides more than in specific actions. In the actual day-to-day living of new schools, people all along the liberal spectrum work together, along with people of all life styles, from "freak" counter-culture to fairly straight. No one advocates setting down a particular political line and making orthodoxy a test for teaching or for admission of students and parents or for curriculum. There are some schools that are political in the narrow sense of being part of particular political movements with their own doctrines. Black Panther "liberation schools" or "children's collective" schools staffed by movement radicals for children from radical collectives are examples. But these are rare exceptions. The great majority of schools have no clear political doctrine and do not present themselves as espousing any particular political line. On the other hand, many people involved as teachers and organizers are quite openly political, often with experience in the civil rights, student, and antiwar movements. It figures that many of the high-school youth involved are anti-Establishment at least culturally, and often politically as well.

Given this situation, there will often be some connection to the various insurgent political activities going on in the community. The curriculum is affected, as was noted in describing the kinds of courses found in the new high schools. The school buildings will often host antiwar or other left-wing activities which are characteristic of the movement in the broadest sense. Almost all the schools are open to all points of view among teachers, parents, and students, and often there is a real desire to involve people beyond the narrow range of the hip progressive middle class. In fact, the new schools cannot but be identified as part of the confused effort to bring about extensive change in American society.

At the far right of this range, there are schools that deviate little from traditional private progressive schools in either clientele or style, but that are consciously experimental in methods, trying out "open structure," new curriculums, etc. At the far left are the schools where the staff and students identify themselves as actively radical and where it is obvious that a person not sharing their views would never get involved. Between these are most of the schools, and within individual schools one can find a mixture of people representing the various shades of opinion.

Earlier in the chapter I gave a highly schematic analysis of the liberal progressive conception of educational reform, broadening the discussion on reformism that began in the first chapter on free school theory and was expanded earlier in this chapter. John Holt has been perhaps the most prominent representative of radical reformism. His educational analysis was radical in its demand for vast transformations of the school and its methods and curriculum; but the general perspective was reformist in that he did not raise large-scale political questions, and framed the position in terms of better schools leading to better personalities, happier children, and more genuine learning. My criticisms of Holt derived in part from my sense that his writings did not really acknowledge the limitations on educational transformation imposed by the needs of the social order.

Recently Holt has expressed a rather different emphasis from the one found in his books, a more highly political perspective, much more radical. His emphasis on the great possibilities of pure educational change has shifted to an emphasis on the social and political contexts within which educational reforms are attempted.

In a free school newsletter which printed letters concerning a free school conference in 1971 at which issues concerning politicization arose, Holt wrote:

> . . . I do not believe that any movement for educational reform that addresses itself exclusively or even primarily to the problems or needs of children can progress very far. . . . I do not think we can treat as separate the

quality of education in a society and the quality of life in general. . . . I am saying that truly good education in a bad society is a contradiction in terms. In short, in a society that is absurd, unworkable, wasteful, destructive, secretive, coercive, monopolistic, and generally anti-human, we could never have good education, no matter what kind of schools the powers that be permit, because it is not the educators or the schools but the whole society and the quality of life in it that really educate. This means that whatever we do to improve the quality of life, for anyone, and in whatever part of his life, to that degree improves education. More and more it seems to me, and this is a reversal of what I felt not long ago, that it makes very little sense to talk about education *for* social change, as if education was or could be a kind of getting ready. The best and perhaps only education for social change is action to bring about that change. The best and perhaps only way to prepare the young to work for a better world is to invite them, right now, to join us in working for it. We cannot say, "We will concentrate *our* efforts on making nice schools for you, and after you get out *you* can tackle the tough job of remaking the world." Nor can we define ourselves as Good People whose task it is to defend children from All Those Other Bad People. There cannot be little worlds fit for children in a world not fit for anyone else.

Once again, I am not saying what people so often say to me—"We must change society before we can change the schools." I am saying that society *is* the school; that men learn best and most from what is closest to the center of their lives; that men being above all else looking, acting, thinking, choosing and acting animals, what men need above all else is a society in which they are to the greatest possible degree free and encouraged to look, ask, think, choose, and act; and that making this society is both the chief social or political *and* educational task of our time.[14]

It is likely that many of the new schools people who found their own concerns and hopes expressed clearly in

Holt's books would be troubled by this analysis. Many reformers would not welcome such an overt politicization of their efforts. At the risk of being repetitious, I want to emphasize that Holt has shifted his *perspective* in significant ways; it doesn't follow that there is a corresponding shift in his recommendations about actions. Free schools should continue to be formed; they can be needed sanctuaries for young people; they should be experiments in how to transcend the limitations of schools as we have known them. But their limitations should be clearly perceived in social and political terms and an emphasis on the necessity for social and political change maintained. Even with this perspective, all of the daily problems of being with young people in a school stay problems.

For many parents their immediate concern is the welfare of their own children, and they do not look at the school issue as a teacher or organizer with a radical perspective might. It may be true that it is the privileged position of the adults involved in most free schools that gives them the opportunity to establish new institutions for their own children; and they may be willing to acknowledge that their actions could be seen as maintaining this privilege, especially if their educational theory is validated and their children do emerge more able, more intelligent, more creative.

But what else can they do, they could reasonably ask. Some parents I know send their children to public schools on principle and become active in trying to change the public schools. Central School in Cambridge, as was described in Chapter 2, attempts to prepare parents for this kind of struggle and refuses to become a free school beyond kindergarten. But this is exceptional. For the parents I have in mind, it matters that their children seem to be in good shape emotionally and intellectually and that the local public schools are far from the worst and most destructive. If these conditions were different, intense concern for the well-being of the children would probably outweigh the abstract political principle.

Realistically, most parents have little hope of bringing about significant changes in the schools in the near future, and for their children the time is now. In some places there are good chances of making substantial changes, and there will be more and more opportunities for free schools that are part of the public school system, with the advantages of financial support, good salaries for teachers, direct contact with the community, and hence a better chance of effecting changes in schools than an isolated private free school has. Something like this has already happened in Berkeley, Philadelphia, and New York. Parent groups have organized in several places with the intention of cajoling, arguing, and pressuring local school boards to open "alternative public schools."

Of course, there are drawbacks to the inside-the-system approach. The complexities of being within the bureaucracy, the compromises that are inevitably made in situations like this, the struggling with opponents of such innovations, the sense of constant hostile evaluation of the project—these conditions can be quite constricting, and some parents, teachers, and students would reasonably place great importance on the almost total freedom of the private free school.

But this has not yet become a serious issue, since the opportunity for such a choice ("public free" or "private free") has hardly existed. The parents, teachers, and students involved in free schools had no choice if they wanted radically different kinds of schools from the ones the public system was offering, and this is still the usual situation today.

Especially with small parent-cooperative elementary schools, politicization can seem beside the point and distracting, if it means trying to act politically by means of the school. Some people oppose the political perspective I have supported because, as noted earlier, they feel that partisan politics are inappropriate to free schools. They see themselves as doing a small good thing, very important for the well-being of their children, and they see other people as free to do the same. They hope they will, and they hope that the public schools will improve too.

Another position along this spectrum accepts the broad political analysis but feels there is no short-range alternative. With some twinges of conscience, people realistically feel that refusing to start a free school and sending their children to the local bad public school, though it may mean they aren't taking advantage of their privilege, does not help change the real conditions. (Similarly, one may give away all of one's income over the poverty line without in any way helping to change the conditions that create the poverty, although one might satisfy one's social conscience.) Such parents might agree that if there were a powerful movement for change within the public schools they would definitely join it, but they don't see this now and they don't see themselves as capable of organizing such a movement. Meanwhile, they have a child of six and, having seen the first-grade class in the neighborhood public school, they just can't let their child suffer *that*, so with a few others, they call a meeting, talk, argue, find a teacher, and start a free school.

A related position evaluates the situation of the small independent free school in a much more positive light both culturally and politically. The idea of experimental schools as catalysts and exemplars is supported by many free school people. From this perspective it is very important that free schools exist as examples and laboratories for people concerned with change. Then, it is claimed, we will be able to see a wide variety of open experiments, far beyond what could be tried within the bureaucratic constraints of even a relatively liberal public school. Furthermore, the desirable possibilities of isolation can be explored. That is, if parents and teachers who share a point of view can work together and let things truly unfold, then the experiments will be *real* experiments.

There is in this perspective a sense of social change by example; a rather untheoretical belief that, in trying to get people to change, one should give them good reasons for thinking that what they might change to is better than what they have. Often accompanied by a cultural radicalism about communalism, sex, family, etc., this position sees the schools as where, in embryo, the vision of the new society, the one that will replace the sick and crumbling society that now exists, can be tried out.

For example, a young woman who is a parent and organizer of a small free school, which includes several people who share a radical perspective on both culture and politics, was asked about the argument that people who hold her values should fight the public school system from within.

> But there are people doing that. Marty's best friend is ———— [a prominent cultural and political radical]. He's doing his thing in the city. And the cities have to be destroyed, but along with destruction has to come building. You've got to have something to replace the system that you're trying to destroy. If you want to get rid of public schools, the best way is to build schools that are your own. Right? I can't see how you can destroy a building unless you've got something in your head that's better. I don't see any sense in it.

She expresses a view that combines both cultural and political radicalism. It is not simply that she wants the free school for her own children; she also conceives of her school and others like it as part of the struggle for radical political and social change.

> I think that the system out there is corrupt. It stinks. And why should we be a part of it? I've seen people try over

and over again. You've got to form the alternatives. You can't just stay out there and scream about what's wrong with it. You've got to start doing something about it. So you drop out and start doing it. The best way to do it is to build a school, because it's propaganda, very honestly, it is. . . . Because the best way to change something is through children, not through the adults. The best way to educate a world is to bring up children educated that way, and for every one child you educate they may educate hundreds. It may sound like a very small way of doing it. But if people do drop out of public school, and I think there should be *endless* private schools, endless schools that take away from the public schools. Because the more kids they remove, the more frightened they get, the more they're going to have to start offering things that are positive alternatives. . . .

It is the *perspective* that is of special interest; because, as with most free elementary schools, little overt political content or activity is possible. In the actual operation, out in the country, with little contact with the non-hip community, the school could easily include parents and teachers who share in the counter-cultural aspects of this perspective without the political dimensions. There are free school people with such a position—cultural radicalism that is ideologically antipolitical. They oppose the political approach, and see in the religious, mystical, spiritual path the only serious orientation to human thought and action. From such a perspective all of the various political approaches I have discussed are considered superficial, detracting from the path of true enlightenment. This position, of course, opposes politicization of any sort, but for very different reasons from the liberal view.

In many schools there coexist elements of all of these views, so that the issue of politics is a source of friction and disputes which can become quite serious. For example, in February 1971, the *New Schools Exchange News-letter* ran a letter from a teacher at the Greenbriar School in Texas, commenting on recent articles that dealt with political issues.

Dear New Schools Exchange People—

I've been following (or at least *trying* to read) these "exchanges" regarding schools, radicalism and political consciousness. It all makes me sad, mad, and disappointed. Simply (!?) *doing* a free school is more than enough for me (and some of the others here)—I mean trying to give yourself fully to kids, helping them find themselves and to fully become (while trying to be and fully enjoying myself, since the two are not that separate for me).

The thing that is most bothersome is that focusing on politics really seems to *interfere* with and *destroy* the free, full growth of children. How can anyone who seriously believes in a "free" school talk of "the use of innovative schools as instruments for social change and political reform"? How can children freely discover themselves if they are being *used as instrument?* Why is the newsletter taking space for such negative rambling. . . .

Yet I know that this is a real struggle for free school people since there are those here at Greenbriar who disagree with me. . . .

What seems more important is that our neighbors, black and white, farmers and ranchers, store owners and gas station folks are coming to accept long hair, beads, "weird clothes" (different life styles) as real human beings just like themselves; not through any direct assault on our part, not through any guerrilla theater in the streets of our nearby town of Bastrop—but just by our being.

The only really relevant political fact is that we have 48 young people who are no longer in the system's schools —that in itself is the most radical revolutionary thing that we can do. What is more, if we turn our schools into heavy political tools, the system is quite capable of wiping us out. Here in Texas, we have a very open school code as regards private schools, a code which the legislature could easily alter to require accreditation or other constricting regulations, as the city of Austin recently did. . . .

Serious arguments arise with such issues as becoming identified with radical political struggles in the community, or public statements by school personnel which can seem to identify the school as politically committed, or attempts to relate to the student and teacher oppositions within the local public schools. This letter represents the people who do not respond to political analyses of the function of education and who are in general apolitical. Their hope is simply to have a nice school for their own children and, as the letter expresses well, they resent the intrusion of politics. They feel that it is difficult enough to establish a school that does well by the small number of children in it without trying to bring in a host of big political issues. The risk of alienating the "straight" community, thus endangering the existence of the school by generating ill-will, is often an important issue, as it was to the teacher who wrote the letter.

These issues can be manifested in many ways. One teacher wishes to have a course on radical social change for ten- and eleven-year-olds; another feels that for such young children this would be indoctrination, and besides would alienate some well-to-do, rather conservative parents who were considering sending their children and giving the school some money. On Moratorium Day some teachers and students want to close the school and have everyone go to the antiwar parade and rally; other teachers feel that the school should go on as usual, but that of course those who want to should go. But they don't see why politics should get mixed up with education.

In conflicts like these, all of the issues we have been discussing in this chapter come out in day-to-day terms. The questions of neutrality, of loading the atmosphere, of taking responsibility for the example one sets, of the meaning of one's commitment both to social change and to good education for these children here and now, keep coming up. They don't get satisfactorily resolved, mainly because they really aren't resolvable. As was pointed out, when issues like these lead to very serious tensions, they are part of the basis for schools splitting into more homogeneous groups.

An eloquent personal statement of these political dilemmas appeared in the journal *Outside The Net*.[15] In a piece entitled "Our School: Struggling and Strategizing Along," Vicki Wirth Legion, a free school teacher in St. Louis, relates the story of how she and some parents, mainly black, started their own free school two years ago. She describes clearly the difficulties of trying to translate free school rhetoric into free school reality. Her main concern in the article is the political question. The initial proposal for the school stated: "We are not trying merely to create one small experimental school for a few children in the community." According to Ms. Legion,

> The school's controlling board of people from the neighborhood was thought of as the nucleus of a well-organized, confident, and experienced parent group that could demand to influence significantly the schools in our community and who could move from their experience to demand that the public School Board begin to make the kinds of changes necessary to provide high quality education for *all* children in the city.

(This is very similar to the view of Central School in Cambridge, described near the end of Chapter 2.) The author explains that her vision of how this would happen was rather romantic—a direct confrontation from a school system threatened and frightened by this free school challenge. At the present time Ms. Legion sees no danger of such a challenge. In fact, she fears that the existence of the school might make it easier on the school system by taking care of the most troublesome and discontented students and parents while providing a good cause for local foundations to support. In this way the school can "lend credence to the popular belief that American society *is* doing right by 'Those People.' "

Ms. Legion emphasizes the importance of the tracking function of American education, and the kind of adaptive socializing the school system accomplishes. Her view is that, especially for poor people, this creates a basic contradiction for free schools. (This is closely related to the discussions of the purposes of schools and the tracking idea I gave earlier.)

> Our school, or any alternative school, bumps right into this giant contradiction: what parents and teachers want for the children is the ability to think creatively and independently, to work for their own reasons, for the satisfaction they get from the job at hand. But what the kids have to be able to do instead, to get by in our country is the exact opposite. Your livelihood and your children's welfare depends on saying "yes, ma'am" and "yes, sir" and giving the answers the boss wants to hear.
>
> Unless we can clearly name this contradiction, and recognize where it comes from, it can reach into the life of a school and tear it apart. In many cases I think, the contradiction appears in the form of tensions between parents and teachers—it certainly did in our school.
>
> . . . Crosswinds like these can tear our hopes apart, and I imagine that many a school has gone down in that struggle—teachers convinced that parents are reactionary and materialistic; parents convinced that teachers are wild and irresponsible. It's easy to forget that the contradiction comes from *outside* the school.
>
> Parents are *not* crass for insisting that the children must be able to grow up and earn a living. . . . The teachers are *not* irresponsible for wanting to work in a way that will help a younger person be excited about what she/he is doing *now*. The present conflict between these two sets

of legitimate concerns is a measure of the sickness of our country under its present economic system.

For this teacher, the dilemma is unsolved. Should the school try to be an active agent of change, with all the expense of energy and commitment and likely defeat, or should it be content to be a good thing for thirty or forty-five children? This dilemma is central, although often ignored or denied. It will be the main concern of the rest of this chapter.

Whatever the disputes on politics, one issue that everyone agrees is fundamental is that of survival and growth. I have noted how marginal the free school phenomenon is at present in actual numbers. It is understandable that people tend to exaggerate the importance of their own activities and accomplishments, and to treat as real what is at best only potential. With free school people, this sort of distortion is especially salient since they spend much time in their own school and talking to other free school people. Because of their perspectives and commitments, they tend to overdramatize the impact of the new schools, and this tendency is reinforced by the relative isolation of the schools from other parts of the community, especially the "straight" educational community.

For some schools, usually Summerhillian or, more recently, counter-cultural, this isolation is desired and deliberate. For them, survival is no more complex a question than for other private schools. Most Summerhillian schools seem quite stable, as is Summerhill. The image they project is clear. They do not attempt to involve themselves in community issues that could make trouble, and they charge substantial tuitions. The theoretical and pedagogical questions are pretty well solved from the start by their commitment to Summerhill. Like the private progressive schools, they provide a particular kind of environment for children; those parents who desire it or find themselves with "problem children" and can afford the tuition will continue to support these schools.

But the main part of the new schools development is not classically Summerhillian. There are relatively few boarding schools and much more focus on conceptions of education that integrate school more into the larger community rather than less, as did Summerhill. There is strong emphasis on parent participation in teaching, choosing teachers, setting policy, using community people and community institutions, and having the children out in the community a good deal, especially high school people. This emphasis transcends the divisions among perspectives on politics, but it is related to political trends in school reform such as the struggles of minority group parents for community control, the concern with "affective education," the encouragement of alternatives within the public school system, and the widespread interest in the "tuition voucher" idea.

For this mainstream of new schools, spanning radical, liberal, reform-by-example, and apolitical "save some children" views, the economic issue is crucial. In describing the schools, I have noted how this problem arises constantly. Most schools are at least tinged with the activist-reformist consciousness of the sixties; and the adults involved, very often quite young and formerly or currently involved to various degrees in the student movement, do not feel comfortable as an almost purely white, middle-class private school, no matter how libertarian the pedagogy. In any case, even for the middle class, the rising costs of education have made it increasingly difficult to think of expensive private schools for all their children. Especially for the people who start free schools, traditional levels of expenditure are impossible, as well as undesired.

In fact, as described in Chapter 2, the social and cultural

conceptions that underlie the rise of free schools make it possible for them to be much less costly than the average public or private school. The small size, the community feeling among staff, the libertarian approach to attendance and behavior mean that the whole apparatus of administrative bureaucracy is eliminated, along with most of the need for administration. Cost for buildings is of course much less, because of the free school idea of what a good environment for learning is. Similarly, costs of expensive texts, testing programs, and expensive furniture and equipment are eliminated, as are other expenses that arise from the standard classroom style of traditional schooling.

The community of the school—parents, teachers, and students—takes on many of the functions that are paid for in normal public and private schools, such as maintenance and repairs, building equipment, transportation of students, bookkeeping, office work, and publicity. Finally, the largest expense for any school is personnel, and the free school philosophy calls for a much, much lower student-teacher ratio than is customary in public schools. The commitment to individual attention, the intimacy of small-group situations, variety of offerings, ability to deal with the individual needs and wants of each student implies a ratio of about 1:5 rather than 1:25 or 1:30, which is the situation in many public schools.

Free schools in general are able to accomplish this aim, and with highly qualified and talented people. For one thing, as noted in Chapter 2, the open form of the institution makes it very easy to use volunteers. Since the problem of a closed institution ruled by a bureaucratic hierarchy with many rules and regulations is eliminated, a volunteer can simply come in and talk to the staff and the children; if he seems all right, that's all there is to it. (Remember the account of the potters in Chapter 3.) There is an abundance of volunteers from the community, especially from nearby colleges and universities. The eternal appeal of working with kids plus the communal and participatory feeling and the culturally familiar atmosphere add up to an enormously attractive opportunity for meaningful volunteer work. In college communities free schools are usually flooded with volunteers, the problem being which ones to accept and how to ensure dependability. As was described, some schools run entirely or almost entirely with volunteer teachers.

In general, many free schools attract mainly teachers who are young and committed politically or culturally to the values represented by free schools. This includes a de-emphasis on material rewards, career success, power, and other incentives to hold jobs that are characteristic of the American system (among others). The value of meaningful, nonalienating, personally satisfying work in a small intense community of like-minded people is so great that many teachers are willing to work for almost no salary, in many cases only room and board. When financial times are bad, which is frequent, even these meager rewards can diminish; I know of teachers who stay involved by living off their savings or taking jobs after school (usually unpleasant and poorly paid).

Since most of the teachers are young and part of the "new culture," this sort of voluntary poverty is possible. Teachers can live together, sharing communally (often with some of the students and parents). In the new life styles little is spent on clothes, housing, and travel.

This situation has enabled many new schools to begin and survive so far. But there are difficulties, which accumulate as the school gets older. One problem of the volunteer or subsistence situation for teachers is that it tends to make it difficult for older people, especially those with families, to work full-time in free schools. It makes for a larger element of young and free-floating people than is desirable. Sometimes commitment is attenuated so that moving on when things aren't going well is not a really big decision. After all, it's not as if you were getting a real salary or working under contract or supporting a family. Also, the inability to pay even what was promised originally cannot but cause some resentment on the part of the teacher.

Most free school people will see a lot of advantages in aspects of the transience that is necessarily part of this situation. New teachers bring fresh energies and viewpoints to a situation where such things are at a premium. A kind of constant experimentation generated by the continuous introduction of new people with new ideas and experiences is also valued.

On the other hand, there are serious problems of continuity. There is often not enough time and opportunity to build a really "together" staff that by working, experimenting, learning from mistakes, and building on past experiences finally develops a *good* school, with a particular individual style, some traditions, even; a sense of continuity and solidity to balance the sometimes restless and frenetic search for newness.

Also, there is a feeling that new schools should reach out to the community beyond those immediately sympathetic, to groups of people who are dubious of the radically different free school style but who could probably benefit greatly from a liberation from the authoritarianism and tracking of the public schools. This applies especially to poor minority communities and white working-class communities. But for this to happen, there would have to be schools with a wider range of styles than is prevalent now. One part of this development would be schools that involved teachers and other adults from these communities, in the manner of the community schools that make up the Milwaukee Federation of Independent Community Schools, or the Roxbury Federation of Community Free Schools, or the Westminster Neighborhood School in St. Louis which Vicki Legion wrote about. In such situations, parent participation and confidence can only be gained by schools that look like they will last so as to be able to really help the children. The sense of easy going experimentation and tentativeness is much more the style of the young hip middle class (even parents) who are both physically and culturally very mobile.

However, even the most hip schools suffer from financial starvation. No matter how low the expenses, much energy has to go into raising money. Without a secure future income it is difficult to attract private donations or comparatively straight affluent people who can pay at the high-rate spots on the sliding scales of tuition which most schools use. Furthermore, even a relatively low tuition eliminates the possibility of many poor people being able to send their children. The lack of money also makes it difficult to get useful equipment and materials, take trips, or find good buildings; and it generates a steady anxiety which can be very draining on people engaged in an activity that requires terrific input of energy even under very good conditions.

I noted in talking about school failures that it is often not the lack of money that is the basic cause of failure. However, poverty causes constant hassles and, besides being often the immediate occasion for failure, is almost always a contributing factor. It certainly discourages people from starting schools, as they look ahead to an unrelieved struggle to collect tuitions, have bake sales, beg from rich liberals, and attempt to interest foundations.

Increasingly, free school people are looking to the possibility of getting some public funding. If they do not, then the evolution of the free school movement will continue to look pretty much as it has the past couple of years. Some free school proponents (like the New Schools Exchange founder mentioned earlier) have seriously exaggerated the numbers and rate of growth and have thus misled people. Basing himself on figures supplied by the

Exchange, Michael Rossman, a prominent radical activist and theorist of new styles and forms of education, published a short essay in the *New Schools Exchange Newsletter* projecting the next few years of the new schools movement. A close parallel is drawn to the "free university" movement in which Rossman was a prominent participant. He constructs a logistic growth curve which he thinks is as applicable to free schools as it is, in his view, to free universities and experimental colleges. (There does not seem to be a decline built in, only a saturation "leveling off" point.) But my own impression is that his figure of 1,000 experimental colleges is inflated. In any case, the number of schools and participants and their prominence on the scene have declined significantly from the peak of three or four years ago, and this is not shown in the analysis.[16]

Rossman sees free schools as in the portion of the curve where the number is doubling yearly, a situation he feels will continue for some years. He conceives of three potential limits to the multiplication of free schools: *"Radical reform in public schools.* Unlikely within this decade. *Political repression.* Not to be expected on a mass scale before about '75. *Economic depression.* Unlikely before '76."[17] He puts forward figures of 7,000 schools and 340,-000 students by 1973 and 25 to 30,000 schools and 2,000,000 students by 1975. (A note at the beginning of the article qualifies the projection by saying that the 1971 figure of 1,600 includes "progressive" schools; that true "free schools" number 500. But in fact this correction was made on my suggestion to Rossman before my own attempt to get an accurate figure had really begun. The truth is that a figure of 350 would have been closer to reality at the time, and this would still have included a good number of schools that should be classified as not truly "free, without qualifications.")

Rossman deduces that free schools will quickly become

a major alternative to the public system, and drain from it more and more of its innovative teachers, responsive kids, and certain classes of parents, hip-liberal in the main. To this extent, the public system will grow even less adaptable; polarization between the system and its alternative will deepen and grow bitter, in style and politics. As it becomes recognized as a "massive Leading Edge," like ecology, the free schools movement will be courted by politicians, and made the subject of major rhetoric and some legislation." Each town, each school district of over 500 students, each ethnic group or neighborhood of over 4,000 persons, has enough predisposed/receptive parents and students to spawn a small free school. A vision of 50,000 free schools is not unreasonable."[18]

Rossman articulates what is believed or hoped for in much fuzzier and inarticulate ways by many free schoolers. My own view is much different, as should be clear by now. George Orwell, in his marvelous essay "Politics and the English Language," critically noted the frequent use of the "not-un" construction. If a vision of 50,000 free schools is "not unreasonable," then maybe it is reasonable. But if one doesn't want to quite commit oneself, one creates an area where something is neither reasonable nor unreasonable.

It is in fact highly unreasonable. The number of schools is not doubling every year; in very fertile areas for free schools, like Rossman's own Bay Area, it is obvious that 60 or 70 in 1971 will not become 120 or 140 by 1972 and 240 or 280 by 1973. In the first place, there will be a tendency to use the existing free schools rather than start new ones next door. In the second place, the difficulty of starting and maintaining schools will become more common knowledge, thus sobering enthusiasms. Also, whether the public school reforms that are happening now are *radical* in Rossman's sense is not really at issue here. In fact, the spread of alternatives within the system is moving rapidly—in theory, as shown by the NEA documents referred to, and even in practice. Rossman's Berkeley is an interesting case where the range of alternatives within the system, supported by a flexible superintendent in a particularly liberal community, is quite broad and is being deliberately expanded, financed by "experimental schools" money from the federal government. (That this process is also corrupting and co-opting has been claimed by knowledgeable observers like Herb Kohl.)

The number of alternative high schools within the system is increasing rapidly, especially in relatively liberal suburban areas. The trend toward allowing parents to help form alternative elementary schools, noted before, will grow and will engage the energies of active parents who might be moved to organize a free school if the public school situation seemed hopeless to them. Instead, it will seem more worthwhile to organize, negotiate, gather parents and teachers and community political support to pressure the school board to allow the experiment. Or, if there is a liberal superintendent, as there have been recently in Berkeley, Philadelphia, Ithaca, and New York City, for example, then it may very well seem worthwhile to work with him, even if some compromises are necessary. The main consideration for parents is that they must think of schools for their young children in a horizon of several years, and the prospect of a school with no tuition, with decent pay for teachers and good equipment, along with parent participation in governance and policy-making and young enthusiastic libertarian teachers, is very attractive. This is especially true for parents and teachers who have the kind of radical political perspective described earlier. The problem of conscience and political analysis go together for this perspective. To be able to have the kind of school they value, which respects the freedom and autonomy of the young people, as well as having no financial troubles and being able to affect school developments in a way that the usual free school isolation prevents, would satisfy both their concern for their children and their political ideals.

The parallel with the free university development is inexact in some important ways. The free universities and experimental colleges were almost completely a product of the student movement. To a large extent, they were parasitic on the regular university in a way that the free schools aren't with respect to the public schools. The free schools are full-time school for the children, and demand a deep and continuous commitment for teachers and parents, commensurate with the responsibility undertaken. Free universities were never so central for the individuals involved. The responsibility is not nearly so great, nor is the commitment. And, revealingly, many of the experimental colleges that seem to be surviving do so because they have become part of the official university scene—that is, they get financial help, give credits, etc., from the host university. The totally independent free universities have had a much higher mortality rate. It seems quite clear now that free universities are not capable of providing a significant alternative to the universities, while the experimental colleges are a not-very-radical, officially sanctioned part of the liberalization of the existing universities.

Thus, in my judgment, Rossman's scenario is mainly fantasy. It won't be political repression nor economic depression that will prevent free schools from becoming a "massive Leading Edge," but the broader social conditions noted before. It is true that financial problems mean there are far fewer free schools than would be formed if there were no such financial pressure. And many of the schools that now exist realize that the financial bind affects seriously their future prospects, their capacity to achieve some real stability, and their ability to expand and attract people beyond the already sympathetic hip-liberal community.

Because of this, there is interest in any possibilities of

breaking the monopoly on public money held by the state public schools. (It is quite obvious that foundations are not now and will not in the future be a significant source of funds for new schools, especially not for the mainstream middle-class-based free school.) The significant new reforms in school financing and governance now being discussed include tuition vouchers and performance contracting. Performance contracting means paying private corporations to do the teaching in schools, under a contract that guarantees certain agreed-upon achievement levels—measurable, of course—or money back. The spread of performance-contracting arrangements opened the education field directly to large "learning corporations" with their "scientific" techniques of "behavior management," their expensive hardware and programmed learning texts. But performance contracting will not help free schools, for it is not very likely that free schools and parent cooperatives will get contracts from school boards. With the emphasis on training large masses of "deprived" youngsters to score "average or above" on standardized reading and arithmetic tests, the approach of small, decentralized, communitarian institutions will be ignored. From the point of view of a centralized bureaucracy, a contract with a company like an "IBM Learning Corporation" or "Behavioral Research Laboratory" will appear much sounder in "ed biz" terms. In any case, the recent negative government report on the results of contracting has dampened enthusiasm considerably.

An innovation in educational financing that has great appeal for new schools people is the tuition voucher plan. The basic idea of the voucher plan is to provide choice to the consumers' of education (the parents) by establishing a kind of market situation. That is, tax money for education would be returned to parents in the form of a voucher. These vouchers would be redeemable by educational institutions, public or private. So, educators could start schools of various sorts, and the parents would choose the school they want and hand in their vouchers. In this way, tax money would be used to support a variety of private schools, thus creating the choice of a market situation. Many organizations of teachers and other public school people have taken a stand against vouchers, and although there has been a federally financed "feasibility study," experiments have not begun as of spring 1972, and even if they do happen, the results will not be in for some years. It is not at all likely, then, that the idea will be relevant to the development of new schools for the next several years, which is about as far ahead as is interesting to look for people doing schools today.

In any case, the idea of vouchers raises some interesting questions. Public school opponents claim that a voucher plan would destroy the public school system (this is assumed to be a bad thing to do). That is, if people can choose what schools to send their children to, and if groups of teachers and parents and learning corporations can start their own schools privately and have them supported by tax money, then the public schools will not only lose their monopoly on public funds but will be unable to compete well. I don't want to discuss the issue in any detail here, though it is very interesting politically and philosophically. (One serious consideration is whether the main beneficiaries would be the large corporations, just as with the performance-contracting plan.)

Another very appealing possibility, though also unlikely to occur in the near future, is the opening up of the public system to include alternative schools. Free schools could be adopted, declared "public," as it were (assuming they fulfilled simple "public" conditions like open enrollment), and granted tax money while being able to retain their spiritual autonomy. Such a plan has the advantage of maintaining education as a public activity with community participation and relevant political discussions and attention. A possible effect of a voucher plan (or performance contracting, to a lesser extent) is the "privatization" of education. By making the provision of schools a matter of private offerings and private choices, the area of education could be depoliticized, eliminated as a subject of public, political concern. (This, of course, was one of the main philosophical and political intentions of the man who proposed the plan, the libertarian conservative economist Milton Friedman, former advisor to presidential candidate Barry Goldwater.)[19]

Whatever the possible educational benefits, privatization will not confront the larger political questions of education which I have emphasized. What might happen is that groups of like-minded people will be able to have the schools they want (assuming that the regulatory guidelines aren't too repressive), while the public *issue* of education would be eliminated. Schooling would be a private matter, like the choice of a family home or automobile. Large and small educational entrepreneurs would provide the kinds of schools that might "sell," and the competitive market would flourish, avoiding state control while providing maximum freedom and consumer choice, just as in the classical theory of the market. The *issue* would be eliminated because criticisms of the schools would no longer be a publicly arguable concern, involving matters such as community organization, school board elections, and public scrutiny of the educational system. In the imaginary system I am discussing, if an individual has any complaints he goes to a different "dealer." If his child isn't doing well, there is nothing to stop the parent from putting him into a different kind of school, and so on. Schools would tend to have like-minded people in them, which, in a way, is part of the original motivation of the idea. In the United States, rich people have always been able to gather their children together in proper private schools; with vouchers, a clear injustice could be righted—

everyone would be able to do this. But it should be considered that the *idea* of a "public school" has much to recommend it. The notion that the educational institutions of the community should be public, including in them a wide variety of people, with the activities being of public concern, discussed and debated within the community, has important advantages over a totally private system.

Another way of putting this point is to emphasize that reformers want their reforms to spread, to convince, to be accepted beyond the original small circle of adherents; and this kind of impact might be facilitated if there were a *good* kind of public school system, one in which there could be experimentation, innovation, variety. The impingement of new education on the general public might be strengthened. Also, the *public* responsibility for providing quality education creates a constantly active public forum in which reformers and radicals have an opportunity to discuss and attempt to persuade large numbers of people to share their points of view.

An illustration of this point is the very recent phenomenon of radical school reform advocates entering school board elections. The survival question puts pressure on almost all alternative schools people, whatever their larger political views, to confront at least the politics of school financing. (Those satisfied with being expensive private schools with "open classrooms" are, of course, exempt from this concern.) Discontent about schools is growing everywhere; the crisis is becoming so manifest that, at the moment this is being written, Dayton, Ohio, is broke; bond issues have been rejected, and the school board is planning to shut the schools for substantial portions of the year, and the outlook for the next year is even bleaker. Chicago faces a similar situation. The increased rate of Catholic school closings will strain the urban school systems even more. All in all, the sense of crisis provides the occasion for talk of radical changes within schools, talk that evokes a positive response in growing numbers of people inside and outside the schools.

Because of this, school board elections have become of interest to free school people. Even quite radical-sounding free-schoolers feel the financial pressures and want public money—in essence, the money they are giving to the public schools through taxation. One way of getting that money loosened up is through political pressure, and this is most relevantly exerted through the school boards. In 1971, in Berkeley and Cambridge, to name places where I had some involvement, free school teachers ran for the school boards on platforms that called for radical reform and public support for free-school style alternatives within the system.

As usual, where radical politics is concerned, Berkeley is ahead of the rest of the country, though, I hope, not far ahead. In Berkeley, there are a relatively large number of free schools both inside and outside the rather liberal public system. (A well-known example inside the system is the high school project Other Ways, begun by Herb Kohl several years ago.) People from the various alternative schools met several months before the school board election, discussed the situation, and decided to form a "New Schools Network" of parents, students, and teachers involved in new schools activity, and to have the Network run a candidate. Joan Levinson, who had been deeply involved in free school activities since their beginnings in Berkeley several years ago and was a teacher at Bay High, a local private free high school, was prevailed upon to enter the race. The feeling about the campaign was very good; many free school people got involved, a lot of people were talked to, literature was distributed. The slogan was "Alternatives cost less, educate more." Although Joan Levinson didn't win, she did very well at the polls; and the people involved felt that the campaign was an effective way to raise community consciousness about the problems and possibilities of free school approaches to education.

I began this discussion by noting Mike Rossman's projections about the growth of the new schools movement and attempting to present a more realistic assessment of the growth and survival situation. I don't think that the Berkeley experience shows that running for school board is *the* answer. It is worth doing, and this kind of grass-roots political activity will increase not only with respect to education. A new perspective on political activity has developed. The eighteen-year-old vote has helped, but the main factor is the "cooling" of the radical movement. This cooling is a complex phenomenon, and deserves long and serious consideration which I will not give it here.[20] My purpose is less to provide a convincing analysis—which I don't feel I have—than to develop a broad framework within which to continue the discussion about free schools and their future.

One meaning of the collapse of an organized "New Left" radical movement, mainly a student-youth movement, is that two seemingly contradictory attitudes held by many radicals over the past few years were both exaggerated. (Rossman speaks for a good part of the cultural-political youth left in expressing both attitudes simultaneously.) What I have in mind are the feelings that, on one hand, apocalypse is close, political repression and fascism are looming on the horizon, and, on the other, that the "new" is breaking out all over and winning adherents at a great pace. (One standard topic of the youth-culture talk is how many people smoke marijuana or drop acid, and how many of the children of big politicians are "heads," and so on.) These attitudes aren't contradictory, since they could not only be valid simultaneously, but the truth of one might even be an important factor in the truth of the other. That is, a ruling group can be expected to react repressively to real challenges to its legitimacy and power, and the more serious the threat, the stronger the repression.

My own sense is that both these attitudes have been exaggerated over the past few years. The apocalyptic sense —the notion that everything was falling apart, that the country was becoming ungovernable, that use of the word "revolution" was appropriate, that discussions of "urban guerrilla warfare" would be useful—didn't uncover the reality under all of the obvious turmoil of ghetto rebellions, campus-building takeovers, increasing dope arrests, increasing violent antiwar activities. The reality was a complex one, but one crucial element was how stable this really troubled country was. The images of critical societal breakdown, such as we recognize in 1917 Russia or 1932 Germany or 1947 China, are inappropriate to our situation. The media concentration on the exciting, exotic, and interesting exaggerated the scope of the oppositional activities. For activists, their own absorption in the intensity of their efforts, combined with their concentration in particular areas like Berkeley or Boston or Chicago, gave them a distorted perception of their strength. Add to this the natural wishfulness of a relatively small number of people who have placed themselves into direct opposition to the power and values of dominant forces of their own country, and the exaggeration is easily understandable.

But the reality was that the country was pretty stable. The great ghetto rebellions of Watts, Newark, and Detroit were not signals for the opening of large-scale black armed struggle the next "long hot summer," as some radicals (often white) predicted, but were, in fact, the end of a particular phase in the rise of the black movement. At the height of the antiwar spirit, no high government official could appear at a major campus without large demonstrations and heckling. But the war has cooled off, at least so far as the American public is concerned; and Nixon has gone to China and Russia. The economy is the main concern now, but it is not an issue that mobilizes demonstrations and sparks a "resistance."

What seems clear is that something happened during the sixties—call it a shift of consciousness. The right did not succeed in becoming resurgent, and does not look like it will be leading the country into a bleak night of American-style fascism, with an underground youth movement fighting back in the "belly of the monster" in the name of revolution.[21] But if the "freezing of America" is a somewhat paranoid fantasy, the "greening of America" is a euphoric illusion. The cultural transformations are real but complex, and their tendencies are not yet unfolded. I'm very confused about the long-run meanings, but I don't feel, despite the spate of new books on Zen and Yoga and gurus and self-serving claims of being very "spiritual," that there is a totally "new consciousness," full of beauty and love and inner peace and transcendence.

What appears now is that the expectations of fast radical changes, either for bad or good, were mistaken. To talk now of a movement for social change is clearly to think in a very long perspective. People who were talking or acting like Weathermen two years ago are back in graduate school today. The students become adults, have children, and worry about the schools. Many radicals are doing political things, but they are scattered, local, and even institutional. Radical social change in an advanced industrial nation like the United States will certainly take a "long march"—but not a military one. There will have to be a lot of gritty day-to-day working within and against the institutions. There will have to be a lot more analysis and original thought, rather than the taking over of an unhelpful Marxism-Leninism for lack of any other theory. There will have to be a sense of how "daily" the lives of most people are—not like the total involvement of the guerrilla or the draft-resister. The whip of repression won't be the means of convincing people of the radical analysis ("the worse the better" argument), nor will the new self-proclaimed spiritual transformation peacefully and effortlessly generate a new consciousness and consequently a new and good society.

These very general and inadequate observations are important to my own active participation and my theoretical sense of the significance and possibilities of the radical-school-reform development today. The school board election description indicates one of the gritty and unglamourous ways in which the work for educational reform has to proceed. The aims will necessarily be more modest than one might wish. "Cultural revolution" without an adequate politics will not bring about the necessary changes. Within America today, cultural changes are open to corruption, commercialization, phony imitation, faddism, and worse. (The Manson affair is a very extreme example of how sour the rhetoric of the counter-culture can go.) One can wear bell-bottoms, grow long hair, smoke dope and drop acid, use phrases like "getting my head together," "beautiful," "far out," "man," and "rip off" and still be a hustler, a manipulator, a male chauvinist, or a crook, all in freak's clothing and spirit.

I am suggesting here, as I have before in this book, that understanding the hard road to social and educational change should lead to more modesty. *We* won't *win* in the near future. Free schools will not sweep the country. Free school candidates will not sweep the school board elections. Many of the new free schools are not wonderful places full of learning, joy, and community. The children and the adults involved are also part of America, and, as John Holt emphasized in the letter quoted before, the whole society and its quality of life are the main educators.

As part of the widespread attempt to improve the society and its spirit, free schools can make a contribution. But the work will be difficult and progress will seem very slow, if measured by the apocalyptic perspectives just discussed. This realization can be discouraging, causing people to give up the struggle, as if the world were to blame for not responding quickly and appropriately to our decency, commitment, and truth. Or, it can be the basis for a serious, unglamorous, gritty, and long-term commitment to continue to organize, teach, start schools, work with public school reformers, criticize our own efforts, talk to people— all with modest expectations for the short term.

The American government and society are solider and more resilient than some radical analysts believed a few years ago, and the movement for social change is less solid and together than it seemed then. The public school system is also more solid than it looks. A disaster in many places—yes, in a sense. Intolerable for many young people and parents—yes, in a sense. Out of money—yes, in a sense. Does this all add up to collapsing? *No.* It is salutary to look at history to find how many "intolerable" situations are tolerated for long periods, how many inefficient, harmful, and unjustifiable institutions and practices continue on and on.

The public school system is large and still has room to maneuver. I've touched on some of the new developments that are in the offing now. There will be some chances for worthwhile small changes, and there will be heightened criticism of old ways and increased interest in new approaches. Free schools can be part of the pressure to push this discontent toward deeper analysis of the way schooling works in American society. Since public schools are the institution of which free schools are the "counter-institution," a close relationship to reform developments there will be necessary for even modestly effective action. My own experience tells me that a splendid and pure counter-cultural isolation so that we can "do our thing" unsullied by the crap of "Amerika" leads nowhere. It can't help the many young people who don't have the same choices, and, in the long run, it doesn't help the people doing it.

The latest theoretical notion in the reform arena is "deschooling." Several articles by Ivan Illich received a good deal of attention when they appeared in the *New York Review of Books*. Books by Illich (*Deschooling Society*) and by his colleague Everett Reimer (*School Is Dead*) appeared in 1971, and Illich has recently been a popular speaker on university campuses. The basic notion is that schools serve to create the illusion that all respectable learning is tied to teaching in official graded institutions which certify competence through degrees and other paraphernalia. This helps produce elitist and hierarchical societies. Schools should be "disestablished," and people should be let free to develop their own informal learning and skill "nets," in which incidental, individually initiated learning encounters can take place. The whole apparatus of school bureaucracies, degrees, and set curriculum should be abolished. All truly radical social changes depend on this. Moreover, Illich thinks that the schools are in fact collapsing and that the need to deschool will become obvious to everyone very soon. (This is an admittedly crude summary, but it gives the basic sense of the analysis.)

I won't present any detailed description and critique of Illich's pronouncements here. What is directly relevant at this point is Illich's critique of free schools. Speaking about "liberated school teachers," he wrote:

> They seem deeply convinced that learning happens only in a "perpetual wedding to the world," yet continue to assume that social man needs a school if he is to be born, and the womb of a free school of gentle people if he is to be born free. Paradoxically, the free school movement risks reinforcing the dominant system of compulsory knowledge and public training for corporate behavior. Free schools tend to be conservative without the redeeming traditional-

ism of the old. Both share a therapeutic orientation, a utopian vision of youth and attitude of condescension. . . .

All schools romanticize the child, whom they burden with the responsibility for the reform of society. Free schools tend to charge children, whose unfettered spirit is taken as the model of tomorrow's unrepressed paradise, with the additional job of liberating their teachers.

John Holt recommended the review from which these passages are taken, stating his agreement, and Peter Marin quoted it favorably in the *New Schools Exchange Newsletter*. I disagree strongly. Both Illich's own ideas and the very favorable response of the sort I just noted seem to me most interesting as a symptom of how hard it is to avoid the temptations of pseudo-solutions and intellectual easy ways out in a tough situation. So far as free schools go, I have been clearly critical of many aspects in which I hope was a complex and fair way, and for some of the same reasons Illich gives. But Illich, on the basis of very little direct contact or experience, characterizes *all* free schools by what is properly ascribed to only some; and in doing so, he rather arrogantly, ignorantly, and condescendingly disparages serious and intelligent efforts by dedicated people. More than that, talk of the "redeeming traditionalism" of the old schools and of their utopian view of children seems silly and an example of the misleading overgeneralizing that characterizes Illich's expositions. (Perhaps Illich should reread Dickens's *Hard Times* to see Thomas Gradgrind's school in action, or look at George Orwell's moving essay on the torments of his school days, "Such, Such Were the Joys," to recapture the "redeeming traditionalism" which leads him to prefer the old schools to free schools—although all schools must be bad.) Illich seems to enjoy making bad parallels which serve mainly to justify his own claim to splendid originality and truth. In fact, according to his own stated definition of schools, free schools aren't schools at all. They might have a lot wrong with them, but it can't be what's generally wrong with schools. Further, Illich neglects mentioning that a large amount of free school activity, including the theory in the form of Paul Goodman, has viewed free schools as a way of getting out of schooling. (I don't find much of value in Illich's writings that wasn't in Goodman's writings years ago.) For good reasons, young people don't want to be in the real *schools,* but the compulsory education laws compel a certain institutional form of getting away—a legal private school. In these places, whatever they are, much is going on. Some of it is as Illich says: bad (and good) therapeutic intervention in the lives of the young people, and so forth. But much is also "learning webs," honest individual contacts, skill teaching, attempts to get out into the world and into real activities, in a society which makes this enormously difficult.

In any case, free schools have about one-tenth of 1 percent of the schoolchildren of the country. In that very small portion, a good deal of questioning, experimentation, self-criticism, and learning is going on, much of it about how to deschool. To say that any place that gathers young people and adults together *voluntarily* (as, for example, free high schools) with the idea of learning more about themselves, the world, how to do things, where many of the adults are not teachers'-college-trained professional teachers but volunteers from the community, skilled and unskilled, people with real lives in the community who have not dedicated their lives to helping children but do this incidentally, as it were—to say that any place like this is a school and has to be bad is absurd. And Illich might agree, claiming he didn't mean he wanted to abolish places like *that.* He wants a society with this as part of a complex variety of learning networks where people learn and teach for their own pleasures and needs and joys and interests, not for degrees, competitive advantages, certification, or creation of winners and losers. Well, as I have tried to show, the most promising aspect of new schools is about this, however confusedly, and Illich's unfair simplifications show a serious lack of knowledge, sympathy, and understanding.

The praise for Illich is a little disconcerting also. Perhaps part of it arises from the feeling of being on the most radical edge of new reform, finding even radical reform unsatisfactory, given its aims, and seeing in Illich a sense of going even farther, transcending the limitations of educational reform. This is just a speculation, and I don't put too much importance on it. What I want to point to is the sense of transcending depressing difficulties which an analysis like Illich's offers, at least to the intellect, and the Illich supporters referred to are intellectuals and writers. In my view, it makes little sense to talk about deschooling a society without emphasizing the necessity of radically changing more important institutions. Schools didn't create class hierarchies, privilege, and vastly unequal distribution of wealth and power. And these conditions can't be abolished by talking about abolishing schools. Schools are one institutional means of reproducing the basic class relationships, privileges, and attitudes characteristic of our society. To imply that we could abolish schooling, degrees, and the grading and tracking functions and so create a decent unschooled society is wrong. There are winning places and losing places in this society; they have to be filled, and those with power and privilege and wealth will use these resources to keep the winning places for their people. There is a consumer mentality, a waste economy polluting the environment, and this cannot be separated from the corporate profit-hungry basis of the economy. With or without schools, these facts determine the basic quality of life and the life opportunities for the members of the society.

Reforming schools can't fix this; I have emphasized that throughout this book. But neither can abolishing schools, whatever that might mean in the real world. (Does it mean that the voucher-type arrangements Illich would make for everyone *couldn't* be used in schoollike institutions, or that a set hierarchy of "quality" establishments wouldn't become widely known? Does he really think that the campaign he urges to make it illegal to ask for educational qualifications in hiring would really change anything? His analogy is the law forbidding questions about race, and I suggest that his proposal will be as effective as a face-to-face interview where the interviewer is forbidden to ask if the person in front of him is black.) As Herbert Gintis points out in his thorough critique of Illich, "in the final analysis 'de-schooling' is irrelevant because we cannot 'de-factory,' 'de-office,' or 'de-family,' save perhaps at the still unenvisioned end of a long process of social reconstruction." (*Harvard Education Review*, Spring 1972).

The tendency for people involved in educational reform to find a big answer for social problems within education resurfaces in a transformed way in the deschooling idea. For example, take the following remarks by Judson Jerome, a participant and spokesman for very experimental colleges who seems to be turning now to deschooling. He wrote, in a letter to the *New Schools Exchange Newsletter*:

> The deschooling movement runs directly counter to the free school movement, of course. . . . To put it somewhat more extremely than I feel it, reform is counter-revolutionary insofar as it helps institutions adapt and prolongs their lives. In the same sense, free schools, because they *are* nice places (when they are) enable parents to avoid facing a number of issues about themselves, their children and society.

This is very confused. The deschooling movement doesn't run counter to anything, of course, because there is no such thing. There is some talk among some intellectuals and writers on education. What the talk can do, as for Jerome, is maybe to get one off the hook, so to speak. Now, since one knows that all schooling is bad, just stop participating. This makes one revolutionary, it seems, while any attempt to make *nice* places, in whatever political perspective, is counter-revolutionary.

The real conditions are that there is a public school system whose functions have been described. It is part of a larger society which increasing numbers of people find could be vastly improved, to put it mildly. The work to bring about this improvement will be difficult and slow, and will take good thought and good action. There are no panaceas and no easy answers—not about what to do about families and sex on the most personal level, nor about the organization of industrial production enterprises on the large-scale institutional level. In education there are also many hard questions, for radicals and reformers especially, since they are committed to going beyond current accepted attitudes and practices which they consider inadequate or harmful. In that good society we are working toward, we will clearly not have schools in Illich's sense because the very definition links schooling into the creation of bad aspects of the society. We will have to think into new forms, as Illich is trying to do in his descriptions of new learning networks and new technologies. And some of this thought should be tried in various practices, as many people in new schools realize. We have compulsory education, which free school people in general oppose; and so whatever we do—in the streets, as apprenticeships, when traveling—will now officially be called a "school." There will be mistakes; there will be manipulators and people who are using the children to try to solve their own problems. But this happens because there are the problems, the damages of contemporary life, not because there are free schools. One could speculate on the bad effects and possible misuses of Illich's suggestions also, if they were plugged into today's society and today's people, with no other serious changes in the larger society.

But this is the crux. There must be other changes for educational reform to do more than alter the surfaces. In *The School Fix, NYC, USA,* a meticulously detailed and concrete study of a public school system informed by a radical perspective that I share and a breadth of experience and judiciousness that I admire, Miriam Wasserman, a high-school teacher and writer on education says:

> . . . until power and status in the schools have been dislodged and relocated—or abolished—the appropriate education question is not "What kinds of educational programs shall we institute to make the schools more harmonious and fruitful institutions?" but "What are the terms and strategy of the struggle to dislodge power and status in the school system?"[22]

I agree with this. One of my intentions has been to show how the new schools movement can be part of a struggle for changes in the public schools as well as an attempt to learn more about the possibilities of learning and doing in a free environment. For me these concerns go together. If free schools are only an escape, then they are an escape for very few, and the millions in the public school system must stay there day after oppressive day. The problems of the free schools are another sign that a willed isolation can be utopian, in a bad sense, leading to a pretense that a happy few can shield themselves and some children from the harsh sounds of a bad world, whereas in all sorts of ways the world keeps creeping in.

Children are compelled by law to undergo a schooling system that hurts them in many ways. Free schools are a very small attempt to get some of them out from the most immediate oppression of the school. The idea of freeing all the children, even to the modest extent represented by the best of the free schools, is a good dream, but a dream nonetheless. It can't be otherwise in a society where the kinds of freedom, social relations, and opportunity for personal development that are part of the dream are not possible for most people, whether adults or children. Part of the important changes in education proper will come from trying to bring about some big changes in the larger society. To the extent that this movement for social change succeeds, we will become more able to transform what now seem like romantic hopes for the lives of a few children into real historical possibilities for all.

NOTES

1 For a very readable exposition of this tradition and its intellectual history in American political thought, see Louis Hartz's now classic *The Liberal Tradition in America* (New York: Harcourt Brace Jovanovich, 1955.

2 For the best recent statement of this position, see the short and readable radical political economy analysis, *The Sick Society: An Economic Examination*, by Michael Tanzer (New York: Holt, Rinehart & Winston, 1971).

3 Good philosophical statements of this point of view can be found in a short essay by that greatest of Enlightenment thinkers, Immanuel Kant, "Idea of a Universal History from a Cosmopolitan Point of View," included in Patrick Gardiner, ed., *Theories of History* (New York: Free Press, 1959). Also, see Kant's essay "An Answer to the Question, What is Enlightenment?"

4 DAVID COHEN and MARVIN LAZERSON, "Education and the Corporate Order," in *Socialist Revolution*, No 8 2, no. 2 (March-April, 1972): 71–72.

5 NEA Center for the Study of Instruction, *Schools for 70's and Beyond: A Call to Action* (Washington, D.C.: National Education Association, 1971), p. 20.

6 Ibid., pp. 71–72.

7 CHARLES SILBERMAN, *Crisis in the Classroom: The Remaking of American Education* (New York: Random House, 1970), pp. 10–11.

8 For an excellent analysis of "tracking" (to which I am indebted for clarification on some important points), see Richard Rothstein, "Down the Up Staircase: Tracking in Schools," in *This*

Magazine Is About Schools, Vol. 5, No. 3 (summer 1971), pp. 103–40; also see Miriam Wasserman, *The School Fix, NYC, USA* New York: Outerbridge & Dienstfrey, 1971).

9 For a good analysis of how the process of maintaining inequality works, see Samuel Bowles, "Unequal Education and the Reproduction of the Social Division," *Review of Radical Political Economics*, 1972; to appear in a Pantheon anthology of essays on education, edited by Wayne O'Neil.

10 In *The School Fix, NYC, USA,* Miriam Wasserman makes this point graphically. She writes: ". . . middle-class parents manifestly would not tolerate an educational arrangement in which their children of average endowment would end up with the postman's, bus drivers', gas station attendants', and receptionists' jobs, or their children of less than average endowment with the charwomen's, porters', supermarket clerks', and messengers' jobs, if not on the welfare rolls. . . . Nor would they tolerate an educational arrangement that produced twice or three times as many qualified candidates for medical school, computer programer jobs, and army officers as there were places, all the less so while not enough people were left to clean the hospital floors, wash the restaurant dishes, and wear the enlisted man's uniform" (p. 98).

11 For a detailed critique of Silberman from a point of view similar to the one expressed here, see Herb Gintis, "The Politics of Education," *Monthly Review*, Vol. 23, No. 7 (December 1971), pp. 40–51; also Miriam Wasserman, "School Mythology and the Education of Oppression," *This Magazine Is About Schools*, Vol. 5, No. 3 (Summer 1971).

12 MARIO FANTINI, ed., *The Reform of Urban Schools* (Washington, D.C.: National Education Association, 1971), p. 8.

13 A clear analysis of the student movement dealing with this issue is Michael Miles, *The Radical Probe: The Logic of Student Rebellion* (New York: Atheneum Publishers, 1971).

14 *KOA—Communications on Alternatives Newsletter*, No. 2 (Fall 1971), pp. 12–13.

15 VICKI WIRTH LEGION, "Our School: Struggling and Strategizing Along," *Outside The Net—A Magazine in Radical Education*, No. 4 (Winter–Spring 1972), pp. 9, 33 for quotations in text.

16 For a sympathetic but critical account of the free university development, see Paul Lauter and Florence Howe, *The Conspiracy of the Young* (New York: Meridian Books, 1971), Chap. 4, "Service on the Campus: The Free University and Educational Reform."

17 MICHAEL ROSSMAN, "Projections on the New Schools Movement," *New Schools Exchange Newsletter,* No. 52, p. 8.

18 Ibid., p. 9.

19 For a definitive study of the voucher ideas currently under study, see *Education Vouchers: A report on Financing Elementary Education by Grants to Parents,* Center for the Study of Public Policy (December 1970).

20 For a clear and balanced analysis of the "movement," its decline, and the current situation and prospects for radical activity, see Christopher Lasch's "Can the Left Rise Again?", *New York Review of Books,* October 21, 1971, pp. 36–41. Lasch writes:

"There are signs . . . that many of those who were demoralized and disoriented by the collapse of the political left and the degeneration of the cultural revolt—including some of the cultural radicals themselves—are once again finding their way back to political action. Some of the academic dropouts have returned to school, with the hope of changing the professions from within. Having tried to survive as independent activists or intellectuals, they are rediscovering the importance of institutional ties. Professional work and organizations turn out to be not purely imprisoning; they also provide some minimal support for the creative use of one's talents, together with the necessary fellowship of one's peers. Nor are the professions completely closed to innovation, as many radicals had supposed. The old guards are still entrenched, but the number of dissidents is growing" (p. 39).

21 This image of the future is dramatically projected in a novel by Marge Piercy, *Dance the Eagle to Sleep* (New York: Doubleday & Co., 1970). A less literary projection of how this might occur can be found at the end of Michael Tanzer's *The Sick Society.*

22 MIRIAM WASSERMAN, *The School Fix, NYC, USA* (New York: Outerbridge, 1970), p. 520.

Allen Graubard helped organize and served as a teacher and director of the Community School, Santa Barbara, California, during 1970–1971, while on leave from M.I.T., where he served as an assistant professor of philosophy in the Department of Humanities. He received his formal education in the public schools of Chicago and Philadelphia and at Harvard, where he received a B.A. and a Ph.D. in philosophy and political science. While at M.I.T. he was active in Resist and the New University Conference. Since leaving M.I.T. in 1971, he has been active in a variety of free school activities.